Reading the Bible as Literature

# Reading the Bible as Literature

## An Introduction

JEANIE C. CRAIN

polity

First published in 2010 by Polity Press
Reprinted in 2010

Polity Press
65 Bridge Street
Cambridge CB2 1UR, UK

Polity Press
350 Main Street
Malden, MA 02148, USA

ISBN-13: 978-0-7456-3507-1
ISBN-13: 978-0-7456-3508-8 (pb)

A catalogue record for this book is available from the British Library.

Typeset in 9.5 on 12 pt Utopia
by Servis Filmsetting Ltd, Stockport, Cheshire
Printed and bound in the United States

For further information on Polity, visit our website:
www.politybooks.com

# Contents

*Preface*                                                                          vi

1  Reading the Bible as Literature: A Way of Understanding        1
2  Style, Tone, and Rhetorical Strategy: A Way of Using
   Language                                                                        22
3  Image, Metaphor, Symbol, and Archetype: A Way of
   Meaning                                                                         43
4  Major Genres: A Way of Seeing                                                65
5  Sub-Genres: A Way of Clarifying and Mapping                          90
6  Character: A Way of Identifying                                            110
7  Themes and Motifs: A Way of Unifying                                   129

Conclusion                                                                          152

*Glossary*                                                                          153
*Notes*                                                                             172
*Index*                                                                             203

# Preface

*Reading the Bible as Literature: an Introduction* advances a specifically useful way of reading, understanding, and assessing the literature
of the Bible.[1] Some generalizations, by now almost "truisms," apply:
like all literature, the Bible embodies and enacts universal or shared
human experience rather than stating or telling about it, inviting readers to enter into and relive a story or poem; focus is upon the whole
text as it exists in its current form, requiring both an analytical and a
holistic approach; the audience addressed is the "common" reader
rather than the specialist; emphasis is upon familiar critical concepts
such as rhetorical devices, figurative and symbolic uses of language,
common genres such as narrative, drama, and poetry, and on characters and themes and motifs. Reading the Bible as literature boils down
to a certain way of reading – reading in the context of the categories
and disciplines of literature – in order to understand better or to cast
light upon its words; it means understanding the features that make the
Bible literature without denying its special role as religious or sacred
text.[2]

The Bible commonly has been understood as made up of two sets of
texts, the Hebraic and the Christian: the "Old Testament," sometimes
referred to as the Hebrew Bible (this more accurately referring to a
collection written in the original Hebrew language), and the Christian
"New Testament," used here without any suggestion that the Old
Testament depends upon the New for its meaning. Both texts belong
within their own respective traditions.

This text presents itself at a basic level for readers who have yet to
acquire many of the tools available for understanding the Bible or literature more generally. This obviously means that the Bible will be read
in translation, an issue that affects a subject normally considered to be
at the heart of literature: the study of style – what an author says and
how the author says it. The translation used will be the New Revised
Standard Version, a translation that describes itself as going back to
the King James Version and as retaining much of the original languages
(Hebrew and Greek) while making them accessible to modern readers.
It provides extensive study notes, timelines, graphs, charts, maps, and
outlines that will aid readers in understanding the Bible in the context
of its own history, culture, and literature, and will help readers avoid
reading anachronistically. It will also identify authors and the approximate dates for when the books were composed.

Reading the Bible "as literature" redirects readers from issues concerning the sacred nature and authority of the Bible to its existence as literature of a particular people: that of the Hebrew nation (the Old Testament) and that of Christianity (the New Testament). With its complex history of composition – the writing of the Old Testament alone taking over a thousand years – the Bible contains much that is unique to itself but shares the mythological, metaphorical, and symbolic language that belongs to literature across the centuries.[3] Written in poetry and prose, much of the Bible reads as a structured narrative abounding in stories, characters, and plots worked out against a backdrop of an ancient people trying to understand its nature, destiny, and place in the universe.

How individuals read the Bible makes a great deal of difference. The way most people read it has come through religious interpretive traditions, Jewish and Christian. With at least some of the texts dating back to the eighth, ninth, and tenth centuries BCE, it should not be surprising to observe that we have documents with original settings and meanings that have come to us through a way of reading, as evidenced in the canonization of the Bible. A direction of modern scholarship has been an attempt to get back to the original meaning of the constituent parts, an approach that has led to a questioning of the traditional authorship, adding to the composition mix a set of editors or redactors, and leading generally to attempts to reconstruct historical context. Noting that much of the traditional meaning that the Bible has had for people has been lost in the search for origins, other scholarship has redirected attention to the existing texts, to the role of readers and their assumptions about meaning, and to literary study.

It should be noted that a textbook originates not in a vacuum, but within surrounding scholarship. This volume alludes briefly to historical analysis and introduces only a basic level of literary analysis. A more advanced course could explore an integration of these approaches and what each has to offer to the other. The potential for this is suggested by an overview of some of the traditions of literary interpretation in the first chapter and by content and biographical notes that supplement the materials in this text. The first chapter, in particular, since it builds the foundation for what follows, refers to a significant number of resources. Additionally, "Preliminary Considerations," addressing theory in each chapter, reference important resources and extend the conversation beyond what has been immediately remarked in the text; these have been included primarily to be used as teaching resources and for continued study. More extensive notes will be found on the web page www.readingthebibleasliterature.com.

The more basic and immediate aim of this book is to introduce readers to some of the common tools of literary analysis, to call attention to close reading in context, to stress the role of interpretation, and, finally, as an outcome of reading and understanding, to appreciate the Bible. Emphasizing unity, coherence, and whole–part relationships and the diversity among the texts themselves, this text invites readers to look at the Bible (and the books in the Bible) as it exists, as a whole. It pays attention primarily to literary elements but presents other information important to building a context for understanding the Bible and for encouraging further study.

Chapters in the book have been organized to demonstrate how authors use language in particular ways to represent and create meaning; how major genres begin with authors' seeing, picturing, imitating, and creating literature that illuminates actual life; how characters reveal identities; and how themes help to create a sense of the Bible as a book. These literary activities – using language in particular ways, discovering meaning through language, and the acts of seeing, classifying, identifying, and unifying – suggest an active rather than passive interaction with the material and point to the requirement of literature that readers engage with the primary text.

# 1 Reading the Bible as Literature: A Way of Understanding

## Outline

Preliminary Considerations
   Definitions
   Form
   Translations
Reading the Bible as Literature
   Appeal and Readership
   A Literary Approach
      Intertextuality, allusion, and typology
      Prophecy
      Macro-plots
      Language
      Meta-narrative
      Monomythic and universal
      Impact on literature
      Experiential
Approaches Taken in Textbooks for Teaching the Bible as Literature
Traditions in Biblical Interpretation
Culture and Religion in Ancient Israel and the Jewish World View
Close Reading
Questions for Reflection

*As readers, you may very well come to the Bible simply wanting to read and understand it more clearly than you have in the past. A textbook, although an intermediary between a reader and the primary text, delays this gratification. Textbooks usually serve as guides, presenting the accepted theories of the discipline and setting out concepts and the analytical methods of that discipline. The discipline in this case involves literature – specifically, the literature of the Bible. "Literature," of course, carries the weight of years of intellectual discussion about what is meant by "literary text," about the appropriate approaches to reading, and about the kinds of tools needed for interpretation.*

*In these chapters, I provide you with the basic definitions and background you need for improving your understanding of the Bible by reading it as literature.* **Literary,** *for example, has generally been defined as a special use of language that intensifies and transforms it from ordinary use. Reading literature poses the special challenge of the* *subjectivity of the reader and the objectivity of the text. Then, of course, scholarship debates whether to focus on the text itself or its historical-cultural context. I have taken the position throughout that I want the Bible to be your primary text and that I want you to engage in close reading. Your reading will always be enriched when you bring as many perspectives to it as you can.*

*I've learned that readers using a textbook want to cut to the core to understand what is required with the materials being presented. In addition to providing, as above, a chapter outline at the beginning of each chapter, I will continue to speak directly to you in italicized sections throughout the book while keeping the materials in the text in the third person to present it more objectively. It's important to know I've written this book for anyone wanting to acquire a more complete and satisfying understanding of and appreciation for the Bible. Both content and biographical notes have been used to provide supplementary information, explanations, and comments and to point to additional references and scholarly work; you should probably disregard these in your first reading of these chapters. As with all literature, I think we can approach the Bible with an expectation that whatever we learn about it will deepen and enrich its meaning for us. We have in the Bible a collection of ancient literature that has been grouped together as an "approved canon" through religious traditions that have made it familiar to a general audience. Apart from its use as religious text, I want you to begin to appreciate it as a unique collection of some of our oldest literature that can be better understood when we use some of the same tools and techniques we would take to reading literature generally. As with any introductory literature course, we will begin by establishing a foundation for our study. In the case of the Bible, we need to begin with some preliminary questions of definition, form, and translation.*

## Preliminary Considerations

### Definitions

The "**Bible**" includes the authoritative Jewish and Christian biblical **canons** and consists not of original manuscripts but "copies of copies of copies" of texts.[1] Many existing manuscripts did not, in fact, make their way into the official canons, which differ in the number and order of the books included. The Roman Catholic and Orthodox churches include the **deuterocanonical** or **apocryphal** books of the Greek **Septuagint** (LXX). The **Jewish Bible** refers to the texts that correspond to the Christian Old Testament, in a different order, as **Tanakh**, a collection including the **Torah** (Law), **Nevi'im** (Prophets), and **Kethuvim** (Writings). Scholars often use the "Hebrew Bible" to avoid taking religious sides in debates about the two **covenants**, but this term properly designates texts originally written in the Hebrew language, excluding the deuterocanonical or apocryphal books. It also refers, more broadly, to the tradition that preserved these texts up to the age of printing.[2] Translated, the Hebrew Bible is known familiarly as the "Jewish Bible."

This text uses "Bible" to refer to the commonly anthologized thirty-nine books of the **Old Testament** and the twenty-seven books of the **New Testament** within the broader frame of different traditions without, hopefully, giving credence to the unfortunate connotations that often accompany these names. "Old" and "New" have not been used to suggest that the Christian faith has superseded (**supersession-ism**), or is superior to, Judaism; nor is there the suggestion that the New Testament merely reinterprets, or distorts, the older tradition.[3] The earliest tradition of referring to both collections in a single book may be attributed to Clement (an early Christian writer around 200 CE).[4] The two collections – written in different languages, at different times, and for different audiences – require sensitivity to different critical frameworks for understanding them.[5] Denominationally grouped canons can lead to preconditioned ways of reading in light of unexamined assumptions.[6] Christians, for example, typically read the Old Testament toward the New Testament, while Jewish people tend to read the same texts in the direction of the **Talmud**, a post-biblical, substantive body of teachings.[7] A more neutral and sensible way of reading looks at two separate traditions in relation to each other. Canonized as a whole and single book, the Bible, despite diversity, evidences a degree of unity that some find remarkable in relation to its parts, character, style, and substance.[8]

*It's important that you understand how the Old Testament references God and why you may see in your translations of the Bible the use of LORD (all in caps) and God. The Bible uses many names for God.*

In Hebrew, the personal and proper divine name, considered too sacred to pronounce, is represented by four consonants (YHWH, known as the **Tetragrammaton**) transliterated as Yahweh (LORD) and appearing about 7,000 times in the Jewish Bible. Synonyms include Yahwe, Yahveh, YHVH, Yahve, Wahvey, Jahvey, Jahweh, Jehovah, and JHVH. A traditional Hebrew reading translates YHWH as Adonai, my Lord, for the sake of reverence (third century BCE, used about 300 times in the Hebrew Bible). Elohim, another reference, denotes "gods" or "divine powers," with emphasis on the plural. The plural form characterizes much of the Hebrew Bible and appears over 2,000 times. Eastern languages used El, the singular form, to refer to God (which shows up about 200 times in the Hebrew Bible). Jehovah refers to the Latin rendition of the Tetragrammaton, to which the vowels from Elohim and Adonai were added. This divine name can be traced to 1518 CE.

*In talking about the origins of the Bible, I refer to historical dates as CE (Common Era) and BCE (Before the Common Era), Common Era meaning the time common to the Judeo-Christian tradition. You may be more familiar with the use of BC (Before Christ) and AD (Anno Domini, in the Year of the Lord). By using BCE and CE, I hope to encourage you to expand your understanding and tolerance for different approaches to the Bible and to acknowledge the general use of these abbreviations in non-Christian contexts.*

### Form

The form in which the Bible exists today does not resemble the form given to it by its original authors; ancient Hebrew manuscripts, for example, made no distinction between prose and poetry, no division of sentences, paragraphs, meter, or speeches in drama, or even separation into words; in fact, ancient manuscripts made no distinction between lowercase and uppercase letters and used neither marks of punctuation nor spaces between words, leading to the possibility for multiple interpretations of strings of letters. By the third century BCE, scrolls were divided into sections, larger sections marked off by a new line, and smaller sections delineated by a gap in the text. This practice was continued with the **Masoretic** text (between the seventh and tenth centuries CE). Stephen Langton, an archbishop of Canterbury (1207–28 CE), developed the chapter division that became a model for other texts. Perhaps as early as 200 CE, the Hebrew and Aramaic **translations** included verse divisions; a Jewish rabbi, Nathan, divided the Hebrew Bible into verses (1448 CE), and Robert Estienne (1555) divided the New Testament into verses.[9] These divisions aid study and reference but, while aptly serving these needs, they interfere with textual unity and reading the Bible in the form(s) in which it originally existed. Readers remain challenged to discover the inherent units within the Bible and to comprehend the literary structure of its books – the use of "book" itself problematic and imposed upon biblical scrolls.

### Translations

*Every translation of the Bible affects meaning in different ways, with translations generally existing on a continuum that runs from literal to moderately literal (form-based), and from moderately idiomatic to idiomatic (meaning-based). Literal translations retain much of the Hebraic and Greek forms of language, including poetic form; idiomatic translations tend to be meaning-based and to convert original languages into modern day language, sometimes to the extent of liberal paraphrase.[10] For this book, I have used the* New Oxford Annotated Bible (NRSV), *a translation that brings together form and meaning, presenting a highly literal translation that goes back to the King James Version authorized in 1611. This translation bases itself upon the critical editions of original texts and subscribes to no particular confessional allegiance. Other versions which I've consulted throughout include the* Jewish Study Bible, *the* New Interpreter's Study Bible *(particularly useful for its identity and discussion of multiple sources), and the* HarperCollins Study Bible.

The difference that a translation makes in reading the Bible can be illustrated by the "Translator's Preface" to *The Five Books of Moses*, a translation that pays careful attention to the rhythm and sound of the original Hebrew language in which the Torah was written, preserving devices such as repetition, **allusion** (a practice of echoing or referring to other works), **alliteration** (repetition of initial consonant sound), and word play. Everett Fox, the translator, believes that readers gain by hearing the literalness of the Hebrew language, and he illustrates this by referring to the **motif** (recurrent pattern/image) of face in Jacob's returning confrontation with Esau.[11] In the NRSV, Genesis 32.20 reads, "For he thought, 'I may appease him with the present that goes ahead of me, and afterwards I shall see his face; perhaps he will accept me.'" The equivalent in the Fox translation reads, "For he said to himself: / I will wipe (the anger from) his face / with the gift that goes ahead of my face; / afterward, when I see his face, perhaps he will lift up my face!" Fox makes the point that the repetition of face signals something of significance, especially when the motif then reoccurs in 32.31, where Jacob wrestles with an angel and is renamed: "Ýakov called the name of the place Peniel / Face of God, / for: I have seen God, / face to face, / and my life has been preserved," and 33.10, where, upon meeting Esau, Jacob says, "For I have, after all, seen your face, as one sees the face of God, / and you have been gracious to me." This difference in translation emphasizes not only the motif but, structurally, the thematic link between the sections, and affects meaning. Fox contends that such meaning would be lost in a translation into idiomatic English. He further gives the example of the Genesis creation (1.3–5) as structurally pointing to the orderliness of God and the creation: "God said . . ., God saw . . ., God separated . . ., and God called . . . ." Another translation, using the principle of translating the Hebrew language in context, renders concretely and realistically the 32.31 passage as "I came out alive." The second passage, 33.10, reads, "you received me in kindness?," reflecting Jacob's surprise.[12]

## Reading the Bible as Literature

*You may be asking, why read the Bible as literature? This question corresponds to ones I've heard students ask in every literature course I've ever taught: Why study literature? I'm always tempted to reply, in the tradition of liberal arts, because . . . it's fun, it satisfies our curiosity, and we learn about ourselves and others and about our world. It deepens and enriches our lives, and it has the potential for making us into better people.[13] What I've taught students about literature applies to reading the Bible: we begin by paying attention to how writers present their content, in what forms and genres; to how they tell stories – develop the plot, setting, theme, and characters; and to how they use language – concretely, symbolically, and rhetorically. This book follows a tradition that makes paying attention to the literary features of the Bible the starting point for all other approaches to understanding its meanings.*[14] *Of course, the critical terms used in a literary approach to the Bible, including " literature," are modern developments, these coming on the scene after the Bible's composition.*

### Appeal and Readership

We know that people read the Bible for many reasons – religious, moral, historical, and literary – and in different ways – literally, figuratively, or symbolically – and consider it "divinely dictated, revealed, or inspired, or as a human creation."[15] The religious texts of the Bible have commonly been thought to represent something more than acts of the imagination and something more than "just literature."[16] Read generally, the Bible has been impacting the lives of people for over 2,000 years; many people, in fact, read it "as religion" and "as Scripture," as a book describing how "to serve God," and find in it an overriding story of the relationship between God and human beings, the story of creation, the nature, behavior, and destiny of humankind.[17] Each of the three major monotheistic religions – Judaism, Christianity, and Islam – find in the Bible a foundational set of texts. Sometimes read as history, and certainly containing history, the Bible reaches before history into primordial and mythical time and projects beyond history into a metaphysical and transcendental future. It raises interesting issues about the subjects of art, fiction, and history.[18] Scholars worldwide, using multiple inroads, have read and commented upon the Bible; in fact, the Bible is commonly described as attracting a greater mass of secondary writing than any other collection of literature.

The Bible has always appealed to a broad readership (with more than 100 million worldwide sales every year and published in more than 450 languages), affecting people in deep and permanent ways, presenting "embodied human experience," telling the stories of people, revealing the best and worst in them, displaying all their raw emotions, and asking "the largest of human questions."[19] As the result of its impact upon people all over the world, and because it continues to reveal new exposures about the human experience, it has been regarded by many as a classic, but *not just a classic*, that deserves to be recognized as among the world's greatest literature.[20]

### A Literary Approach

Reading the Bible "as literature" invites readers, minimally, to focus on reading and appreciating the books of the Bible as they exist.[21] Introductory literature courses traditionally have focused upon existing texts, paying attention to the acts of reading, understanding, and assessing.[22] They emphasize unity, coherence, and whole–part relationships, looking at a text as having a beginning, a middle, and an end. Introductory courses require readers to gain a sense of the "whole" text and to read in this context.[23] Such courses exist to help students acquire some basic tools for reading and understanding individual works; students have been told that literature embodies human experience and that they can learn from reading literature much about themselves, others, and the world itself.[24] They have been encouraged to read with an attitude of curiosity, particularly for diversity, and an open mind, engaging self-criticism and discovering that asking questions may be more important than committing to answers.[25] They learn that texts have life away from their origin and that meaning becomes inextricably bound to the act of reading.[26] Reading becomes the foundation for analysis, interpretation, and reassembling a text as "a whole."[27]

### Intertextuality, allusion, and typology

Biblical canons evidence purposeful organization through traditions of collection, and, published as books, they evidence literary principles at work that hold them together and suggest that they can be read as books.[28] One such principle can be described as the **intertextuality** of the Bible: its use and reference of other texts to influence meaning.[29] This principle should not be confused with **typology**, the search for deeper and fuller meanings within texts (especially the Old Testament) in light of God's work in history.

Biblical writers clearly used earlier biblical texts; they looked back as they created text and recast language and themes found in earlier writing, and they borrowed phrasing, imagery, and sounds without explicitly stating the source. For example, Joshua retells the calling of Abraham to the encampment before entering into Canaan. In some ways, Joseph's story echoes the Genesis account of brothers, and the exiles (Assyrian and Babylonian) recall the exile from Eden. Deuteronomy and the Prophets in the Old Testament make much use of the stories in Exodus. This allusive nature of biblical narrative opens up the possibility of reading always within the context of an even greater narrative or story and for reestablishing beginnings, middles, and ends. For example, biblical scholars refer to two major narratives in the Old Testament: the Primary Narrative (Genesis through Kings) and the Secondary Narrative (Chronicles, Ezra, and Nehemiah), this later tradition retelling and reinterpreting the story of Israel.

New Testament writers freely allude to, or consciously echo, other Old Testament texts.[30] Since the Scripture they referenced had no chapter and verse divisions, New Testament writers identified the quote or paraphrase by place, such as Moses at the burning bush (Luke 30.27), by time, such as in the days of Abiathar (Mark 2.26), or by words (Romans 11.2). The New Testament contains a total of almost 300 direct quotes from the Old Testament, and, if including indirect and partial quotes, the number jumps to about 1,000. In some instances, the Greek Septuagint (and writers of the New Testament wrote in Greek) was quoted literally, but quotations were also altered or corrected.

The kinds of quotations include the formulaic and composite as well as some that occur without acknowledgement or introduction. **Formulaic quotation** uses introductory formulas such as "saying," "writing," "what says the Scripture," "it is written," "the Scripture has said," "that it might be fulfilled," and God, Moses, or Isaiah "has said." **Composite quotations** simply combine two or more quotations taken from one or more sections of the Old Testament. Jewish writers in the first century CE knew large portions of the Hebrew Bible by heart, and a clause, a phrase, or a word could point to a wider Old Testament context and ideas; the writers of the New Testament had minds richly filled with Hebrew history and allude to it constantly.

A popular strategy of reading, **typology**, explains the characters and events of the Old Testament in terms of the New. For example, it sees Adam as a type of Christ; it understands the story of Jonah as prefiguring Jesus' resurrection; it understands the exodus as a type of baptism. In short, it understands the Old and New Testaments as a unified story which presents Jesus as a descendant of David and a fulfillment of Davidic covenant. The Gospel writer Matthew introduces Jesus as the new Moses; he sees a correspondence between Moses as the prophet of the Old Covenant (Israel) and Jesus as the prophet, priest, and king of the New Covenant (universal). This form of interpretation, found especially in the early church leaders, lost ground after the Reformation (a sixteenth-century religious movement) summoned people back to the Scriptures themselves as a counter to ecclesiastical interpretation.[31]

*Prophecy*
Much of the Bible consists of **prophecy**, a biblical genre sometimes defined futuristically, a direction not supported by scholarship. It may be more easily defined indirectly through a definition of prophets – individuals taking on the role of spokespersons for God, even when their utterances were to be taken ironically; they acted as intercessors between God and the people.[32] Scholars generally understand Israel's prophets as typically focused on their immediate political and social worlds and concerned about impending crises, such as the Assyrian military threat or the Babylonian destruction of Jerusalem. A distinction should also be made between "prophecy" and "apocalypse." Daniel in the Old Testament and Revelation in the New address coming "end times" signaled by God's "sudden breaking into human history and terminating it."[33] The New Testament consistently references both the Law and the Prophets in the sense of "speaking before," foretelling, forth telling, and predicting the future.[34] Critics have argued that prophetic interpretations force upon the past an unintended and largely reconstructed meaning.[35] Christianity counters by arguing that texts carry a deeper or fuller meaning than what the authors themselves perceived or intended, and attribute this to divine inspiration and divine direction.

*Macro-plots*

Another principle that holds together parts of the Bible can be recognized in its macro-plots, a narrative process whereby several layers of stories function as a single entity.[36] An example of this can be found in Genesis and the accounts of beginnings, the founding father Abraham, and the Jacob and Joseph cycles. To illustrate, the book received its name from a Greek translation of the Hebrew world "toledot," which literally means "beginnings."[37] Genesis 2.4 says: "These are the generations of the heaven and earth when they were made." Two genealogical registers (5.1, 10.1) present the descendants of Adam and the descendants of Noah's sons, followed (in 11.10) by the descendants of Shem, leading to Abraham. Genesis 25 presents the descendants of Ishmael and Isaac, Abraham's two sons. Yet another chapter (36) presents the descendants of Esau. Genesis concludes with the Jacob and Joseph cycles, the latter linking directly to Exodus and the descendants of Jacob in Egypt. The narrative presents these genealogies as intertwined and related. All generations lead to Egypt, the wilderness wandering, the possession of Canaan, and the birth of the nation of Israel.

*Language*

Perhaps the strongest unifying principle consists of the imagistic, **metaphorical**, and **symbolic** uses of language (discussed as images of relationship in the third chapter) that belong to the creative imagination and to literature in general. Since the Enlightenment (beginning in the seventeenth century), a world view has been favored that emphasizes factuality, the scientifically verifiable or historically reliable facts.[38] The Bible, however, belongs solidly with the religious rather than the secular view: it presents an experiential reality in which the boundaries between self and world, between subject and object, between realities (the finite and the infinite), soften to allow an experience of connectedness.[39]

A few examples will illustrate how understanding the Bible metaphorically brings it solidly into the tradition of literature. First, there is the notion of journey that underlies its macro-plots: Egypt and bondage, and the Babylonian exile and return.[40] The journey carries with it the possibility of discovering greater realities. There are the Christological metaphors that point to Jesus as the Word of God, the Son of God, and the Wisdom of God: the "I am" the light, the way, the truth, the life, the vine, the resurrection, the door, the Good Shepherd.[41] To these should be added the symbolic uses of light and darkness, all with ancient, archetypal, and cross-cultural meaning.[42] The "kingdom of God," important to both the Old and New Testaments, carries several metaphorical meanings, having social overtones of God's coming kingdom as being one of righteousness and social justice (distributive and egalitarian in contrast to humanly kingdoms of oppression).[43] Simply consider the Lord's Prayer, with its "Thy Kingdom come" (Matthew 6.9–13 and Luke 11.1–4). Birth metaphors abound with hope of this idealized future. And, as one final example, note the mythical redemption (and transformation) of human beings from between beginning and ending time presented in the images of motion, sight, and wakefulness.[44] The metaphors of death and resurrection in the New Testament, in fact, express this transformation as a process of decentering (death) and recentering (resurrection).[45]

*Meta-narrative*

The fact remains that the anthologized sixty-six books of the Bible have traditionally been read as one book.[46] As a whole, the Bible reveals a loose chronology and overarching **meta-narrative** that tells a story about the past and the future, with the New Testament reinterpreting the Old Testament.[47] It has also been regarded as containing four acts: creation and fall, Israel, Jesus, and the Church.[48]

As story, the Old Testament provides a dramatic account of origins, with roots in primeval and mythical time.[49] This ancient story presents a God creating the world and pronouncing it good up until the creation of humankind in his own image – a creation that exercises its own will to determine what is good. The stories that follow present an ongoing struggle with God.[50] The history of Israel, as has often been noted, follows a pattern largely of promise unfulfilled on account of human rebellion; in time, Israel falls to the Assyrians, Judah to the Babylonians, with the Persians, Greeks, and Romans over the horizon. A surviving remnant looks to the future for an anointed one, the Messiah, who will reestablish the Jerusalem that has been destroyed. The pattern repeats: Jerusalem built, Jerusalem destroyed.[51]

Christianity tells a similar story and looks to a future in which God's people will be united in a climactic and heavenly Jerusalem that serves as the counterpart to the earthly Jerusalem. Revelation describes the creation of a new heaven and earth in which God's presence fully abides with humankind: it achieves this by depicting a marriage in which heaven and earth become one; it then describes the creation of a New Eden, a new Tree of Life, and a New Jerusalem. In this way, the New Testament reinterprets tradition in terms of its own hope for a world that expresses divine will.

*Monomythic and universal*

Reading the Bible as literature also opens doors to discovering what within it belongs to literature generally. One finds, for example, in Jesus and Moses the monomythic and universal hero types. **Monomyth** refers to a basic pattern in which a hero begins in the ordinary world but receives a call to enter into an unknown and mysterious world of strange powers and events, where he must face tasks and trials alone or with assistance. Recognizable features include a miraculous birth, initiation at a young age, withdrawal, trial and quest, descent, resurrection and return, ascension, apotheosis, and atonement.

A mythic approach would describe Christianity as combining several aspects of mythology: the virgin birth (Mary, for some, as goddess and Queen of heaven, thought to be a take-off from Asherah and Ishtar), the dying god, the sacrifice, the hanging on a tree, the meeting of time and eternity, and the resurrection. The Asian god Attis is hung on a tree; the Norse Odin hangs on a tree to learn of the mysteries. Indo-European mythology provides a background for understanding the use of triads or threes in the Bible: the goddess as maiden, mother, and crone. Adam and Eve represent the first man and woman, with associations that exist in the mythical, such as the mother goddess.[52] The motif of war in heaven can be found in Babylonian mythology. The water of life and baptism can be found in Mesopotamian myth: the god Enki sends water of life to comfort the suffering goddess Ereshkigal. Greek mythology presents Zeus and other sky gods. Like Genesis, the Greek story of creation begins with chaos and void out of which came Gaia (Mother Earth), Eros or Desire, Uranos or sky. When the Gospels describe Jesus as descending to the underworld, the motif has appeared in Greek in Herakles, Orpheus, or Theseus. Death, the antagonist of life, has mythical overtones: the Greek Pandora opens her box and death comes into the world; the Sumerian Ereshkigal is goddess of the underworld.

While literalist readings of the Bible may fear the **mythological**, the fact that myth addresses death, the changing seasons, the passage of the sun and moon, and the origin of the universe and life may provide enhancement and appreciation for the Bible as literature.[53] It should be stated that the Bible has also been approached in yet another way – as history – this generally contrasted to the Bible as mythology, and this approach leads to a discussion of truth and fiction. Actually, mythology predates scientific method and the discipline of logic and may, in fact, provide the foundation for them.

*Impact on literature*

Reading the Bible as literature provides a way to bridge what has been described as a gulf or a gap of "ignorance" between it and general literature.[54] Today's reader, for example, cannot be counted upon to have much general understanding of the 3,000 or so men and women described in the Bible; the more important characters, some of these no longer familiar, would include the Patriarchs, the kings (especially of the monarchy), non-Israelite leaders such as Pharaoh and Nebuchadnezzar, the original human beings, the priests Aaron and Zadok, the Old Testament hero Moses and the New Testament Jesus, and the mothers, especially Sarah, Rebekah, Hannah, Elizabeth, and Mary.

English literature has been described as having its richest sources in the Bible, the latter contributing to the language, style, expression, and very tone of literature.[55] Knowing the Bible well aids readers in recognizing titles, stories, characters, allusions, genres, images, and plots in literature generally that have been drawn directly from it.[56] Archibald MacLeish's play *J.B.* borrowed its characters and story directly from the Old Testament Job; Milton's *Samson Agonistes* draws on the character of Samson; Robert Frost in *A Masque of Mercy* makes Jonah a character in modern New York. The Bible remains the major source and influence for modern writing, running through all of Western literature.[57]

*Experiential*

The Bible speaks in images that arise out of bodily experience, appealing to and being shaped by the imagination and the emotions.[58] Images exist first and then build into a connected pattern of metaphor, symbol, and archetype, these all contributing to meaning within the universal, shared language of culture.[59]

That the Bible images reality and truth, rather than stating it in abstractions and propositions, "puts us on the scene and makes us participants in the action";[60] it enacts human experience instead of telling about it; it expresses a truthfulness to the human experience, this distinct from propositional truth and ideas that are true or false.[61] This affects how people read the Bible: the test of truth in literature occurs when readers say about its portrayal of life that life is like this.[62] In a sense, the Bible must be rescued from theology, abstractions and propositions; it must also be rescued from scholars – both the conservative scholar, who organizes it into theological outlines and proof-texts, and the scholar who traces the text from its original to its existing state.[63] While the Bible certainly lends itself to abstract ideas and propositions, as literature it should not be reduced to these; rather, it invites a different approach. Its truth can be uncovered by tracing images and patterns of images, an approach appropriate to the visual and sensory, emotion, and imagination. Human beings have been described as being by nature "image-makers" and image users.[64]

Transient life on earth plays out its drama of birth and death in natural time under the unending cycles of the sun and moon, day and night, these cycles providing the frame for the ongoing drama of human life and death and passage into another state. Building on this experiential grounding, figurative language conceptualizes to greater abstractions and enables human beings to talk about ideas such as God and conformity "to the image of God."[65] Metaphor, the basis of all language and literature, builds an interactive relationship between the contingent world, the subject, and the eternal.[66] Jesus as presented in the New Testament epitomizes an ideal conformity between the human body and the divine. Paul, in Romans 5, speaks of Adam, the first earthly being, as a type for Christ, the heavenly being, yet to come.[67] God, throughout the Bible, is personified to speak and to reveal himself through words and deeds; in Genesis, God walks; in Hosea (2–3) he is pictured as a loving husband; in Isaiah (49.15) he is presented as a mother tenderly caring for the child of her womb; and John (10) introduces Jesus as the Lamb of God and as a Good Shepherd.[68]

Carl Jung, emphasizing the symbolic dimension of spiritual references and events of the Bible, develops Christ as an archetypal image of the unified, whole personality, the Self; he particularly liked the Johannine theme of Christ as symbolizing love, the life of the Spirit, salvation, and reconciliation.[69]

## Approaches Taken in Textbooks for Teaching the Bible as Literature

*In this section, I explore some key distinctions among approaches that have been taken to studying the Bible relevant to literature. Textbooks get written, as we know, to serve as a resource critical to student learning and as a teaching tool for faculty. We have varied needs and different teaching contexts. We may all begin by wanting to understand the Bible or even wanting to understand the Bible as literature, but we can get to our destination through different ways. Understanding something about different approaches can give us a better understanding of what our options are and of the Bible itself – and certainly can enliven our engagement with its content. This book, in introducing the Bible as literature, pays attention to what a text is saying and how it says it.*

During much of the twentieth century, reading the Bible has been part of the college curriculum, with three general approaches being taken: the literature of the Bible, the Bible in literature, and the Bible as literature.[70] The literature of the Bible tends to employ a narrowed definition of literature and to extract narratives (tell a story in a particular way) that seem independent and capable of standing on their own, thus acknowledging that some parts of the Bible may be literature but not making this claim for the whole, and usually setting aside consideration of the Bible as religion.[71] Multiple anthologies of literature in the Bible appeared in English classes in the 1900s. The teaching of the Bible as literature became popular in high school and college classrooms in the 1970s. This approach resulted from the recognition that the Bible provides "a framework for Western literature" and that it should be taught early in literature classes. [72] The Bible in literature approach explains how literature has used the Bible, directing attention to its influence.[73] The Bible as literature emphasis treats the study of the Bible in similar ways to the study of any other literature, insisting that it possesses the same traits as literature generally and that it can be admired for its literary beauty.

The Bible as literature faces some very significant challenges.[74] First, it has roots in an antiquity not always acknowledged by current practitioners; in modern scholarship, "Bible as literature" has actually often referred to the critical approach of source criticism, perhaps even serving as a "code-name" for it; if it ignores sources, it puts itself at odds with the work literary critics set out to do in investigating the original historical setting and authorship (especially at advanced and scholarly levels); it sometimes, too, attempts to pass off the Bible as literature in the same sense as other world literature; and, finally, it may say something about the Bible and a way of reading that some consider wrong.[75] It may very well be that the study of the Bible as literature straddles approaches that remain, in some ways, irreconcilable: the Bible in the sense that it has traditionally been read, up until a century or so ago, and the Bible that we now have. That it may be regarded "as something other than Scripture" drives the choice of preposition and leads to reading the Bible as history, as morality, and as having literary value. Americans, in particular, have separated sacred and secular, many such arguments dominating the courts in the nineteenth and twentieth centuries, with the result that the Bible can be allowed in classrooms if taught from perspectives other than religious.[76] Since a "symbiotic relationship exists between the Bible and Western literature," making "sharp" distinctions between these approaches to reading the Bible may not be possible, but it should be possible to avoid forcing readers to make either/or choices, just as it should be possible to avoid using "Bible as literature" as a disguise for religion.[77] Most everyone will agree that readers have interest in the Bible and that how they read it – religious, moral, literary, historical – certainly does make a difference.[78]

Reading the Bible as literature, a preoccupation of scholars with roots in the 1800s, realized significant growth during the 1900s that continues into the current century. Matthew Arnold (1822–88) first used the phrase "the Bible as literature," but Richard Green Moulton popularized the term in *The Bible as Literature* (1896) and *A Short Introduction to the Bible as Literature* (1901).[79] Moulton argued that the Bible treated as literature has a place in liberal education.[80] When in 1984 Ryken published his *How to Read the Bible as Literature and Get More Out of It*, he talked about "a growing awareness that the Bible is a work of literature and that the methods of literary scholarship are a necessary part of any complete study of the Bible."[81] Foster Kent published his *The Songs, Hymns, and Prayers of the Old Testament* in 1914 and Laura H. Wild her *A Literary Guide to the Bible: A Study of the Types of Literature Present in the Old and New Testament* in 1922. In 1927 F. R. Webber explored symbols in the Bible, while in 1931 Charles Allen Dinsmore wrote a book on *The English Bible as Literature*.[82] Robert Alter and Frank Kermode brought rigor and seriousness to the study of the Bible as literature through their *The Literary Guide to the Bible* (1987). In 1993, Leland Ryken and Tremper Longman III published *A Complete Literary Guide to the Bible*.[83] A 1993 publication, *A History of the Bible as Literature*, by David Norton contributes significantly to understanding the many complex positions that have given rise to the idea of the Bible as literature.[84] Varsity Press published *The Dictionary of Biblical Imagery* in 1998. These important titles and historical trends point to only some of the significance of the study of the Bible as literature and make the case that study of the Bible as literature is not new.[85]

Much of what has been written about the Bible as literature takes an approach other than strictly literary. Stephen L. Harris addresses the historical and cultural environment and follows the canonical order of the Hebrew Bible.[86] J. Benton White and Walter T. Wilson, in *From Adam to Armageddon*, introduce a religious document through the religious communities that created it.[87] John B. Gabel, Charles B. Wheeler, and Anthony D. York, in *The Bible as Literature*, view the Bible as a religious document significant for the religious communities that created it and conduct a literary-historical examination as well as providing introductory chapters on the literary aspects. Robert Alter and Frank Kermode, in *The Literary Guide to the Bible*, provide a book in literary textual criticism.

*I have written this textbook with an assumption that a literary approach to the Bible rightfully should begin with reading, understanding, and assessing.[88] A literary approach invites us to pay attention to the familiar tools used in literary analysis – story, theme, genre, plot, character, setting, and point of view – and looks at form and technique. Generally, reading literature involves a holistic approach to a book that finds unity and coherence supplied by an author's voice, themes, and motifs, and an interlocking system of allusions and echoes, a common core of events and images.[89] Opposition to holistic readings emphasizing large-scale unity and coherence grew out of the scholarship, from 1900 to 1975, that moved away from arguing for the Bible as the foundation for introductory literature courses (with anthologies including selected parts of the Bible) to a focus on criticism – literary, redaction/editor, source, and form – and analysis, discovering indeterminacy, complexity, and ambiguity.[90]*

*I believe that we can still make a case that the authoritative canon, the Bible as we know it, while tortuously decided over time, evidences selection and arrangement that lend a degree of unity and coherence among its parts, books, and, indeed, to the two covenants.[91] The Bible, for example, contains repetitions and events that seem to foreshadow others and key words and themes that repeat themselves. It also appears to tell a single story: the past and the future (interpreted differently within the context of the Jewish Bible or the Christian New Testament), with human history its subject. Even when approached through several traditions of authoring and editing, the Bible still presents itself as containing unity and coherence, in degree, both within and across these traditions.[92]*

## Traditions in Biblical Interpretation

*You may be asking, "Why can't I just read the Bible? Why do I need to know anything about criticism?" Literary criticism may be called a science, though we know it as belonging to the human sciences, its conclusions based on close reading and examination of texts. Generally, criticism introduces us to a variety of techniques used to help us study the meaning of our primary text. Simply answered, we analyze the Bible to understand it, and we can learn from the work of others and what they have written about their own analyses. Furthermore, analysis will, in the end, bring readers back to putting it all together again.*

**Biblical criticism** should be understood as an umbrella term for the study and investigation of biblical writings. A critical approach to any text certainly requires careful reading and discerning and discriminating judgment.[93] Biblical criticism generally requires readers to ask questions about the origin, preservation, transmission, and message of biblical texts. Scholarship of the Bible has taken two approaches: textual criticism refers to the study and analysis of existing manuscripts to determine evidence on which to base a text and to eliminate error, while biblical, historical, and literary criticism, the second approach, investigates the date and place of a composition, its author or authors (including editors, this known as redaction criticism), and reconstructs the historical situation out of which a writing arose.[94]

Growing out of the eighteenth-century Enlightenment, much biblical criticism prides itself on striving for objectivity, presenting the Bible as a collection or anthology produced over many years by multiple authors and editors, or redactors; it looks at the Bible as the product of the human mind, and the anthology as containing texts composed over a long period, growing out of an oral tradition and multiple sources.[95] It asks how the Bible came into existence, who were its authors and what their purposes were, when the various pieces of the Bible were written, and what the social settings were.[96] An underlying assumption of this criticism suggests an evolutionary development of the Bible: from oral to written and then to collected and canonized, or authorized, as the books of the Bible.[97] It emphasizes its composite nature and the historical setting.[98]

These scholars have sometimes been criticized for engaging in intricate analysis, looking behind the final text to find earlier stages of its existence; for asking questions about the integrity, authenticity, and credibility of the texts that compose the Bible, and for continually challenging and debating each other. The criticism has been accused of circular reasoning (assuming existing hypotheses, then using these to identify origin), using arbitrary aesthetic principles (duplication, contradiction, disjunctions) to analyze sources, and leading away from the final canonical text.[99] It has also been disparaged for making reading and interpretation of the Bible the sole province of scholarship. The approach, some think, denies the Bible to individuals unequipped with an understanding of ancient languages, cultures, and sophisticated exposure to literary criticism. Opponents suggest that this criticism is overreliant upon scientific method and Enlightenment reason in its search for historical truth, excludes the contemporary milieu, and obscures the significance of the Bible for contemporary culture.[100] Considered positively, this criticism has contributed significantly to what can be learned about the formation of the Bible, its content and history, particularly when the pieces have been put together in a synthesis that brings attention back to the Bible as a whole.[101]

Critics interested in the literary aspects of biblical texts have focused on their final form as the primary object of study. A type of literary criticism, **narrative criticism**, insists on close reading and looks at the particular way a story is told in relation to complex literary structures such as plot, characterization, and closure.[102] A traditional literary reading of the Bible takes a basic approach, not ignoring the many complexities associated with the origin and composition of its books or of the Bible itself, glossing over textual problems such as duplication, omission, interpolation, or contradiction, or homogenizing the voices, styles, points of view, and messages. It considers the Bible in its current form and asks questions about the what, the how, and the correct reading of existing texts. It looks at the collection as a whole and its interwoven parts, and it points out that literary and theological continuities exist between the Old and the New Testament.[103] The direction of literary criticism generally has been away from genres and structuralism to strategies for reading and an emphasis upon stories and narrative.[104] As remarked in the Preface, the approach taken in this book invites a broad category of readers to use the common tools of literary analysis – the study of symbolic and rhetorical uses of language, themes, genres, and characters – for reading and understanding the Bible, a collection of sixty-six books, as a whole.

A literary approach can assist readers to understand the complexity involved in reading and understanding the Bible and help them resist the idea that there exists only one correct interpretation of a particular passage.[105] Interpretation of the Bible, as with all literature, requires fitting all the details together in the context of the whole to suggest meaning; in the end, an argument can be made for the most economical explanation, the one that appears to add least to the text.[106]

## Culture and Religion in Ancient Israel and the Jewish World View

*Any study of the Bible raises questions about the people, their physical world, and their history. In this section, I provide an abbreviated, condensed sketch of the culture and religion of the ancient Israelites. I introduce briefly their origins, migrations, and development into a nation, and their subsequent defeat by other nations. Generally, biblical history can be divided into four periods: the Patriarchs; Settlement in the land of Canaan; the Monarchy; and Post-Exile and Intertestamental/ New Testament.[107] An important contribution of this ancient people is the monotheism (by some accounts, overworked) that has provided the foundation for the Jewish, Christian, and Islamic religions.*

Genesis, the first book of the Bible, generally has been described as containing two main sections: primeval history (1–11.26) presented in four main events: the creation of the universe and humankind, exile from Eden, a universal flood, and a scattered people; and patriarchal history (11.127–50) presented through Abraham, Isaac, Jacob, and Joseph.[108] The earlier section presents original human beings who choose quickly the path of procreation and mortality.[109] They face the inevitable dangers of extinction – this presented in the flood story and in their becoming a scattered people. The second section begins the cultivation of a family who will become Israel. These ancestors migrate to Egypt and become numerous enough to cause concern; they leave Egypt, travel through the wilderness, and eventually enter Canaan, where they settle according to tribal allotments. A herding and farming people, they are ruled by non-royal leaders until the monarchy (1000 BCE). The development of these people can be traced structurally through events surrounding the First and Second Temple.[110]

Isaiah describes Abraham, the father and founder of the Hebrew nation, as redeemed by God (Isa. 29.22), a description that opens up, for some, the intriguing possibility that Abraham, called by God to leave his country (in a timeframe of 2100–1500 BCE) and take up residence in Canaan, may have left Mesopotamian society because it had reached a spiritual impasse.[111] That view gives Abraham historical reality and sees his departure from Mesopotamia as one from a polytheistic religion followed by a journey to monotheism.[112] Others see polytheistic religions as already evidencing a complex sense of a transcendent God and a universal and inclusive monotheism.[113]

From Mesopotamia, Abraham brought with him regard for the limitless sky and its recurring drama. He also brought with him the Sumerian cosmology that viewed the earth as "a flat circle attached at its perimeter to the dome of heaven." In the air, between heaven and earth, hung the moon and sun, visible to humans and predictive of life on earth; "below the circle of earth lies the realm of Death, a sort of basement to the sea of chaos that surrounds the earth and heaven on all sides."[114] In the primitive mind, the sun and moon were gods and the earth was thought of as mother. Air was mediator between heaven and earth, and the most important god; the sea was unpredictable and challenging. Everything was cyclic – the phases of the moon, the changing seasons, the cycle of a woman's body, the cycle of birth, sex, and death. Abraham responded to this same cosmology, but the developing religion is clearly monotheistic. A sovereign God creates in an orderly, linear, and purposeful way; the sun, moon, and sea are all physical objects rather than gods.[115] Humankind bears the image of its Creator and has a clear destiny. The Bible provides a connected sequence of episodes and stories that present the traditions of these people uniquely in relationship to God.[116]

Canaan, the land the Israelites possessed, lies between the eastern end of the Mediterranean Sea and the inland deserts, an area approximately 150 miles long and 70 miles wide; in the second century CE it was renamed Palestine by the Roman Hadrian.[117] As far back as the third millennium BCE, Canaan was known as a geographical designation. Its landscape varies. The western region, a coastal plain, 20 to 30 miles wide, provided the chief route to Egypt; inland, a limestone region less fertile than the plain runs north–south, extending from Beersheba in the south to the Lebanon mountains in the north, and broken in the north by the Plain of Megiddo; between the mountains and the Transjordan east, the Great Rift Valley runs from north to south, providing the channel for the Jordan River, which flows 65 miles south to empty into the Dead Sea, a salt lake 1290 feet below sea level; east of the Jordan, the Transjordan is a mountainous terrain cut by deep canyons, averaging about 1500 feet above sea level. Radical differences among the four areas in which the people lived isolated them from adjacent lands. Occupations included farmer, shepherd, and commercial city dweller. Archaeologists have confirmed a resettling of the land in the Iron Age, beginning about 1200 BCE.

*As I mentioned in the lead-in to this section, biblical history can be divided into four broad periods: the Patriarchs, Settlement in the land of Canaan, the Monarchy, and Post-Exile and Intertestamental/New Testament). Briefly, the Babylonian exile ended in 539 BCE when the Persian Cyrus (Babylonia fell to the Persians that year) allowed the captive people to return to their homeland and to rebuild the walls of Jerusalem and construct a new temple – this completed in 515 BCE.*

*Several points should be made about this sketch of culture and religion in the ancient world and its relationship to the New Testament which builds upon this foundation. First, Palestine was transformed in many ways by the Persians, the Greeks (Alexander the Great in 336–323 BCE), and the Romans (150 BCE to 150 CE). A certain continuity of Jewish belief and worship continued, although it was impacted by syncretistic influences of these contributing civilizations. Without the apocryphal books, a gap of 400 "silent" years exists between the ending of the Old Testament and the beginning of the New Testament. This is the Intertestamental period.*

*During this time, dramatic and sweeping changes were occurring. This is the time of the Ptolemies, who ruled over Egypt (323 to 30 BCE) and the Seleucids (referencing the time when Seleucus, one of the sub-commanders under Ptolemy, captured Babylon in 311 BCE and set himself up as a sovereign independent of Ptolemy). Both the Ptolemies and the Seleucids began with generals of Alexander (who died in 323 BCE). Around 170 BCE, the actions of Antiochus IV Epiphanes contributed to the Maccabean revolt in 167 BCE. The names of important leaders include the priest Mattathias of the house of Hasmon and his five sons, "Maccabean," meaning "hammer," a title given to the oldest son of Mattathias. A short-lived independent Jewish state resulted from this rebellion, which ended when the Roman general Pompey succeeded in adding Judea to the Roman province of Syria. During Hasmonean rule, the titles of both priest and king were contested, and groups known in the New Testament as Pharisees and Sadducees questioned leaders' claims to the office of high priest. The Herods, familiar in the Gospels, emerged as a result of Roman civil war. The fall of Jerusalem and the destruction of the Temple in 70 CE ended the priesthood.*

## Close Reading

*To complete the following exercises, you will need to reference a web page constructed to supplement this book; the tables below will be found at www.readingthebibleasliterature.com.*

*Exercise 1*
Using an idiomatic translation of Genesis 4 (for example, the *Living Bible* or *Today's English Version*) and a literal translation (NRSV), what characteristics mainly distinguish the two?

*Exercise 2*
Explain how the Old Testament follows a pattern of unfulfilled promise.

*Exercise 3*
Read Isaiah 53 without imposing a New Testament context. How does the meaning change?

*Exercise 4*
Explain how the apocryphal books complete the 400-year gap between the Old Testament and the New Testament.

*Exercise 5*
Scan Genesis. Identify each event on a continuum from nonhistory/prehistory to history, explaining your choices.

*Exercise 6*
Explain how different languages, laws, political structures, social classes, and groups in the two Temple periods contributed to a different understanding of how God was dealing with Israel.

*Exercise 7*
Read at least one apocryphal book and explain what differences you find between it and books in the Old and New Testament with which you are familiar.

## Questions for Reflection

1 What is "the Bible"?
2 How do New Testament writers identify quotes or paraphrases from the Old Testament?
3 What connotations render BC and AD or BCE and CE preferable in specific contexts?
4 What is supersessionism, and why should it be avoided in discussions about the Old and New Testaments?
5 What attitudes in reading literature generally should be taken to reading the Bible as literature?
6 What literary principles hold parts of the Bible together?
7 What is meant by intertextuality?

8  How does typology connect (or does it?) the events and persons of the Old Testament to those in the New Testament?

9  What distinguishes formulaic and composite quotations?

10  What is meant by the "backward way" of reading the New Testament?

11  What is meant by macro-plot?

12  What distinguishes story and narrative?

13  How does "the Bible as literature" differ from "the Bible in literature" and the "literature of the Bible"?

14  How is it that the Bible can be described as an "anthology" of ancient texts?

15  How does reading the Bible "as literature" introduce an apologetic in approach?

16  What primary directions have been taken in textbooks on teaching the Bible as literature?

17  What arguments exist for making reading the appropriate emphasis in introductory literature courses?

18  What is meant by "biblical criticism"?

19  What is the relationship between "lower" and "higher" criticism?

20  What is redaction criticism?

21  What are some of the major types of literary criticism?

22  What primary objections have been raised to "biblical criticism"?

23  Why is it important to read the Bible in the context of its own history and culture rather than our own?

24  What significant differences exist between concepts of time in the biblical and the modern world?

25  What are the two covenants and how should they be viewed in relation to each other?

# 2 Style, Tone, and Rhetorical Strategy: A Way of Using Language

## Outline

Preliminary Considerations
   Style, Tone, and Strategy
   Translation
Comparison, Association, and Arrangement of Words
   Comparison and Association
   Arrangement of Words
A Sampling of Rhetorical Devices
   Simile and Metaphor
   Personification, Metonymy, and Synecdoche
   Anthropomorphism and Zoomorphism
   Merism and Oxymoron
   Quotation, Allusion, and Foreshadowing
   Irony, Rhetorical Question, Amplification, and Euphemism
   Repetition, Recursion, Inclusio, and Chiasm
   Signs and Visions
   Close Reading
   Questions for Reflection

*In early writing classes, you will commonly encounter rhetorical devices in an alphabetical list, with definitions, and be told that using these will help you to improve the effectiveness, clarity, and enjoyability of your writing. They have a practical nature that suggests they can be mastered with lots of use and practice. My reason for introducing style, tone, and rhetorical strategy early in this book is that they play a significant role in your being able to read and understand the Bible. I want this text to introduce the Bible as being extremely rich in its extensive use of rhetorical devices. Studying these, you will learn quickly that the Bible is about more than theology and doctrine and that it is not reducible to science, natural science, or history.*

*About definitions . . . since Aristotle, "defining" has been explained as a process that determines what necessary and sufficient conditions (essence) make an object to be a particular kind of thing.[1] Correct definition, the identity of "kind," involves putting things into categories and organizing categories, and this then becomes critical to how we know anything. A complication arises in understanding "essence situated" – whether in the mind or in the world, and what, thus, constitutes "real." Beginning a chapter on the Bible as literature with definitions of rhetorical devices means using the common-sense notion that kinds of rhetorical devices can be recognized and defined and that doing so helps us understand literature.*

## Preliminary Considerations

Remarkably, the Bible, given its complicated composition history, multiple authors, and many translations, presents itself as a whole, creating in its readers a sense of its style(s). It requires a hermeneutics in which its meaning must be discovered in its most minute part, while, at the same time, attention must be paid to its meaning as a whole. It has been described as being on a continuum that runs from understanding it as a disparate collection of original texts in various languages, without a single author, to, at the other extreme, a harmonious and unified whole, sometimes thought to be authored by the Holy Spirit.[2] In this same vein, one of the experts on the use of figures in the Bible says that figurative language in the Bible provides the "Holy Spirit's own markings."[3] The other position counters that such views are reductionist and that they oversimplify complex interpretive traditions.

*Earlier I said that the Bible is about more than theology, but I probably also need to tell you that theology and literature share a sense of the power of language to talk about realities. The Bible, for example, talks about heaven (ascended to) and Sheol, a Hebrew word translated in the KJV as Hell and in other translations as "the place of the dead" (descended to). Literature, more generally, talks about the place of human beings in the universe, their sense of inclusion or exclusion, their mythologies of ascent and descent, and the way mythologies and metaphorical language provide a counter-balance to the historical and scientific.[4]*

### Style, Tone, and Strategy

Style, tone, and strategy, closely related concepts, give additional force, life, intensified feeling, and greater emphasis to the manifold forms, words, and sentences in the Bible.[5] **Style**, derived from the Latin word for a tool used for writing (*stilus*), refers to how something is written, to the mode of expression, or to the author's choice and arrangement of words and phrases into sentences and paragraphs. **Tone**, similar to mood or emotion, names and describes the manner in which an author expresses attitude, the intonation of the voice that expresses meaning. The tone can be, for example, solemn, serious, objective, ironic, humorous, sarcastic, or tongue in cheek. **Rhetorical strategies** manage language to achieve specific effects. Narrowly interpreted, rhetoric means persuasive speech; more broadly, it includes the use of cultural conventions and expectations (ways of thinking, writing, and speaking) and the manipulation of these to achieve effects. Rhetoric defines "**schema**" (Greek) as a deviation from the ordinary pattern or arrangement of words and uses "**trope**" to refer to a rhetorical figure of speech that deviates from the ordinary pattern or signification of a word (thought). A "**figurative**" (from the Latin *figura*) use of language departs in either thought or expression from the ordinary and simple method of speaking. The Bible, though grounded in concrete images, uses figurative or rhetorical devices liberally.

## Translation

Readers of the Bible rely upon those who know the original Hebrew and Greek languages to construct appropriate translations. The work of translation requires a macroscopic view of the whole and a microscopic attention to words, sentences, and paragraphs, the building blocks of style. Literal Bible translations, such as the King James Version, tend to translate idioms or figurative language word for word. For example, the NRSV translates 2 Peter 1.13, 14, from the Greek as "I think it right, as long as I am in this body, to refresh your memory, since I know that my death will come soon . . .," adding a note that body refers to "tent," while the KJV retains the figurative "tent" and describes death as "putting off the tent." Beauty and suggestion exist in the KJV that the NRSV does not capture. "If any book requires special attention to style when translated, then surely, it is the Bible."[6]

*Looking at the Bible as literature does not mean overlooking its own distinctive characteristics. The first overall notable feature is that the Bible uses narrative or storytelling with the advantage that it draws readers into the events, characters, and stories to experience them rather than be told about them. The Bible expresses itself in "extraordinary concreteness," as opposed to abstract and propositional thought, many of its images rooted in the human body or, more generally, within human experience.[7] It uses a formal literary language, only occasionally deviating into slang, dialect, or idiolect, suggesting you should pay particular attention when this occurs (consider Gen. 25, where Esau "gulps" the "red stuff" like an animal). The Bible employs a "limited vocabulary" which gives to it a sense of overall simplicity, but it also chooses these words with the "nuanced" precision of artistic expression.*

*Another prominent characteristic of the Bible is "**parataxis**," or the use of parallel clauses linked by "and." This contributes overall to the "additive" nature in the way its content is presented. This additive nature carries over into the linkage of ever greater parts within the Bible so that discrete or micro-events occur in series linked together into chains of like words, actions, and stories. As part of the linkage, the Bible throughout presents its stories as episodes, part of but distinct from a greater whole, such that it has been a general practice to pull out different parts as stories and episodes and to look at them individually. The Bible's narrative prose, however, almost always reads as part of a sequence, a link in a chain.[8] The thrust of this text will be to put stories back into the greater* *whole, a direction taken up in the chapters on genres. This chapter looks more minutely at the rhetorical devices common to literature generally and found throughout the Bible, which, if recognized, can lead to more informed reading and understanding of its content.*

## Comparison, Association, and Arrangement of Words

*I have put only a few rhetorical devices in the next paragraphs into bold text because my purpose here is to present two basic processes out of which these devices originate. The first is the use of comparison and association; the second is the arrangement of words. I have also given you examples to stimulate your thinking about how often the Bible uses rhetorical devices.*

### Comparison and Association

Rhetorical devices occur so frequently in the Bible that ignoring them means not using the literary tools readily available for understanding it.[9] These grow out of, at a basic level, comparison and association. Comparison includes simile, metaphor, **implication** (this last without the "like" or "as" of simile, and without the verb of metaphor), parable, allegory, vision, sign, type, shadow, example, image (discussed in the next chapter), impersonation (or **personification**), and **condescension** (used when God is spoken of as a human being). The Bible further incorporates hundreds of associations, related to **metonymy**, where one noun becomes associated with another and meaning derives from the association produced in the reader's mind, such as in the "death, body of" (Rom. 7.24) and the following examples: deception, spirit of (1 John 4.6); freedom, law of (James 1.25, 2.12); fury, wine of (Rev. 18.3); gloom, caverns of (2 Pet. 2.4); promise, children of (Rom. 9.8; Gal. 4.28); revelation, spirit of (Eph. 1.17); salvation, day of (2 Cor. 6.2, 2); injustice, wages of (2 Pet. 2.15); life, tree of (Rev. 2.7, 22.2, 14, 19); mercy, vessels of (Rom. 9.23); peace, gospel of (Eph. 6.15); peace, God of (Rom. 15.33, 16.20; 2 Cor. 13.11; Phil. 4.9; 1 Thess. 5.23; Heb. 13.20).

Association includes **appellation**, using a quality, office, or attribute for a proper noun, such as when God is spoken of as "the Majesty" (Heb. 1.3), when John the Baptist is called Elijah, because he came in his spirit and power (Matt. 17.12; Luke 1.17), and when Jesus is referred to as Lord, Teacher, Rabbi, Son of Mankind, Prophet, Christ, Lord, and so forth.

Another common device, **circumlocution**, uses a descriptive phrase in place of a name in order to emphasize the association: born of woman (human) (Matt. 11.11; Luke 7.28); the product of the grapevine (wine) (Matt. 26.29); the city of David (Bethlehem) (Luke 2.11); those sitting on the surface of the entire earth (humanity) (Luke 21.35); terrestrial tabernacle house (body) (2 Cor. 5.1); those about to be enjoying the allotment of salvation (the saved) (Heb. 1.14); in this tabernacle (alive) (2 Pet. 1.13); my tabernacle is to be put off (I am to die) (2 Pet. 1.14); He Who is sitting on the throne (the Deity) (Rev. 4.2, 10, 5.1, 7).

## *Arrangement of Words*

Other recognizable figurative uses of language come from the arrangement of words: omissions, additions, parallelism, prominence, and reversal; the repetition of words, ideas, sounds, and word-play. **Variance** deviates in meaning from what is literally said and includes **irony** (meaning just the opposite of what is intended, as in calling Christ "king" while he is being crucified); **double meaning** (a statement that is literally and figuratively true) underlies a statement such as "one should die for the sake of the people" (John 11.50); **belittlement** (the use of a weak term to express a contrary fact) occurs in "Bethlehem in no respect least" (Matt. 2.6); and **incongruity** (statements incorrect when taken literally) can be seen in "fruit of the lips" (Heb. 13.15).

## A Sampling of Rhetorical Devices

*In this section, I introduce simile and metaphor briefly in their role of making explicit and implicit comparisons; I will return to metaphor more broadly in the next chapter. You will recognize immediately the role metaphor and simile play in helping you imaginatively to see, hear, taste, touch, and feel, thus contributing vividness to the act of reading.*

*Of course, all rhetorical devices give additional force, more life, intensified feeling, and greater emphasis to what we read. If we remember that language itself consists of symbols, we should understand that figurative language expands and adds layers of meaning to what we read. This means, too, that we will not always agree in our interpretations of literary writing intended to invoke or provoke a subjective response in the reader. All language has magic, but literature makes a special use of language to arrest, preserve, and allow readers to re-experience life in all its varied forms.*

## *Simile and Metaphor*

The importance of paying special attention to style in the Bible can be illustrated in the distinction between **metaphor** and **simile**, figures of speech respectively defined as implied comparison using "is" and explicit comparison using "like" or "as." Familiar similes in the Bible compare mortal life to grass: "All flesh is like grass" (1 Pet. 1.24) and to trees: "He shall be like a tree planted by rivers of waters" (Ps. 1.3). A metaphorical, implied comparison, easily recognized, says, "The LORD God is a sun and a shield" (Ps. 84.12). For interpretation, stating that one thing "is like" or resembles another differs substantially from saying that one thing "is" or represents the other.[10] The familiar metaphor "The LORD is my Shepherd" links two unrelated nouns – "Lord" and "Shepherd" – these coming together in some point in which they agree. Language and metaphor, in particular, have important implications for theology.[11] "This [bread] is my body" (Matt. 26.26) links two distinct things, "bread" and "body," both of which must be taken absolutely literally as two things in which the meaning of one carries across and transfers to the other as representation.[12]

Readers will encounter in the first two chapters of Genesis a metaphorical use of language that speaks to the very heart of the Hebrew understanding of the relation between heaven and earth, God and man. The first account makes use of metaphors: God is Creator (craftsman) and humankind is a creation or created object.[13] The "Creator," by definition, has power and authority over the object of creation, and the "created," by definition, is dependent upon the artisan. By the same account, humans made in the image or with the likeness of God (1.26, 27) stand erect as a special order of creation in relation to other creatures (fish, birds, cattle, wild animals, creeping things). The fact that the Creator speaks creation into existence suggests an ordering principle in language and a connection between God above and human beings below.

In the second account, God forms human beings from the dust of the earth, the metaphor still being that God is Creator (potter) and human beings are clay, formed, shaped, and given life by the breath of God, where breath is soul and life. In this account, Adam, not a proper noun but a reference to the earthly origin of the created, names the other creatures (2.19), demonstrating that humans share language as an ordering principle. In fact, the metaphor of "language is creation" runs throughout Genesis, creating a tension between the creative acts of human beings and the creative act of God. It should not surprise readers to hear Eve in Genesis 3 use language to interpolate the specific command given by God not to eat of the tree of knowledge of good and evil; she adds that God has said they should not touch it.

*I have used simile and metaphor, figurative language with which you are already familiar, to suggest how paying attention to detail may enhance your reading and understanding of the Bible. You will discover that the Bible, from Genesis to Revelation, makes extensive use of figurative language that appeals to the imagination; using comparison, the imagination adds surprise, force, and beauty to the ordinary. You must, of course, begin with the literal meaning of a word, usually one meaning and constant; the figurative departs from this meaning and introduces diversity and variability. To say figuratively that "God is light" does not state a literal fact; rather, in the infinite realm, God compares, in some ways, to physical light in the existing finite world.[14] The law of comparison means that two objects must be unlike in the main but similar in one or more particulars.[15] In the next chapter, I extend our discussion of imagery and return to simile and metaphor as imaging devices and to a broader discussion of archetype and the universal patterns of human experience.*

### Personification, Metonymy, and Synecdoche

The Bible contains multiple examples of **personification**, where things are represented or spoken of as persons. The book of Job provides an example of the personification of an ear and an eye. Job, speaking in soliloquy, recalls the good old days and laments his current condition of having lost everything except his flesh, with even this inflamed by open sores from head to foot. When he was in his prime, the decision-makers of society respected him: "The ear that heard me acclaimed me; the eye that saw, commended me" (9.11). This is more than **metonymy**, or using the ear and eye to represent anyone who uses the ear to hear or the eye to see; here, the ear hears like a human being and the eye sees. The use of breath to represent life in Genesis 2 is a metonym, breath standing in for life. Psalms 5.9 makes use of metonymy when it says "their throats are open graves." Here, throat stands for the thing affected by it, speech. Isaiah 55.12 personifies mountains and hills when the writer says they will burst into song and that trees will clap their hands. In **synecdoche**, a whole or totality is represented by naming a part. Psalms 35.10 introduces a synecdoche in which all the bones speak for the person: "All my bones shall say, 'O LORD, who is like you?'" Genesis 6.12 uses synecdoche when it says "all flesh had corrupted its ways upon the earth" – flesh associated with people.

*In the next section, I address a figure of speech wherein God is given the characteristics of human beings; a reverse process occurs when human beings give themselves the characteristics of God. In Genesis 3.22, after the original human beings had eaten from the tree of knowledge of good and evil, God uses a simile: "See the man has become like one of us; and now, he might reach out his hand and take also from the tree of life, and eat, and live forever." To prevent this, God sends them out of Eden. The Bible repeatedly develops the motif of human aspiration to move into the role of maker (if confined to the earth), with this creativity potentially capable of setting itself up as a rival to the Maker (God).*

*You may have read or heard at some point of the philosopher Nietzsche's Zarathustra, who teaches that the once greatest blasphemy (against God) ended when God and the blasphemers died. Zarathustra counsels human beings to stay true to the earth, discarding super-earthly hope. He urges them to dare to become the Superman ("Zarathustra's Prologue and Zarathustra's Discourses"). It would be a wrong interpretation to say that Nietzsche encourages human beings to become God, not when he stresses giving up even the hope of such an extra-earthly Being or Reality. I believe, however, the concept of Superman does illustrate the potential for moving in the direction of making a god of human beings. Traditional Judaism certainly teaches against human beings competing with the creative power of God.*

## Anthropomorphism and Zoomorphism

The Bible throughout uses the figurative device of **anthropomorphism** to attribute many of the characteristics of human beings to God. For example, consider the following: God is given a soul (Lam. 3.20), a body and head (1 Cor. 11.3), a face (Ps. 16.11), eyes (Zech. 2.8), ears (Ps. 31.2), nostrils (Job 4.9; Exod. 15.8), a mouth, lips, and tongue (Num. 7.8; Job 11.5; Isa. 30.27), a voice (Isa. 30.30), arms (Ezek. 15.16; Job 40.9), hands (Job 10.8), a finger (Exod. 8.19), a heart (Jer. 19.5, 6; 1 Sam. 13.14), bowels (Isa. 43.15; Luke 1.78), a bosom (John 1.18), and feet (Isa. 60.13). God is further granted all the attributes of humankind – rejoicing (Ps. 104.31), repentance (Gen. 6.6), jealousy (Exod. 20.5), zeal (Isa. 9.7), displeasure (Zech. 1.15), pity (Joel 2.18), remembrance (Exod. 2.24; 1 Sam. 1.19; Pss. 78.39, 103.14), thought (Pss. 92.5, 6, 139.17; Jer. 29.11), breath (Gen. 2.7), laughter (Ps. 2.4), speech (Gen. 1.1; John 1.1); and God acts like human beings: sitting (Mal. 3.3), seeing (Ps. 11.4), hearing (Gen. 16.11; 1 John 5.14), smelling (Gen. 8.21; Phil. 4.18), tasting and touching (Hos. 4.4; John 4.32, 34), walking (Deut. 23.14, 15), riding (Isa. 19.1), and so on. Genesis explains that God created human beings in his image (Gen. 1.26). Imitating God figures importantly in Jewish faith, just as imitating Christ plays a central role for Christians.[16]

Reversing the biblical description of "humans created in the image of God," thinkers through the ages have claimed that "all gods are projections of the human personality": God → image → people: people → image → God. The Bible returns constantly to a motif of human beings as users of language and creators aspiring to become Creator. The Tower of Babel story illustrates this in the Old Testament and the Day of Pentecost returns to it in Acts 2.

A closely related figure of speech, **zoomorphism**, attributes the features of an animal to a different species. The Psalmist says, for example, "In the shadow of your wings I used to rejoice" (Ps. 63.8). Applied differently, "If I take the wings of the dawn, and settle in the remotest part of the sea" (139.9) compares the rays of the sun to the wings of a bird and makes the point that God is always present.

*Understanding figurative language can help you not to misread the Bible. The next figurative devices illustrate the importance of close reading. I will give you several examples of the figurative use of merism, beginning with early ones in Genesis. It may take practice for you to recognize merism (ideas expressed together to suggest greater wisdom) and oxymoron (the pairing of contradictory words such as "eloquent silence" and "cold fire").*

## Merism and Oxymoron (Gen. 1, 2)

"**Merism**" is a special use of synecdoche which uses the word "and" to join together contrasting parts to express totality. Close reading will enable you to find this figure of speech throughout the Bible. Genesis

1.1 says God made heaven and earth – polar opposites. The totality expressed is that God made everything that was made, the entire world. How important is it not to read this figure of speech literally? When Genesis refers to knowledge of good and evil (literally, bad), "evil" should not be taken to connote immorality.[17] Rather, recognizing the use of merism, the reader should interpret this to mean "everything" or "the ultimate." Furthermore, in Hebrew, "knowledge" literally means "intimacy" or "sexuality," not intellectual or ethical knowing. Recognizing the figure of speech and using a good Bible translation helps readers understand the linkage between sexuality (procreation) and the aspiration to divinity or immortality, perhaps the real reason the original humans were sent out of Eden.

Old Testament poetry uses merisms extensively. These include light (day) and darkness (night), and the "greater" and "lesser" lights of Genesis 1; life and death, beginning and end, and even, perhaps, heaven and hell. Man and beast (Ps. 36.6) refers to all living creatures; "as far as the east is from the west" (Ps. 103.12) expresses absence of boundaries; and the concept of God knows "my downsitting and mine uprising" (Ps. 139) means God knows everything about me. Deuteronomy (6.7) uses merism in the expression "when you lie down to rest and when you get up" to express the idea that we are to meditate continually. Job 11.6 employs it to express vertical and horizontal totality in the heights of heaven and depths of the underworld. Another merism suggests itself in the question from God "Who is this that darkens counsel by words without knowledge?" (Job 38.1); another occurs in yet another question, "Where is the way to the dwelling of light, and where is the place of darkness?" (38.19). Jeremiah (7.20) uses the tree of the field and the fruit of the soil to express the totality of the cultivated and the uncultivated. Ezekiel (17.24) employs the green tree and the dry tree to refer to all of nature.

The New Testament also uses this particular figure of speech, often with implication for theology. Consider Matthew (5.17–19):

> Do not think that I have come to abolish the law or the prophets; I have come not to abolish but to fulfill. For truly I tell you, until heaven and earth pass away, not one letter, not one stroke of a letter, will pass from the law until all is accomplished. Therefore, whoever breaks one of the least of these commandments, and teaches others to do the same, will be called least in the kingdom of heaven; but whoever does them and teaches them will be called great in the kingdom of heaven.

Here, merisms appear in "not to abolish" but "to fulfill," in "heaven" and "earth" and, interestingly, in "law" and "accomplished," and, finally, in "least" and "great." Together, these suggest all is being "fulfilled" or "summed up." Ephesians (3.18) pairs opposites in "breadth and length" and "height and depth." Another use of this figurative expression occurs theologically in Ephesians 2.13–17, where the writer picks up "near and far," "creating one new humanity," and "putting to death hostility" to express that humanity is one rather than two (Jew and Christian). Revelation describes Christ as the mediator of peace between two groups. It may very well be that the Bible, as organized, functions as a merism, beginning in Genesis with Eden lost and ending in Revelation with the "New Jerusalem" gained, these two referring to the entirety of human history and representing the "Alpha and Omega" (Rev. 21.6) of God's sovereignty. Revelation 11.17 extends merism to the triadic "one who is, was, and is coming." Finally, while it may be to stretch a point, it might be said that the "Old Testament" and the "New Testament" form a merism that represents all of God's word and the "Bible" as totality.

**Oxymoron** comes from combining two Greek words meaning "sharp" and "dull." It refers to a locution that produces an incongruous, seemingly self-contradictory effect and can be recognized in putting together contrasting words or ideas. The device can be used to show that something normally foolish can, upon consideration, be exceedingly wise. God's wisdom through the ages has been esteemed as foolish by humankind but turns out to be wise beyond human comprehension.

The Bible has much to say about false wisdom and wise folly. Jeremiah sets before human beings a choice between two ways: "And to this people you shall say: Thus says the LORD: See, I am setting before you the way of life and the way of death." Proverbs 14.12 warns that "There is a way that seems right to a man, but in the end it leads to death." Matthew 16.25 says, "Those who want to save their life will lose it, and those who lose their life for my sake will find it." This would appear to be extreme foolishness: to save your life, you must be willing to lose it! That the Bible works on two levels at once, material and spiritual, helps to reveal the wisdom here: one must be willing to lose physical life in order to gain spiritual life. The **undisputed letter of Paul** (1 Corinthians 1.25) puts together contrasting ideas for special effect: "For the foolishness of God is wiser than man's wisdom, and the weakness of God is stronger than man's strength." Another undisputed letter, 2 Corinthians, more directly illustrates contradiction: "When I am weak, then am I strong." Other than oxymoron, differences noted in the description of Paul may result in varying assessments: in the pastoral 1 Timothy 1.15, 16, the writer describes Paul as "the chief of sinners"; in Ephesians 3.8, the writer says Paul is "the least of all saints"; yet, in 2 Corinthians, Paul describes himself as not behind the chief of apostles.

*In reading the Bible, you will want to pay attention to speeches (what characters say) and to narrative reports (what others report people as having said). Such quotations serve the purpose of helping represent people's thinking and acting. It should not come as a surprise to find the New Testament quoting frequently from the Old Testament. The Bible uses allusions and foreshadowing for "looking back" to the past and for "looking forward" to the future. Thus, the New Testament alludes to the Old (but the Old Testament also alludes to itself at many points throughout); Christians have interpreted the Old Testament as looking forward to the New Testament.*

### Quotation, Allusion, and Foreshadowing (Heb. 1; Gen. 18.16–33)

The New Testament has been explained by some as reinterpreting the Old Testament to portray Christ as its fulfillment.[18] However one reacts to this statement, the New Testament clearly quotes the Old Testament frequently, with chapter and verse divisions, enabling an easy cross-referencing of materials quoted or alluded to – for example, Matthew 3.3, Isaiah 40.3, John 12.34, Psalms 89.36, Acts 2.19–20, Joel 2.30–1, and so forth.[19] Quotations sometimes repeat directly word for word; at other times, composites (made up of different parts) join into one passage, and elsewhere the quotations **allude** to or make only a brief reference to material. With allusions added to the number of quotations, references in the New Testament to the Old Testament climb even higher. Revelation alone, for example, has been described as making more than 350 allusions to the Old Testament.[20]

These references create an interlocking set of events, images, and doctrines that contribute to the idea that Bible has unity and coherence.[21] Consider how John 12.38 quotes Isaiah 53.1, making a compelling case for the connection of the "Suffering Servant" of Isaiah and the life of Jesus, particularly the suffering on the cross. Or, again, recall how the Gospel (John 19.37) quotes Zechariah directly: "They shall look on him whom they pierced (12.10). Matthew (2.13–15) quotes Hosea (11.1) to link historical Israel to Jesus as the head of "New Israel." Sometimes, the linkage comes through events. The feeding of the 5,000 in John (chapter 6) alludes to the feeding by manna in the wilderness.

The power of allusion exists in its being able to use a few words, to echo a theme or motif, to stimulate the mind to understand a greater meaning; indispensable to literature and remarkably dense in its presence in the Bible, it activates one text by another.[22] For example, consider how Moses in the ark of reeds (Exod. 2.3) recalls Noah in the ark (Gen. 7). Or, again, consider the two hospitality stories of Lot in Sodom (Gen. 19) and the concubine in Judges 19. In both cases, strangers are taken into hospitality; the populace wants to rape them, and the host offers women instead. Since allusion presupposes the temporal priority of one text to another, the question naturally arises relative to the dating of texts. The Judges account would seem to come later, since it elaborates on the language in Genesis and actually makes the moral judgment more explicit. There would seem to be evolution and a suggestion that humankind could return to the morally depraved state of the people of Sodom.

Hebrews in the New Testament, although attributed to Paul, was probably composed after 60 CE and before 95 CE and clearly reflects a Christian commitment. The book illustrates how meaning can be expanded through an intricately connected and skillfully created set of quotations and allusions. It makes three theological points: Jesus Christ, as superior to the prophets, to the angels, and to Moses; Christ's priesthood, as superior to the Levitical priesthood; and Christ's sacrifice, as superior to those offered by the Levitical priests.[23] The first chapter provides an example of the style of the book. The author skillfully sets up a series of contrasts between "long ago" and "in these last days," our ancestors and us, the prophets and the Son, and the same God speaking then and now.

**Foreshadowing** advances plot by providing subtle hints about developments that will come later in a story. The hints expand the meaning of one text into that of another. Done in reverse, this amounts to reinterpretation. Hebrews, written as Christological reflection, reinterprets the earlier earthly priests who "offer worship in a sanctuary that is only a shadow of the heavenly one" (8.5) as foreshadowing a superior "high priest, one who is seated at the right hand of the throne of the Majesty in the heavens [Jesus]" (8.1). The writer refers to older priestly rites as "sketches of heavenly things" (9.23) and to the Old Testament law as "only a shadow of the good things to come and not the true form of these realities" (10.1). The writer advances the notion of Christ as "the culmination of the tradition of Israel" by having him say, "See, God, I have come to do your will, O God (in the scroll of the book it is written of me)" (10.7), quoting Psalm 40.6–8. In the Old Testament, repeated occurrences have sometimes been interpreted as foreshadowing.[24] Abraham and Joseph both go to Egypt as the result of a famine (Gen. 12, 41); in both cases, the Pharaoh is struck with disease or plague such that he urges the Hebrews to be taken away; in both cases, Abraham and Joseph leave Egypt with much material wealth to return to their own land and to worship God.

*You will need to read the Bible with an eye to its potential for being misread and misinterpreted. You may find yourself asking whether God (as well as prophets, priests, and kings) means what he says. What happens, for example, if you ask whether God really meant that the first couple should not eat of the tree of knowledge of good and bad. Does Job really mean it when he tells his friends that wisdom will die with them? Did Jesus really mean it when he said he came not to call the righteous but sinners to repentance? Did the writers of the ascription set up over the head of Jesus at the cross really mean "This is Jesus, the King of the Jews"?*

## Irony, Rhetorical Question, Amplification, and Euphemism

*Irony (Gen. 22; Heb. 11; Job 11, 12; Matt. 27.37; Mark 15.26; Luke 23.38; John 19.19; 2 Sam. 6.20; Amos 4.4; Matt. 22.16)*
**Irony** uses words to suggest the opposite of their literal meaning; dramatic irony exists when others know what the characters do not know.

The near sacrifice of Isaac by Abraham begins with the important words "God tested Abraham" (Gen. 22.1). When God tells Abraham to sacrifice Isaac, the reader knows, as Abraham does not, that God is testing him to see whether he will conform to God's will. Furthermore, Abraham knows what Isaac does not: that Isaac is the intended sacrifice. The **irony** of the near sacrifice of Isaac includes Abraham's failure to recognize that God never intends that he should sacrifice Isaac.

Abraham may be forgiven for acting quickly on what he thinks is divine command: "Take your son, your only son, whom you love, and go to the land of Moriah, and offer him there as a burnt offering . . ." (22.2). For Abraham, God's word was not a laughing matter; it was meant to be acted upon, and he could not test God: he could not say, OK, I will sacrifice Isaac in order to see if you will raise him from the dead in order to fulfill your promise that he will become a great nation. After all, when Sarah was told that she would have a son in her old age, she had laughed. Abraham remembers God's asking him, "Why did Sarah laugh? . . . Is anything too wonderful for the LORD?" He remembers that Sarah, being afraid, had denied the laughter and that God had replied, "Oh yes, you did laugh." Hebrews 17 says, "By faith Abraham, when put to the test, offered up Isaac." Hebrews 10.8, 9 states that Christ, as an embodiment of God, neither desires nor takes pleasure in sacrifice but, rather, wants conformity to God's will. An Abraham conforming to God's will would be tested but not required to carry through the sacrifice. Irony exists on yet another level when Abraham tells Isaac, "God himself will provide the lamb" (Gen. 22.8). Isaac has no way of knowing that he is to be the burnt offering, but he does not test his father's answer.

One of the best-known examples of irony in the Bible demonstrates that Job's so-called friends have no more knowledge than Job and that they have no right to sit in judgment. Job has endured the first cycle of speeches from his friends: Eliphaz, who tells Job he must have sinned; Bildad, who tells Job to repent; and Zophar, who tells Job that God is lenient and exacts "less than your guilt deserves" (11.6). Job effectively says, "So, you're the people who know everything, and wisdom will die with you" (12.3). He goes on to say, "I have understanding . . . I am not inferior." Romans 2.1 picks up on this theme of judgment: "Therefore you have no excuse, whoever you are, when you judge others; for in passing judgment on another, you condemn yourself, because you, the judge, are doing the very same things."

*Rhetorical Question (Job 38.4; Isa. 40, 66; Matt. 5.34, 35; Acts 7.44–50)*
The Bible brilliantly uses **rhetorical questions** – often one set asked by God and another by the human creature.[25] In Job (38.4), the LORD answers him out of a whirlwind with a question that suggests divine sarcasm, "Where were you when I laid the foundation of the earth?"[26] The Bible, in fact, constantly reminds the creature of the Creator, the temporal of the Foundation, the one in relation to the One and the Last.

In the face of the Eternal, Isaiah quotes the LORD as saying, "Heaven *is* My throne, And earth *is* My footstool" (66.1). Matthew quotes this, adding Jerusalem: "But I say to you, do not swear at all: neither by heaven, for it is God's throne; nor by the earth, for it is His footstool; nor by Jerusalem, for it is the city of the great King" (5.34, 35). Acts ties together the Old Testament and the New Testament by reminding people that God does not dwell in human temples.

In Isaiah 40, rhetorical questions multiply: Who has measured? Who has directed? With whom did he take counsel? Who taught Him knowledge and showed Him the way of understanding? To whom will you liken God or what likeness will you compare to Him? Have you not known? Have you not heard? Has it not been told you from the beginning? Have you not understood from the foundations of the earth (40.12–21)? A series of answers follows the series of questions:

> *It is* He who sits above the circle of the earth,
> And its inhabitants *are* like grasshoppers,
> Who stretches out the heavens like a curtain,
> And spreads them out like a tent to dwell in. (40.22)

The answer is followed by yet another question: "To whom will you compare me, or who is my equal?" (40.25). The answer suggests the absurdity of any comparison: "The Creator of the ends of the earth neither faints nor is weary. / His understanding is unsearchable. / He gives power to the weak" (40.28). The questions are repeated yet again, and answered again: "Have you not heard? / Has it not been told you from the beginning? / Have you not understood from the foundations of the earth?" The chapter concludes: "Those who wait upon the Lord shall renew their strength, they shall mount up with wings like eagles, they shall run and not be weary, and they shall walk and not faint" (40.31).

A further passage from Isaiah illustrates why the rhetorical question works well to emphasize a difference in two ways: God's way and the way of human beings, the way of Creator and the way of creation:

> For my thoughts are not your thoughts,
> nor are your ways my ways, says the LORD.
> For as the heavens are higher than the earth,
> so are my ways higher than your ways
> and my thoughts than your thoughts. (55.8, 9)

Job asks, "Where shall wisdom be found?" concluding that human beings do not know the way to it, that it is hidden, and that only God understands the way to it (Job 28:12, 21, 23). As already suggested, much of literature treats the subject of the unending quest for the meaning of human experience. Literature usually takes the search to the language of metaphor; the Bible tends to suggest that, in the last analysis, wisdom comes to human beings only as a divine gift, and that it belongs to the very nature of God himself.

*Amplification (Gen. 40)*

**Amplification** is the rhetorical device that refers to using more words than the grammar requires. The Bible contains many redundancies that engage the mind and emphasize, intensify, enhance, or amplify what has already been said.[27]

Repetitions can also include affirmative and negative statements. A story in Joseph's life (Gen. 40) illustrates how repetition can be used to emphasize an original statement, to call very special attention to it, and to point out how quickly human beings tend to forget favors. The chief baker, after hearing a favorable interpretation of the cupbearer's dream, states, "I also had a dream: there were three cake baskets on my head . . ." (40.17). Joseph answers, "This is its interpretation: the three baskets are three days; within three days Pharaoh will lift up your head – from you! – and hang you on a pole; and the birds will eat the flesh from you" (40.18, 19). On the third day, Pharaoh restored the chief cup-bearer but hanged the chief baker (40.20–3).

*If you've ever used the words "darn" or "heck," you will recognize that you are substituting a supposedly good word for one deemed less acceptable in public use. "Pass away" rather than "die" has been the pre-ferred good word to talk about physical death and, perhaps, connotes a theological position. A person has merely "passed away" from this life and entered into life somewhere else, eternally. Bible translations will substitute one language and culture's euphemisms for those of another, but care must be taken to make sure that the new culture requires the euphemism. For example, would we really need the biblical euphemism "covered his feet" when we want to talk about individuals going to the bathroom or relieving themselves?*

*Euphemism*

While the Bible generally uses plain language and plain subjects, it also uses **euphemism** to soften delicate sentiments for human beings. Ruth, for example, requests that Boaz spread his skirt over his handmaid for "receive me in marriage" (3.7–11). The passage carries a slight overtone of sexual intimacy, since feet, in Hebrew, can be a euphemism for genitals.[28] Humans use euphemism to make a word or phrase less offensive, disturbing, or troubling to the listener than that which it replaces. For example, death may be called a friend, or the dead described as joining a majority. The Bible also speaks directly: it describes Abraham as breathing his last; he dies "in a good old age, an old man and full of years, and was gathered to his people" (Gen. 25.7). Jacob describes his death as "I am about to be gathered to my people" (49.29). God, unlike human beings, calls death a calamity, the enemy, the last enemy, the king of terrors, and this is the sense of death that Bildad brings to Joseph, already intensely suffering: "By disease their skin is consumed, / the firstborn of Death consumes their limbs. / They are torn from the tent in which they trusted, / and are brought to the king of terrors" (Job 18.13, 14).

This death evidences the unvarnished reality of what happened in the Garden of Eden: "And the LORD God commanded the man, 'You may freely eat of every tree of the garden; but of the tree of the knowledge of good and evil you shall not eat, for in the day that you eat of it you shall die'" (Gen. 2.16–17). This is the death that the final Christian book of the Bible destroys: "Then Death and Hades were thrown into the lake of fire" (Rev. 20.14). This destruction inaugurates a new age with a victorious God: "See, I am making all things new . . . It is done! I am the Alpha and the Omega, the beginning and the end" (21.5, 6). This ending, and conclusion of the story, is repeated: "I am the Alpha and the Omega, the first and the last, the beginning and the end" (22.13). For Christians, the Bible closes with finality. Death no longer needs euphemism; its reign of terror has ended!

## Repetition, Recursion, Inclusio, and Chiasm

**Repetition,** arguably the Bible's most important literary device, is a favorite Hebrew literary form in both narrative and poetical literature, whether of words and phrases, actions, images, motifs, themes or ideas. At the broadest level, the theme of exile – loss of home, native place, family – holds together several sections of the Old Testament: the expulsion from Eden (Gen. 3), the banishment of Cain (Gen. 4), confusion of language and scattering of people (Gen. 11), family strife (Gen. to 2 Kings).[29] The larger story of exile can be found in the lives of Moses and Joshua and the fate of the nation of Israel.

Repetition serves as the basic compositional device in the New Testament book of Revelation.[30] A series of seven visions presents an incrementally growing conflict between good and evil forces. This repetition of sevens begins early and continues throughout the book: seven stars, seven golden candlesticks (1.1), seven churches (1–3), seven seals (5–8), seven angels (8.2), seven signs (14) and seven plagues (15), and, of course, there is the echo of creation in seven days. Appearing at the end of the collection of sixty-six texts, it rounds out a story that extends from creation to apocalypse.

**Recursion** refers to the deliberate shaping of narrative events so that key elements are repeated from one narrative to another. Two examples from Genesis demonstrate the importance of this technique.[31] A parallel exists in the way the Genesis account presents creation and the restoration of the land after the flood (7.24–9.17). Both address the "face of the deep" and "the great deep" (1.2, 7.11). Once the deep is broken up, first land (1.9 and 8.11) and then vegetation (1.11–12) appears. Next, seasons are noted (1.14, 8.13). In good time, living creatures enter the scene (1.24, 8.17). God next encourages their multiplication (1.22, 8.17) followed by the appearance of man (1.26, 8.18), also blessed and told to reproduce, to rule over the fish, birds, and every living thing and to use them for food (1.29, 9.3). The parallel suggests a deliberate shaping of the text to emphasize order and pattern.

Another example of recursion occurs in the stories of the fall (Gen. 2–3) and the incident of Noah's drunkenness. The parallels exist in the garden (2.8) and the orchard (9.20), the eating from the fruit of the tree (3.6) and the drinking of wine (9.21), the nakedness (3.7, 9.23), the "knowing" as a result of the action taken (3.7, 9.24), the curse (3.14, 9.25), and the presence of the three sons (4.1–2, 24; 9.25–7).

The same technique accounts for other repetitions in Genesis. The flood account, for example, repeats much of the pattern and order of the first creation, evoking a deliberate shaping of narrative events to suggest design and plan. Noah follows a pattern similar to that of Adam and Eve. His account involves three sons, Shem, Ham, and Japheth, just as Adam's sons were Cain, Abel, and Seth; in Noah's case, Shem's descendants are favored over those of Canaan and the Canaanites. Abraham's journey into Egypt (chapter 12) is repeated in Israel's sojourn in Egypt (46, 47, 11, and 12).[32] A famine triggers both events. In another example, Abraham declares to Sarah his intention in much the same way that Joseph addresses his brothers; Pharaoh takes Sarah into his house, just as Joseph is taken into the Pharaoh's house. Abraham acquires sheep and cattle; Joseph is put in charge of the Pharaoh's livestock; the Israelites acquire property in Egypt and are fruitful and increase. The Pharaoh sends Abraham from Egypt; the Pharaoh calls Moses and Aaron to take the Israelites out of Egypt. Abraham grows rich; the Israelites acquire much livestock, silver, and gold. Abraham returns to the altar and worships God; the Israelites celebrate Passover.

**Inclusio** uses repetition to mark off the beginning and ending of a section, framing or bracketing the material it contains. The repetition can be a word or phrase, a sentence, or even two concepts, their use being that they bind parts together. Translations may note this with an explanation of what words were used in the original language. An example of the use of this device can be found in Psalm 73, which begins with "God is good" and ends by saying, "it is good to be near God." Other examples in Psalms include same sentences (8.1, 9, and 145.1–2, 21); words or phrases (69.1, 35); and concepts (1.1 and 2.12).[33] Psalm 6 also uses this device to contrast the blessed who do not walk "in the counsel of the ungodly" and the ungodly who "will perish." The Song of Moses in Deuteronomy seems to use inclusio to describe "all people of the earth" in contrast to "one people of God." One of the most familiar books in the Bible making use of this device is Ecclesiastes (1.2, 12.8): "'Vanity of vanities,' says the Preacher; 'all is vanity.'" Inclusio is used to advance the argument that Genesis 1–2.4a and 2.4–3.24 belong to two different original sources, the first story framed by the word pair "heaven . . . earth (1.1) and "Such is the story of heaven and earth when they were created" (2.4a).[34] An example from the New Testament can be found in James in the question, "What good is it" and "what is the good of that?" (2.14–16). Finally, the Gospel of Mark uses a symbolic inclusio to frame the precise beginning and end of the career of Jesus: at baptism (1.10) and at the tearing of the veil (15.38).[35]

Another form of repetition, **chiasm**, juxtaposes, reverses, or contrasts words, dialogues, episodes, scenes and events with the most important idea in the apex, middle, or crossover in the story.[36] A simple example can be found in Mark 2.27: "The Sabbath was made for humankind, and not humankind for the Sabbath." Isaiah 6.10 uses the following structure:

| | |
|---|---|
| A | Make the mind of this people dull, |
| B | and stop their ears, |
| C | and shut their eyes, |
| C | so that they may not look with their eyes, |
| B | and listen with their ears, |
| A | and comprehend with their minds, |
| | and turn and be healed. |

*This device, some believe, exists in the Abraham story in Genesis, the travel story of Luke, the whole of Ruth, and the Gospel of Matthew. Other examples include the following:*

*Isaiah 6.10*
*Make the heart of this people fat, and their ears heavy, and shut their eyes;*

*lest they see with their eyes, and hear with their ears, and understand with their hearts, and turn and be healed.*

*Genesis 11.1–11*[37]
    *"the whole earth had one language" A (v.1)*
        *" there" B (v. 2b)*
      *"to each other" C (v. 3A)*
  *"Come, let us make bricks" D (v. 3b)*
*"Let's build for ourselves" E (v. 4a)*
*"a city and a tower" F (v. 4b)*
    *"And God went down to look" X (v. 5a)*
      *"the city and the tower" F (v. 5b)*
    *"which the sons of men built" E (v. 5c)*
      *"Come . . . let's confuse" D (v. 7a)*
*"each man, the language of his neighbor" C (v. 7b)*
        *"from there" B (v. 8b)*
    *"the language of all the earth" A (v. 8c)*

## Signs and Visions (Dan. 2, 4, 5; Rev. 12)

A special rhetorical device, a **sign**, refers to an actual occurrence that carries significance beyond its surface meaning. The kiss of Judas, for example, signifies betrayal. In Revelation 12, the woman and the male child take on meanings beyond themselves:

> A great portent appeared in heaven: a woman clothed with the sun, with the moon under her feet, and on her head a crown of twelve stars. She was pregnant and was crying out in birth pangs, in the agony of giving birth (1, 2)... And she gave birth to a son, a male child, who is to rule all the nations with a rod of iron. But her child was snatched away and taken to God and to his throne. (5, 6)

In the New Testament, people constantly ask Jesus to perform signs to show that he is who he says he is.

A **vision** in the Bible means seeing beyond human sight and real existence, and carries, like parable and allegory, symbolic meaning. In Revelation, for example, the throne stands for rule and the Temple for religion, the Lamb for the sacrifice of Christ, and the wild beast for the opposing powers. The New Testament, in particular, relies upon visions to carry meaning.

*You may be in a place now to understand that taking the Bible as either completely literal or wholly figurative creates a serious divide in the way individuals regard its truth; a more insightful approach will regard these as a continuum and pay attention to the idiom of the original languages (Hebrew and Greek) as well as that of the language into which the Bible is translated; it will take into account the literalness of the word(s) as well as the appeal to the imagination. It will understand that metaphor expresses truth beyond logic and proposition and that interpretation need not be restricted to physical realities. The Bible must be experienced in such a way that disregarding what it says figuratively simply no longer makes sense. What may be most at issue will be whether the "experience" of the Bible results in religious choice; but religious choice should not be made upon the basis of simplistic approaches to language.*[38]

## Close Reading

*Exercise 1*
Read Genesis 1–2. What rhetorical device links the various acts of creation? To what degree does this same rhetorical strategy help to organize chapter 2?

*Exercise 2*
Read Proverbs 1. What rhetorical device operates (most clearly seen in verse 20) to make an abstract idea concrete?

*Exercise 3*
Read Psalm 23. What rhetorical device enables the reader to grasp some of the personal qualities of God?

*Exercise 4*
Read several chapters in Revelation. How does it use symbolism to portray characters and events?

*Exercise 5*
Read Revelation 4 and Ezekiel 8. How do these passages operate on a visionary level?

*Exercise 6*
How does vision work in Isaiah 1?

*Exercise 7*
Read Genesis 12. How does archetype function in the calling of Abraham (Abram)?

*Exercise 8*
Read Mark 1 and 15. How is inclusio used to frame the beginning and end of the career of Jesus?

*Exercise 9*
Read several chapters in Hebrews, especially chapters 8–10. How does the author use quotations, allusions, and comparison to make his point about the "New Covenant"?

*Exercise 10*
Read the book of Amos. How does it use visionary writing to express future judgment?

## Questions for Reflection

1 How do multiple authors and editors affect the style, coherence, and unity of the anthology of books in the Bible?
2 Why does the Bible require special attention to style?
3 How does the tension between a literalist and a figurative interpretation of the Bible affect meaning?
4 Is it possible for a text to be taken as literally false but figuratively true?
5 What is the primary difference between metaphor and simile?
6 How does paying attention to detail enable an enhanced reading and understanding of the Bible?
7 Is it possible that not understanding the presence of a figurative device can contribute to missing the whole point of meaning?
8 What makes Psalm 23 an allegory?
9 What are the differences between metonymy and synecdoche?
10 Why does the Bible present God anthropomorphically?
11 How is oxymoron important to figuring out some of the theological mysteries of the Bible?
12 What primary differences exist among quoting, alluding to, and foreshadowing in the Bible? How do these work in the context of the Old Testament? The New?
13 How does irony resolve the paradox of a loving and just God who commands that Abraham sacrifice his son, or does it?
14 How do rhetorical questions relate the limited and finite to the infinite?

15  Do you consider the Bible to contain mostly meaningful or mostly mindless repetition?

16  Does God speak euphemistically about the plight of human beings?

17  What tensions exists between figurative and literalist interpretations of the Bible?

18  How does a literalist or an idiomatic interpretation of the Bible help or hinder the understanding of meaning?

19  How does the Bible use vision to create connections between history, the present age, and the future?

20  What does it mean that ancient texts of the Bible cannot be taken as science, natural science, or history?

# 3 Image, Metaphor, Symbol, and Archetype: A Way of Meaning

## Outline

Preliminary Considerations
Two Unifying Images
    Light, Darkness, and Fire
    Water
Five Metaphors of Divine–Human Relationship
    The Metaphor of King and Subject
    The Metaphor of Judge and Litigant
    The Metaphor of Husband and Wife
    The Metaphor of Father and Child
    The Metaphor of Master and Servant
Archetypal Encounters of the Divine and Human
    Mount Horeb/Sinai
    The Mount of the Skull
    Close Reading
    Questions for Reflection

*You may find this chapter challenging, requiring from you mental effort and concentration. That's because the structure of the Bible reveals itself in interlocking patterns of myth, metaphor, and typology richer than the descriptive language of fact and evidence.[1] At the same time, you may find your enjoyment heightened by language that quickens the imagination and appeals to spiritual discovery and revelation. The figurative uses of language in literature and religion invoke vision and offer revelation of a reality greater than time and space.[2] Literature, unlike religion, generally neither affirms nor denies the reality of the vision. Another reason you may find this chapter difficult is that you will have to move beyond the literalism that has resulted from our modern world's emphasis upon empirical fact and history.*

## Preliminary Considerations

*You may want to note that I have used an organizing principle in this text of moving from the particular arrangement of words to larger patterns, and from patterns to the more encompassing genres and themes that help to organize texts.[3] The next section illustrates this principle.*

A literary approach to reading the Bible means understanding how it uses language, both literally and figuratively, to present human experience in a connected pattern of images, metaphors, motifs, symbols, and archetypes; these often overlap and sometimes can be used interchangeably. An **image** names a **concrete** thing (such as tree or house) or action (such as running or threshing) and requires readers to experience literally and connotatively what the image evokes. Metaphor and simile (previously discussed in the roles of comparison and association) function much like **symbol**, an image that stands for something in addition to its literal meaning. **Archetype** refers to a recurring image or pattern representing the universal elements of human experience. The following examples illustrate these meanings.[4]

- *Image* – water, with the first level (the literal properties) of meaning primary.
- *Metaphor* – implied comparison, "I planted, Apollos watered" (1 Cor. 3.6), speaks of a figurative planting and watering.
- *Simile* – direct comparison, "like cold water to a thirsty soul, / so is good news from a far country" (Prov. 25.25).
- *Motif* – an unfolding pattern such as the arrival of a man from a foreign country, the appearance of the woman at the well to fetch water, the dialogue between a man and a woman, the drawing of water, the woman running home to tell her family, the inviting of the stranger into the home of the betrothed in hospitality and welcome (Gen. 29.4–12).
- *Symbol* – "Whoever drinks of this water shall never thirst" (John 4.14), with the second level of meaning, salvation, as primary.
- *Archetype* – universal pattern in image or symbol (mountain top, city), plot motif (crime and punishment), and character type (jealous sibling). "Archetypes are the universal elements of human experience."[5]

*You should be aware that the issue of determining what is real involves a complicated history of philosophy which assigns "reality" to the external world, to the mind, or to some interaction of the two. The first level of image described above suggests that an actual something called a "tree" exists in the world and that an image of it exists in the mind and corresponds to the literal and actual object. This remains the common-sense understanding of how human beings obtain information about the world and use it to make intelligent decisions and to reason and be guided by moral principles. It is a view, however, that studies in the cognitive sciences have begun to question. These studies describe conceptualization and thought as deeply seated in human beings and their modes of interacting with and shaping their world. They point out that reason itself relies centrally upon imaginative capacities – primarily metaphor – and that meaning can never be purely objective or subjective.[6]*

*Throughout this text, I have called attention to the importance of the mythological and metaphorical and to the image-making capacity of the imagination – these originating at the foundation of societies and literature.[7] It should be noted that the Bible belongs at the threshold of the emergence of Western philosophy and that image and metaphor exist in abundance in its primal understanding of the world.*

## Two Unifying Images

(Gen. 1.1–5, 2, 13, 19.11, 20, 26; Isa. 6.9–10, 29.9–10, 43.8, 45.7; John 1, 4; Rev. 1.15, 2.10, 21, 22.1–2; 1 John; 2 Peter 2, 3.5–6; Exod. 10, 13, 24, 25, 27; Judg. 16, 19; 2 Sam. 23; Job 2; Luke 8.22–5; Ezek. 47; Jer. 2.13; Matt. 14, 15.14, 23.16–17, 19.24, 26; 2 Kings 6.18, 25.7; Acts 9; Deut. 28.28–9; Rom. 1.21)

### Light, Darkness, and Fire

Master images recur in the Bible and serve as links between the Jewish Bible and the Christian Bible, between creation and the **new creation**, between physical reality and spiritual reality, the real and the ideal; these images connect metaphorically to a mythology addressing the nature and destiny of human life, its place in the universe, and its sense of an infinitely bigger other.[8] Two of the most familiar images are light and water, often occurring in shared proximity. These images begin in the literal and concrete: Genesis describes the essential stuff of life as beginning with the primal elements of light and water; Isaiah describes the sole God as the one who formed light and created darkness (45.7). Revelation uses these primal images figuratively in its vision of a **New Jerusalem**, a city that "has no need of sun or moon to shine on it, for the glory of God is its light, and its lamp is the Lamb" (21.23). John sees a "river of the water of life, bright as crystal, flowing from the throne of God and of the Lamb through the middle of the street of the city" (22.1, 2).

*The first five books of the Old Testament, traditionally thought to have been written by Moses, have been thought by some scholars to have been composed by a series of editors out of four traditions: Jahwist, Elohist (these two written around 1000, 8000 BCE), Priestly (587–500 BCE), and Deuteronomic (600 BCE). I discuss these (also known as multiple-author theory or the Documentary Hypothesis) more fully in chapter 4.*

"In the beginning when God created the heavens and the earth, the earth was a formless void and darkness covered the face of the deep, while a wind from God swept over the face of the waters," followed by, in this Priestly account, God saying, "Let there be light" (Gen. 1.1–3). God creates light, sees that it is good, and calls it day, and the darkness, night (1.45). Light and darkness form contextual polarities relative to the life that will spring from them; likewise, God separates the water and the land, calling the land earth and the water sea (1.10). On the basis of these two separations, God makes the necessary preparations for life itself. For biblical writers, the blazing sun could scorch the land and bring drought. In the account of Noah, the windows of heaven could also open up, the fountains of the deep break forth, and the floodwaters encompass the created order. Second Peter describes a world deluged by water that perished, and he warns: "The present heavens and earth have been reserved for fire, being kept until the day of judgment and destruction of the godless," a version of **retributive** justice (3.7). This judgment will come in God's time, a time in which one day is like a thousand years (3.8), an explanation perhaps growing out of a frustrated and unfulfilled **eschatology**. God forestalls judgment, Peter says, "not wanting any to perish, but all to come to repentance" (3.9). The literal images, thus, take on universal meaning and evocativeness. Light, as a source of life, goodness and blessing, and truth, becomes a symbol of God, representing the Messiah, and the Church. The Psalms describe God as preparing the light and sun (74.16), as covering himself with light (104.2), and as making darkness as light (139.12).

Light emerges as one of the Bible's major and most complex symbols, appearing nearly 200 times between the moment of physical light springing forth as the first created thing and the obliteration of darkness in Revelation's New Jerusalem.[9] The Gospel of John and 1 John, more than any other book in the Bible, use light figuratively to speak of Jesus as the life and light of all people, a light that shines in the darkness and cannot be overcome by it. John connects spiritual creation with the original creation in which God created light and life, speaking the world into being through the Word that now reveals itself as the "true light." The book of 1 John not only connects light with the Christian walk but identifies it with the Great Commandment to love. Revelation concludes that there will be no need for the sun or moon in the New Jerusalem, "for the glory of God is its light" and "The nations will walk by its light, and the kings of the earth will bring their glory into it. Its gates will never be shut by day – and there will be no night there" (21.22, 23). Revelation concludes that the New Jerusalem will have no more night and no need for light of lamp or sun (22.4).

Darkness, light, and fire provide primal images symbolizing God's absence or presence. In Exodus, Moses stretches out his hand over a dense darkness in the land of Egypt that lasts for three days, this darkness offset by the Israelites' having light where they lived (10.23). When Pharaoh lets the Israelites go, they set out with the LORD going in front of them as "a pillar of cloud by day . . . and in a pillar of fire by night . . . Neither the pillar of cloud by day nor the pillar of fire by night left its place in front of the people" (13.21–2). In the tabernacle, seven lamps give light (25.37). The lamps burn continually (27.20). In Leviticus, Aaron sets up the lamp "to burn from evening to morning before the LORD regularly; it shall be a statute forever throughout your generations" (24.3). Luke presents Simeon as taking Jesus in his arms and declaring he has seen "a light for revelation to the Gentiles / and for glory to your people Israel" (2.32). Paul in Acts experiences a light from heaven flashing around him that identifies itself to him as Jesus (9.3); Peter is delivered from prison by an angel that appears as a light that shines in his cell (Acts 12.7).

Light functions throughout the Bible to uphold right action and behaviors in contrast to the less reputable shenanigans of darkness. The Gazites in Judges waited all night to kill Samson, but Samson, at midnight, destroyed the doors of the city gate: so they circled around and lay in wait for him all night at the city gate (16.2, 3).

In a further illustration of using darkness to cover evil deeds, Judges tells the sordid story of an all-night abuse and rape of a Levite's concubine: the concubine from Bethlehem leaves her master to return to her father. The husband pursues her, receives the hospitality of his father-in-law, and they leave together after five days to return home. On the way back, the husband chooses, tragically, to stop in Gibeah, which belongs to Benjamin. An Ephramite residing in Gibeah greets them and hospitably takes the master, his concubine, and his servant to spend the night among the Benjamites. That night, the men of the city demand to have intercourse with the men. The Ephramite offers them instead his own virgin daughter and the Levite's concubine. The Levite redresses this violation by sending parts of the concubine's body to all twelve parts of the tribal confederacy.

The Bible often describes human reaction to life in terms of light and darkness. David, in his last words, describes his model for just rule in terms of light, while Job can only lament the day of his birth as darkness. David says, "One who rules over people justly, ruling in the fear of God, is like the light of morning, like the sun rising on a cloudless morning, gleaming from the rain on the grassy land" (2 Samuel 23.3–4). Job, on the other hand, curses his life and yearns for darkness and death as a way out of a miserable existence.

Related to light, sight and blindness figure prominently in the Bible: recall, for example, the Sodomites groping around Lot's house; the dim-eyed Isaac tricked by Jacob; Samson's eyes gouged out; a troupe of blinded Syrian warriors being led to Samaria; the man blind from birth and healed by Jesus.[10] Congenital or acquired, this lack of light makes individuals physically vulnerable; Israel occasionally blinded neighboring nations (2 Kings 25.7) but not their own. Even God temporarily blinds individuals and groups (Gen. 19.11; 2 Kings 6.18; Acts 9). By extension, physical blindness becomes related to spiritual blindness and the inability to recognize and face truth (Isa. 43.8; Deut. 28.28–9; Isa. 6.9–10, 29.9–10; Rom. 1.21; Matt. 15.14, 23.16–17, 19, 24, 26). Matthew and Luke both describe Jesus as a light coming into darkness, and Christians celebrate his birth as coming at the winter solstice or time of deepest darkness.[11] In Luke's account of the conversion of Paul, light is associated with revelation and transformation.

The extinguishing of light becomes a notable archetype in the apocalyptic visions of the end of time. Isaiah poetically describes the day of the LORD as a time when "the stars of the heavens and their constellations / will not give their light; / the sun will be dark at its rising / and the moon will not shed its light" (13.10). Jeremiah writhes in pain as he envisions an earth that lies in waste and void: "I looked on the earth, and lo, it was waste and void / and to the heavens, and they had no light" (4.23). Matthew sees the coming of the Son of Man, after the Desolating Sacrilege, as lightning coming from the east and flashing as far as the west (24.27). In that day, he quotes Isaiah, the sun will be darkened and the moon will not give it light. Amos (5.20) and Ezekiel (32.7–8) both associate the loss of light with God's final judgment. Revelation, describing the overthrow of Babylon, says "the light of a lamp will shine in you no more" (18.23).

*In following the use of light as image, metaphor, symbol, and archetype, you discover the theological themes of creation, fall, exodus and migration, destruction (deluges in the past and apocalypse in the future), and redemption; literature addresses these themes through the heroic quest.[12] Theologically, light symbolically depicts the* **transcendence** *and* **immanence** *of God: from above, but permeating everyday life, it functions critically to transform the human and earthly with the transcendent splendor that is God. Second Corinthians 4.6 describes this transformation: "For it is the God who said, 'Let light shine out of darkness,' who has shone in our hearts to give the light of the knowledge of the glory of God in the face of Jesus Christ." Literature would be more comfortable talking about a journey leading to expanded awareness through the* **imagination**.

### Water

Water imagery in the Bible triples that of light, appearing over 600 times, functioning in three main ways: as a cosmic force of life that can be controlled only by God; as a source of life; and as a cleansing agent.[13] Recurrent water images in the Bible include springs, wells, cisterns, seasonal rains, floods, the crossing of waters, the drawing and carrying of water, and ceremonial cleansings with water. Water brings life and death, blessing and affliction, order, and chaos. In Genesis, God commands, and the waters separate into waters "under the dome" and waters "above the dome" (1.7). Speaking, God gathers together the waters under the dome into seas (1.9, 10). Second Peter 3.5–6 ascribes these remarkable accomplishments to the word of God: "by the word of God heavens existed long ago and an earth was formed out of water." The word that mastered primeval water is the divine Word that in the gospel of John appears in the flesh (1.1–5).

The unifying motif of water appears many times in the Old Testament. Genesis speaks of the creation of a mist out of dry ground and "A river flows out of Eden to water the garden, and from there it divides and becomes four branches" (2.10). While the generation of Noah is destroyed by flood, the children of Israel cross the Jordan into the promised land of Canaan. Lot chooses to settle in the well-watered plain of the Jordan (Gen. 13). In Ezekiel's vision of the New Temple, water flows from below the threshold to the east and south (47). In the New Testament, an angel shows John "the river of the water of life, bright as crystal, flowing from the throne of God and of the Lamb through the middle of the street of the city (Rev. 22.1, 2). Revelation also unites the images of light and water when it describes the exalted Christ standing among the seven golden lampstands with a voice like the sound of many waters (1.15).

The Bible makes a distinction between stale (cisterns) and living water (springs, wells). Jeremiah speaks figuratively when he says, "my people have committed two evils: they have forsaken me, the fountain of living water, and dug out cisterns for themselves, cracked cisterns that can hold no water" (2.13). Both Joseph and Jeremiah are thrown into dry cisterns. In Genesis, the waters bring forth living creatures (1.20). Isaac's servants dig in the valley and find wells of spring water (Gen. 26.19). Accustomed to the Jewish practice of keeping themselves aloof from Samaritans, the Samaritan woman at the well is surprised that Jesus, a Jew, asks her for a drink. Jesus tells her, "If you knew the gift of God, and who it is that is saying to you, 'Give me a drink,' you would have asked him, and he would have given you living water" (John 4.11). Jesus explains to her that physical water quenches physical thirst for only a short time; speaking of water metaphorically, he tells her about a water that satisfies the spirit: "The water that I will give will become . . . a spring of water gushing up to eternal life" (4.14), this referring to the movement of spirit within the individual, mysterious, ever renewed, and upwelling in fullness of life.

As described in chapter 1, water in the Old Testament invokes a special **cosmogony**: a flat earth, a dome of heaven, and, below the earth, the realm of death and the sea of chaos. The sea, the original enemy of God at creation, must be conquered. The mastery of water, familiar in Moses' leading the Israelites out of Egypt at the Red Sea, appears in the New Testament in the story of Jesus' commanding the waters to be still (Luke 8) and his walking on the water of the Sea of Galilee (Matt. 14). In the biblical world, the seasonal rains could stop and the wells, springs, and cisterns dry up. These images contribute to the contingency of earthly life subject to eternal forces and always threatened by extinction. The need to husband water becomes a prevailing **motif** throughout the Bible, an act accomplished by God: in Revelation, God sits enthroned above a crystal sea, imaged as calm, smooth as glass, and subdued by the master's voice (4.6, 22.1).

Water plays a predominant role in preparation for entering into Canaan and then afterwards in Israel's repentance and restoration. Conversion (of the Gentile) to Judaism required a once-for-all ritual washing: full immersion, followed by circumcision.[14] John gave the

Jewish immersion a new interpretation, calling it a baptism of repentance, a decisive act in which the person receives symbolic purification. The Gospel writers link this baptism to the Exodus conquest; it includes a call back to the wilderness and to the Jordan. Christian baptism symbolizes a passage from death to life: a descent into water based on the premise of reversion to watery chaos, dissolution, new creation, and new life.[15] Christians further associate baptism with the death, burial, and resurrection of Jesus.

*The final chapter in this book addresses the divine–human relationship as a central theological theme of the Bible: the relationship of human beings to God and the relationship of human beings to each other. Here, I address this theme in the context of metaphor, or "A is B." Metaphor achieves what ordinary language cannot: the union of ordinary experience and the ineffable God as Supreme Being through what cognitive psychology explains as empathetic projection. Metaphor makes possible a discussion of the reality of the non-human personality: God is king, judge, husband, father, and lord or master.[16]*

## Five Metaphors of Divine–Human Relationship

In the category of human character, many metaphors describe the divine–human relationship, the five most frequent being those of king and subject, judge and litigant, husband and wife, father and child, and lord or master and servant, all implying an obligation in the relationship.[17] Each metaphor begins with the literal, physical image but, beyond the literal image, each represents in some way a characteristic of God. Both metaphor and simile move the reader to a second level of reading where king, judge, husband, father, and master stand for something more than the literal and concrete, and call for interpretation. Ignoring either the concrete, physical image or its figurative meaning impoverishes the reader's experience of the Bible. The archetypal level addresses the primal stuff of common humanity, the immemorial patterns of response to the human situation in its permanent aspects.[18] The Bible uses the recurrent patterns of king, judge, husband, father, and master to express the infinite character of God.

### *The Metaphor of King and Subject (Deut. 17.14–20; 1 Sam. 8.4–18, 12; Exod. 15.2, 18; Judg. 8; Isa. 6; Ezek. 1; Rev. 21.1–6; Isa. 38)*

The Bible depicts two royal images of kingship: one human and one divine. On both levels, the king ideally projects an image of protection, justice, mercy, power, and authority. Deuteronomy, a central portion of the book dating to documents discovered in the Jerusalem Temple archives during the reign of Josiah (621 BCE), focuses on the special covenant relationship based on the law as summarized in the Ten Commandments, these laws forming the basis for community. After they have taken possession of the Promised Land, the people request a king from a wrong motive: to be "like all the nations that are around me" (Deut. 17.14). Deuteronomy records a concession to the demand for kingship, limiting choice to "a king whom the Lord . . . God will choose" (17.14). Additionally, the king may not be a foreigner (17.15), must not accumulate horses (17.16), wives, or wealth (17.17); more positively, he must have a copy of the law written for himself, and he must keep and obey it (17.18–20). Moses, in his celebratory song for deliverance from Egypt, captures ideal kingship as that of Yahweh and no other: "The LORD [Yah] is my strength and my might . . . my salvation . . . my father's God . . . Yah is his name . . . The LORD will reign forever and ever" (Exod. 15.2, 18). The warrior Gideon in Judges refuses kingship: "I will not rule over you, and my son will not rule over you; the LORD will rule over you" (8.23).

Deuteronomistic history, which most theorists suggest includes Joshua, Judges, Samuel, and Kings, explains Israel's history relative to keeping and abiding by the covenant relationship. Without surprise, the kings of the monarchy, and later in the divided kingdoms of Israel and Judah, fall short in one or more of the requirements outlined by Deuteronomy. The Bible sets the precedence for this in the very first king, Saul, who progressively reveals himself to be proud, disobedient, a liar, and, potentially, a murderer of David (1 Sam. 18.10). From the beginning (1 Sam. 8.4–8), God clearly warns the people about the oppression they can expect from their king: he will establish for himself a military and make servants of their sons; he will take their daughters to serve as perfumers, cooks, and bakers; he will take a portion of their fields and produce; he will take their slaves and their possessions. Samuel warns the people that they will eventually cry out from the oppression, but God will not answer.

The people, despite the stern warning, refuse to listen, telling Samuel, "we are determined to have a king over us, so that we also may be like other nations (1 Sam. 4.19, 20), so the LORD says, "Listen to their voice and set a king over them" (4.22). Ironically, the LORD listens, an act his rebellious subjects have rejected; humankind, made in divine image, rejects Yahweh as LORD of creation, including human beings.[19]

*The Kingdom of God, and God's reign as king (60 percent of the references to throne), serves as a central, unifying motif in the Bible, accompanied by all the imagery of kingship, including the throne:[20] Physically, kings sat upon the throne (1 Kings 2.19, 10.18, 18; 2 Chron. 9.17, 18, 23.20; Esther 5.1; Acts 12.21); the lion symbolizes the king's power and authority and, on the human level, the most common reference is to the throne of David, a king known for exercising righteousness and justice. This throne also references the Davidic covenant: God's promise that descendants of David would always sit upon the throne (2 Sam. 7; 1 and 2 Kings; 1 and 2 Chron.; Isa.; and Jer.).*

The Bible uses thrones to symbolize God's sovereignty, power, and splendor. Two memorable references to the heavenly throne occur in

Isaiah 6 and Ezekiel 1. Isaiah describes God as sitting on his throne, high and lofty, the hem of his robe filling the temple (6.1), attended by seraphs, each with six wings, flying with two wings and covering their faces with another two and their feet with the last two, crying, "Holy, holy, holy is the LORD of hosts; / the whole earth is full of his glory" (6.3). Ezekiel describes a fantastic vision of God's throne: he begins with a stormy wind coming out of the north, a great cloud with brightness around it and fire flashing forth continually, in the middle of which are four living creatures (1.4–5). The creatures manifest human form, each with four faces (human being, lion, ox, eagle), four wings, their legs straight, and the soles of their feet like those of calves' feet; they have human hands and move straight ahead, without turning as they move. In the middle of these creatures, something that looks like fire burns, torches move to and fro among them, and the creatures dart like lightning into the fire. Ezekiel sees a wheel, one for each of the four, their construction being something like a wheel within a wheel (1.16). The wheels move in any of four directions, their rims full of eyes all around. Ezekiel describes a dome over their heads, shining like crystal; the creatures' wings issue the sound of mighty waters, like the thunder of the Almighty, like the tumult of an army. Above the dome, Ezekiel sees a throne, its appearance like sapphire, and something seated in it with the likeness of human form (1.26). From what appears like loins, Ezekiel sees something gleaming amber, something that looks like fire, generating a splendor all around, akin to that of a rainbow. Ezekiel, stretched in his attempt to express himself metaphorically, summarizes, "This was the appearance of the likeness of the glory of the LORD" (1.28).

Isaiah, Ezekiel, and Revelation leave little doubt that throne imagery may be one of the Bible's most glorious and evocative images.[21] The writer of Revelation (21) sees a new heaven and earth, the old passed away, a holy city, Jerusalem, coming from God, prepared as a bride, and hears a loud voice from the throne saying, "See, the home of God is among mortals" (21.3). A voice from the throne says, "See, I am making all things new" (21.5).

Other images of the throne include the LORD surrounded by the host of heaven (1 Kings 22.19; 2 Chron. 18.18), a rainbow like emeralds (Rev. 4.3), twenty-four other thrones (Rev. 4.4), a crystal-clear sea of glass (Rev. 4.6), countless numbers of angels (Rev. 5.11), a holy throne (Ps. 47.8) glorious in appearance (Isa. 63.15; Jer. 14.21, 17.12; Matt. 19.28, 25.31) and eternal in duration (Pss. 9.7, 45.6, 93.2; Lam. 5.19; Ezek. 43.7; Heb. 1.8; Rev. 1.8, 5.13).

### The Metaphor of Judge and Litigant (2 Sam. 12.1–15; Judg. 4.4–16, 17–22; Exod. 18.13–27; Ezra 7.25–8)

The final chapter in this book describes justice as the thematic corollary of God's steadfast love and mercy.[22] As is the case with king, judge has both a human and divine face. The Bible presents God as the perfect and patient judge, a forbearing God who pleads constantly, who warns degenerate humankind continually that rebellion leads to final judgment. The judgments of God, remaining mysterious, set the standard by which all other justice must be known: God remains the ultimate authority, the ultimate justice.[23] Metaphorically, an ideal human judge imitates God's righteousness (Luke 12.57; John 7.24) but does not attempt to usurp God's role as the final judge (Deut. 1.17). The judges depicted in the Bible, in fact, do not really belong to the legal profession as such; rather, they function as deliverers, prophets, kings, and priests.

The book in the Bible which carries the name "Judges" actually uses the word "judge" only once – in the case of Jephthah as deliverer. Before a successful battle with the Ammonites, he tells them, "Let the LORD, who is judge, decide today for the Israelites or for the Ammonites" (11.27). Despite this clear understanding of God as the absolute, ultimate, and completely just judge, the Bible displays many portraits of human beings exercising this role. One of the best examples is King Solomon's rendering a just judgment in the case of two women claiming the same child. Other judges on the human level include David, Deborah, Moses, and Ezra.

The book of 2 Samuel presents King David in an act that displeases God and the prophet Nathan who must condemn him. The well-known story tells how David commits adultery with Bathsheba, the wife of Uriah, one of David's elite thirty warriors. Learning that Bathsheba is pregnant, David, to cover up his involvement, brings Uriah home from battle, thinking he will have sex with Bathsheba; when the ploy fails, David sends Uriah into the heat of battle to be killed (11.14).

Nathan presents the case to King David in the form of a legal case: he tells him the story of a rich man who had very many flocks and of a poor man who had but one pet lamb; when a traveler stops at the rich man's house, instead of taking one of his own flock to fulfill his duty of hospitality, the rich man instead takes the lamb of the poor man and has it prepared for the guest. When David hears this story, he reacts as a just king and judge: angry about the rich man, he declares, "As the LORD lives, the man who has done this deserves to die; he shall restore the lamb fourfold, because he did this thing, and because he had no pity" (12.5, 6). Nathan tells David, "You are the man!" (12.7). Nathan makes clear to David that he is the rich man – the man that God himself anointed king using the elders (1 Sam. 5.3), a man rescued from King Saul and given his wealth and all of Israel and Judah; he is also the man who has destroyed the family of Uriah, committing adultery with his wife and having Uriah killed (2 Sam. 12.7–15). As a result of divine judgment, David experiences trouble within his own house in his sons Amnon, Absalom, and Adonijah (1 Kings 1), and his new-born son from Bathsheba dies. David repents, but repercussions continue, just as they continued for the repentant Saul (1 Sam. 15.30); the Bible presents these outcomes not as predestined acts, but as the resulting consequences of poorly made decisions and moral flaws. Nathan will remain David's adviser, partly because David recognizes the truth of Nathan's judgment and repents.

The Bible presents Moses as a prophet and judge who legislates ad hoc, case by case, in advance of the codes that issue from Mount Sinai. Moses' father-in-law, Jethro, also called Reuel in the Old Testament, observes Moses sitting as judge for the people from morning until evening (Exod. 18) and suggests that he look for able, trustworthy men who hate dishonesty and set them as officers over thousands, hundreds, fifties, tens; he tells Moses to let them sit as judges in minor cases. Moses will still serve as main counsel, hearing all the important cases. Moses follows his father-in-law's advice and appoints several judges.

Deuteronomy describes the appointment of judges and officials throughout the tribes to render just decisions for the people (16.18). One of these, Deborah, one of the very few women identified as a prophet (others being Miriam, Exod. 15.20; Huldah, 2 Kings 22.14–20; and Noadiah, Neh. 6.14), instructs Barak to take warriors from the tribes of Naphtali and Zebulun and to post themselves at Mount Tabor, where Deborah will draw out Sisera, the general of Jabin and the Canaanite forces (Judg. 4). Barak agrees to lead the army but insists that Deborah accompany him; Deborah agrees but tells Barak the road will not lead to his glory, for the LORD will sell Sisera into a woman's hand. True to prophecy, Barak destroys the army of Sisera, but Sisera flees in panic to the tent of Heber the Kenite; Heber's wife, Jael, meets him, takes him into her tent, and provides him with water and milk; he falls soundly asleep, and she drives a peg into his temple. A recounting of the story in poetry has Deborah singing glory to Jael:

> Most blessed of women be Jael, . . .
> she struck Sisera a blow,
> she crushed his head,
> she shattered and pierced his temple.
> He sank, he fell,
> he lay still at her feet;
> at her feet he sank; he fell;
> where he sank, there he fell dead. (Judg. 5.26, 27)

After the Babylonian captivity and return, Ezra the priest performs many of the functions of a judge, his most controversial action being the initiation of divorce for those men who had married foreign women. The Bible describes Ezra as having power (given from God) to appoint magistrates and judges who know the laws of God to judge the people; like Moses, he teaches those who do not know these laws (Ezra 7.25–8). Those who know and do not obey must be judged for death, banishment, confiscation of goods, or imprisonment; the retributive justice model prevails: disobey, be punished.

## *The Metaphor of Husband and Wife (Ruth; Hosea 1–3; Jer. 3.1–5; Eph. 5.21–33; Rev. 21; Matt. 1.18–25; Luke 2)*

The most pervasive metaphor of relationship/unity in the Bible, beginning with Adam and Eve in Genesis and concluding with Christ and the Church in Revelation, is that of marriage. Marriage, metaphorically, describes an ideal unity, a relationship built upon mutual love and realized in a permanent form. Isaiah, in a promise of assurance to an exiled people, tells the barren and desolate to burst into song, "For your Maker is your husband" (54.5) and "the children of the desolate will be more than the children of her that is married" (54.1). Operating on two levels at once, marriage points to the possibility of both physical and spiritual creation: Paul describes all of creation in a birth image as groaning in its pain to be liberated from bondage (Rom. 8.21, 22) and, in one of the most beloved chapters in the Bible, Jesus tells Nicodemus that he must experience a **new birth**: "Very truly, I tell you, no one can enter the kingdom of God without being born from above . . . without being born of water and spirit . . . [for] what is born of the Spirit is spirit" (John 3.3–7). The Shema's "Hear, O Israel, The LORD is our God" (Deut. 6.4) calls for a responding love and conduct from a people wedded to God. God's love throughout the Bible, particularly in the Deuteronomic tradition, results in the liberation and ideal community of God's people: God continues the life cycle and fulfills the promise and obligation of a permanent, bonded relationship.

The Bible provides numerous portraits of the relationship between husband and wife: Adam and Eve, Abraham and Sarah, Isaac and Rebekah, Jacob and Rachel, Ruth and Boaz, Solomon and his Shulammite bride, Esther and the king, Mary and Joseph – all founded on the basic principle of two becoming one.[24] Boaz and later Joseph, the husband of Mary, emerge as ideal husbands. And, in less than ideal relationships, Hosea and Ezekiel (16) picture men capable of loving, forgiving, and restoring the unfaithful.

A literary approach to the book of Ruth often treats it as a short story appreciated for its dialogue, succinct prose, character development, and pastoral setting. A Bethlehemite family, parents and two sons, sojourn in Moab after escaping a famine. In Moab, the sons marry; in time, the father and two sons die, leaving Naomi and her daughters-in-law, Ruth and Orpah. Naomi chooses to return home but urges them to stay in Moab, an option Orpah chooses. Ruth, on the other hand, travels with Naomi to Bethlehem. Once there, she gleans in the wheat fields to support herself and Naomi. In the fields, Boaz takes notice of Ruth. Naomi identifies Boaz as kinsman and urges Ruth to pursue him more actively. Ruth makes two requests of Boaz: the request of marriage for herself and redemption for Naomi through his responsibility as near kinsman.

Here, the motif of kinsman-redeemer is about more than **Levirate** marriage, a custom whereby the brother of a deceased man must provide progeny and protection for the family's land.[25] Boaz informs Ruth that a more closely related kinsman has the first obligation to act as kinsman-redeemer; Boaz agrees to act in his appropriate role as "next-of-kin" (Ruth 3.11–13). At first, the more closely related kinsman agrees to purchase the parcel of land that Naomi has chosen to sell but, upon learning that Ruth must also be acquired, he excuses himself, explaining that he would be damaging his own inheritance (4.6). Boaz then, under no compulsion of duty, fulfills the responsibility of kinsman-redeemer.

The concept of kinship relates to the formal or written covenant or agreement belonging to the institution of marriage; from the eighth century BCE onward, the covenantal relationship between Yahweh and Israel is compared to marriage.[26] The same use can be found in Hosea 1–3 and in Jeremiah 3.1–5. The ideal unity involved in the covenantal marriage evolves out of mutual love, respect, and fidelity. The kinsman-redeemer motif in Ruth portrays a God defending his people when he sees no one else coming to their aid; in Isaiah, he comes as "Zion Redeemer" to those in Jacob who turn from transgression (59.20). Combining the kinsman-redeemer metaphor, the New Testament pictures Christ as redeemer and marriage as the bond between the community and God (Eph. 5.21–33; Rev. 21.2).

In the New Testament, Joseph, the husband of Mary, demonstrates a similar story of love and loyalty. Matthew's genealogy legitimizes both the human and divine origins of Jesus as the Messiah and traces that genealogy through four Gentile women, including Ruth. As told by Matthew, "Mary had been engaged to Joseph, but before they lived together, she was found to be with child from the Holy Spirit. Her husband Joseph, being a righteous man and unwilling to expose her to public disgrace, planned to dismiss her quietly" (1.18, 19). Joseph's engagement to Mary means that the couple had entered into a formal "permitted" relationship with each other that had not yet been consummated sexually. Mary's being "found to be with child" and Joseph's unwillingness to expose her suggests a love and loyalty that prevail over social custom. The righteous Joseph learns through a dream that the son will be born "to fulfill what had been spoken by the Lord through the prophet" Isaiah (1.23). He awakes from his dream and follows the commandment from the angel of the Lord to take Mary as his wife but "had no marital relations with her until she had borne a son; and he named him Jesus" (1.25). In addition to loving, protecting, and providing for Mary, the righteous Joseph obeys the messenger of God.

*Fertility, perhaps related to pagan mythology and the idea of sacred marriage, functions in the Bible as a metaphor for blessing, miracle, joy, and it extends into the idea of resurrection and spiritual life.[27] Physically, husband and wife share the same human identity before God, becoming united in "one flesh" (Gen. 2.24). Together, man and wife complete each other, discovering companionship and intimacy and, together with God, produce children (Gen. 4.1). Mary is the archetypal young woman who gives birth, but she represents something more, for she rejoices that "the child to be born will be holy; he will be called Son of God" (Luke 1.35); "for the Mighty One has done great things for me, and holy is his name" (1.49). At some point in the New Testament, the imagery of mother gives way to that of bride, with Revelation imaging Christ as Bridegroom and the Church as Bride.*[28]

### The Metaphor of Father and Child (Matt. 6; Rom. 5.12–14; 1 Sam. 2.29, 34; 3.10–14; 2 Sam.13; Gen. 21, 25, 37)

In the Bible, fatherhood provides a general theology and a major archetype, occurring over 1,000 times.[29] On the human level, the Bible presents fathers as progenitors of descendants, agents of blessing, heads of their clans, overseers of the economic fortunes of their families, authorities, and, at their best, spiritual paragons.[30] Physical fathers, however, fail abysmally. They do not protect their children, they show preferential love, bumble in handling family discord, neglect to discipline, allow their children to be overcome with secular concerns, and, all too often, demonstrate their own flesh-and-blood vulnerabilities. Against these images, God the Father provides the example of what an ideal father should be.

The Old Testament uses "son" as a symbol for Israel (Exod. 4.22–3), describing Israel as first-born son; throughout, it depicts an ideal fatherhood that culminates in the image of the relationship between God and the Son in the Christian Bible. The Gospel of Mark presents Jesus as the Son of God (1.9–11). The New Testament, in fact, makes at least 150 references to Christ as "the Son," "the Son of God," or "the Son of Man."[31]

The Lord's Prayer, discussed in the chapter on sub-genres, acknowledges divine paternity; Jesus teaches the disciples to pray to the Father as "Our Father in heaven . . ." (Matt. 6.9). Through the metaphor of Father, the concrete and finite world is connected to the eternal and infinite. The Creator is father of all children who participate in the Father's kingdom: "Your kingdom come. Your will be done, on earth as it is in heaven" (6.10). The prayer then pictures the ideal care of the Father, who provides daily bread (6.11), who forgives failures (6.12), and rescues his children (6.13).

*The Bible, as one would expect, presents a catalog of fathers: Adam, Noah, Abraham, Lot, Jacob, Isaac, Manoah, Eli, David, Solomon, Job, Joseph (the father of Jesus); likewise, Psalms and Proverbs address fathers generally and prescribe their responsibility for the upbringing of children.*[32] *These fathers illustrate humanity's failure generally to live up to any ideal set for itself: Adam leaves a legacy of disobedience to his children; Eli, a priest, cannot control his sons, who scandalize the Israelites and God, and Eli himself loves his sons more than God; King David cannot control his own children (a daughter, Tamar, is raped; he does not discipline Amnon; and he cannot reconcile himself to Absalom); Abraham loves Isaac over Ishmael; Isaac dotes on Esau rather than Jacob; and Jacob loves Joseph more than his other sons.*[33]

### The Metaphor of Master and Servant (Gen. 18, 24; 1 Kings 8; Mal. 1.6; Matt. 20; John 13; 1 Peter 2.16; Rev. 19)

Beginning with Genesis and continuing through Revelation, the Bible demonstrates the relationship of servant to master. When the LORD appears to Abraham in the form of three men, Abraham extends full hospitality as a servant, providing them water to wash and giving them bread (Gen. 18.3–5). Rebekah extends similar hospitality to a servant sent by Abraham to find a wife for Isaac; when the servant asks for a drink of water from her jar, she replies, "Drink, my lord," and offers to draw water for his camels also (Gen. 24.18, 19). Jacob, when he encounters Esau, many years after stealing his birthright, refers to Esau as lord and himself as servant (Gen. 32). Moses is identified as the servant of the LORD. Solomon describes his father David as a servant and himself as the servant who will build the temple for God that his father aspired to build (1 Kings 8). Malachi says, "A son honors his father, and servants, their master" (1.6). When the mother of James and John ask that they be permitted to sit one at Jesus' right hand and the other at his left, Jesus turns the concept of servant on its head by telling her, "whoever wishes to be great among you must be your servant, and whoever wishes to be first among you must be your slave; just as the Son of Man came not to be served but to serve, and to give his life a ransom for many" (Matt. 20.26–8). John 13.16 says that servants are not greater than their master. 1 Peter 2.16 instructs the servants of God to live as free people. In Revelation, John falls down before the angel who has brought the "true words of God" but is reprimanded: "You must not do that! I am a fellow servant with you and your comrades who hold the testimony of Jesus" (19.9).

*It will be helpful at this point to recall the definition of archetype at the beginning of this chapter as representing the universal elements of human experience – expressed in patterns, in images, or in symbols. These often reveal themselves in a pair of opposites: the ideal and the un-ideal; wish fulfillment and anxiety; and longings and fears. I introduced also Northrop Frye's idea that the Bible symbolizes a wide imaginative unity that includes creation, fall, exodus, migration, destruction of the human race in the past (deluge) or the future (apocalypse), and redemption – patterns within mythology that give rise to an infinitely greater order. I want to discuss now the image of ascent into this greater order by looking at two archetypal images involved with mountains, one in the Old Testament and one in the New Testament. The corollary of ascent is descent, and both can be connected to an experience of intensifying consciousness.*[34]

## Archetypal Encounters of the Divine and Human

(Lev. 1–7; Hebrews; Exod. 3.1–2, 19, 20; Deut. 1.6, 4.10; 1 Kings 19.8–18; Mal. 4.4; Matt. 4.8, 5.1, 17.1–8; Mark 3.13, 9.2–8; Luke 4.5, 9.28–36, 23, 24; Acts 1.10–12; Jer. 17)

*Two dramatic encounters of the divine and human occur on Mount Horeb and at Golgotha; both represent symbolically the coming together of the infinite and the finite. On Mount Horeb, Moses receives two tablets of law, one addressing the relationship of human beings to God, and the other addressing the relationship of human beings to human beings; Christianity has interpreted Jesus' death on the cross as a bearing of the curse of God incurred by continued disobedience to the law (Gal. 3.13–14).*

### *Mount Horeb/Sinai*

*The different names for the mountain have been explained as resulting from multiple strands of tradition being wound together to produce the first five books of the Old Testament (discussed in chapter 4).*

There are over 500 references in the Bible to mountains and hills, an image conveying physical place, inspiring awe, and sacred site.[35] Individuals experience theophanies, the revelation of the transcendent God, on mountain tops: God appears to Moses on Mount Horeb (Elohist and Deuteronomist sources, Exod. 3.1–2); and the Israelites experience God on Mount Sinai (Yahwist and Priestly sources), an encounter accompanied by fire, smoke, and earthquake (Exod. 19). When Jezebel kills the prophets of God, Elijah flees to Mount Horeb and encounters God in the form of a voice (1 Kings 19.8–18). In the New Testament, Jesus refutes the temptation of Satan on a mountain (Matt. 4.8; Luke 4.5), is transfigured (Matt. 17.1–8; Mark 9.2–8; Luke 9.28–36), teaches from a mountain (Matt. 5.1; Mark 3.13), and ascends from the Mount of Olives (Acts 1.10–12).

The motif of the Mountain of God unites the Old and New Testaments: first in the form of Mount Sinai, and then in its displacement as the dwelling place of God in Mount Zion.[36] The two mountains share similarities – associated with God's appearance and dwelling, the place of the law, covered by cloud and fire – and differences – people stream to Mountain Zion rather than being fenced away ("Set limits around the mountain and keep it holy"; Exod. 19.23). Holy presence is comforting rather than threatening; Zion becomes a synecdoche for the entire city of Jerusalem and land of Israel, and, in Revelation, a symbol for the Church of God (14.1). The two mountains, taken together, can be argued to trace an important theological theme throughout the Bible: the progress of redemption.

Exodus 19 sets the stage for the giving of the Ten Commandments in Exodus 20. Moses goes up to the LORD, who calls to him from the mountain, instructing him in relation to what he is to tell the Israelites, who have just entered the wilderness of Sinai. He is to remind them of the covenant: "if you obey my voice and keep my covenant, you shall be for me a priestly kingdom and a holy nation." Moses keeps faith and sets before the Israelites the word of God (19.7). He consecrates the people, preparing them for the descent of God to the mountain: on the third day, "Mount Sinai was wrapped in smoke, because the LORD had descended upon it in fire; the smoke went up like the smoke of a kiln, while the whole mountain shook violently" (19.18). Moses is instructed to set limits around the mountain and to keep the people away from the holy site. After giving Moses the Commandments, God then forbids the making of gods of silver and gold, requiring that they make only "an altar of earth and sacrifice on it your burnt-offerings and your offerings of well-being, your sheep and your oxen; in every place where I cause my name to be remembered I will come to you and bless you" (20.23, 24).[37]

The importance of mountains to the establishment of community has two contexts: one is the Law (Sinai), and the other is sacrifice, the means through which communion with God is established. It was on Moriah that Abraham had been commanded to sacrifice Isaac. Although ancient cultures used sacrifice as a way of winning divine favor, the more common use in the Bible invokes the sense of a gift offered to God and symbolizes that human beings owe their very lives to God, the sacrifice standing in the place of that obligation.[38] The images of sacrifice include blood, fire, and smoke, with the animal sacrifices always involving blood because "the life of the flesh is in the blood; . . . as life, it is the blood that makes atonement" (Lev. 17.11). In a similar way, Christians understand Jesus' death upon the cross as, once and for all, a sacrifice and atonement for transgressions. This notion of atonement has broad theological meaning, proposing a separation or estrangement that is overcome in a reconciliation.[39]

Hebrews, perhaps more than any other book in the Bible, explores the relationship between the Hebrew sacrificial rites and the sacrificial death of Jesus, uniting many of the images of the Old and New Testaments. Christ is seen as the high priest (9.11) entering into the tabernacle (9.11) and finally into the Holy of Holies to offer his blood for eternal redemption (9.12). In Romans, Paul has already used sacrifice to explain a way of Christian living: "I appeal to you therefore, brothers and sisters, by the mercies of God, to present your bodies as a living sacrifice, holy and acceptable to God, which is your spiritual worship" (Rom. 12.1, 2). The writer of Hebrews makes Christ the mediator of a **New Covenant**, connecting this covenant to the covenants made with Abraham, Noah, Moses, and David, and proclaiming it the culmination and purpose of the prior covenants.

### The Mount of the Skull

All four Gospels vividly detail the crucifixion of Jesus. The imagery of the cross becomes an expression of suffering, commitment, self-denial, and the bridging of the gap between humanity and God, the breaking of the barrier between Jew and Gentile, and the restoration, in fact, of the entire cosmos.[40]

The New Testament, whether or not one agrees with its theology, interprets the Old Testament sacrifice to expiate sin typologically: all sacrifices are made in anticipation of the supreme sacrifice (1 Cor. 5.7; Eph. 5.2; Heb. 10.1, 11, 12). 1 Corinthians 5.7 says, "Clean out the old yeast so that you may be a new batch, as you really are unleavened. For our paschal lamb, Christ, has been sacrificed." Ephesians 5.2 makes a similar interpretation: "Therefore be imitators of God, as beloved children, and live in love, as Christ loved us and gave himself up for us, a fragrant offering and sacrifice to God." Hebrews, as previously pointed out, delineates this theology even more completely: the law is only a shadow of the things to come; by a single offering, Christ perfected for all time the sanctified, completing the act, and sitting down at the right hand of God (10.1, 11–14). As type, all earlier sacrifices represent the archetype, the original pattern (the last is first), and, in this case, the sacrifice of Jesus becomes the atonement sacrifice (Lev. 16.15, 16, with Heb. 9.12, 14), the Passover lamb (Exod. 12.36, 46, with John 19.36; 1 Cor. 5.7); the peace offering (Lev. 3.1 with Eph. 2.14, 16); and the sin offering (Lev. 4.23, 12, with Heb. 13.11, 12).

Blood figures prominently in the crucifixion as a source of life. As pointed out already, Leviticus describes the "life" of the flesh as being in its blood. David, in battle with the Philistines, thirsts for water from the well of Bethlehem, yet refuses to drink it when provided, saying, "The LORD forbid that I should do this. Can I drink the blood of the men who went at the risk of their lives?" (2 Sam. 23.17). In Mark, on the first day of the Feast of Unleavened Bread the disciples make preparation for the Passover, at which Jesus celebrates, taking the cup and explaining, "This is my blood of the covenant, which is poured out for many. Truly I tell you, I will never again drink of the fruit of the vine until that day when I drink it new in the kingdom of God" (Mark 14.24–5). At the crucifixion, one of the soldiers pierced Jesus' side with a spear, and at once blood and water came out. The book of 1 John interprets this symbolically: "This is the one who came by water and blood, Jesus Christ" (5.6–8).

Although extremely literal, rooted in concrete human experience, the Bible always stands for something in addition to the literal; it is laden with symbolic meaning. This can be illustrated in the use of trees, which figure prominently in their natural state: they present images of majesty, beauty, stateliness, affording places of security and rest; they bear abundant fruit, their deep roots resisting drought. In an arid land, the generic references to trees, at least 250 times, point not to their abundance, but to their special significance.[41] They thrive when well watered, and they offer protection and shade; they also provide fruit in their season.

Metaphorically and symbolically, trees take on greater significance. For example, Jeremiah laments the green trees and high hills on which the children of Judah have offered sacrifices to gods other than Yahweh; as a result, God's anger is described as a fire kindled against them (17.4), his judgment as reducing them to shrubs in the desert and the uninhabited salt lands of the wilderness (17.6); contrasted to these, those who trust in God enjoy his provision: "They shall be like a tree planted by water, / sending out its roots by the stream. / It shall not fear when heat comes, / and its leaves shall stay green; / in the year of drought it is not anxious, / and it does not cease to bear fruit" (17.8).

Trees symbolize strength, power, glory, wealth, honor – qualities that, in human beings, can lead to pride, exaltation, and arrogance (Isa. 2.13); all too often, they come to represent a divinization of the natural order, leading to the orgies of nature religion described by the prophets where idols are worshipped "under every spreading tree and oak" (Ezek. 6.13; 1 Kings 14.23). Used in their positive sense, trees represent a renewed, created order: Psalms says, when the LORD is king, "Then shall all the trees of the forest sing for joy" (96.12); Isaiah describes a time when the desert will be replanted with cedar, acacia, myrtle, olive, pine, fir, and cypress trees (Isa. 41.19) and "all the trees of the field shall clap their hands" (Isa. 55.12–13).

In the beginning of Genesis, the tree of life symbolizes life and immortality, and in Revelation the tree of life connects the creation of the world to the re-created world that is to come.[42] Adam and Eve eat from the tree of knowledge of good and evil, interpreted by some as God's mercifully preventing them from eating of the tree of life and, as a result, dooming themselves to endless physical life in an imperfect world. Alienated, the tree of life provides an image of loss and nostalgia not restored until Revelation: "On either side of the river is the tree of life with its twelve kinds of fruit, producing its fruit each month; and the leaves of the tree are for the healing of the nation" (22.2). Thus, Genesis and Revelation envelop other images of trees, especially in Proverbs, that represent fullness and blessing. Both the tabernacle and the lampstand have been linked to tree images.

At the center of these two trees of life, the cross comes to symbolize curse and blessing, judgment and healing.[43] As mentioned before, Galatians 3 describes Jesus as publicly exhibited in the crucifixion (3.1), links this to a discussion of law and faith, then describes how Jesus became a curse: "Christ redeemed us from the curse of the law by becoming a curse for us – for it is written, 'Cursed is everyone who hangs on a tree'" (3.13). The reference draws upon Deuteronomy, which explains that an executed person hanging on a tree represents God's curse (21.23). This curse brings about the renewal of life and immortality, illustrating how a single image contributes to unity and coherence in the Bible as a whole. Rather than thinking of the Old Testament as "old" and the New Testament as "new," it should be possible to explain them as providing a full metaphorical and archetypal picture of the envisioned ideal world realized in the final descent of a new heaven and earth.[44]

## Close Reading

*Exercise 1*
Read several chapters from the Gospel of John. The book has often been described as addressing two realms: earthly and heavenly. How does reading at a literal level help with understanding "earthly" meaning? Discuss figurative language as moving reading to a symbolic level and presenting the "heavenly" or infinite realm.

*Exercise 2*
Read selections from the following, then explain how the images of light, fire, and darkness work on both the literal and the symbolic level. Gen. 1.1–5, 1.20, 2, 13, 19.11, 26; Isa. 6.9–10, 29.9–10, 43.8, 45.7; John 1, 4; Rev. 1.15, 2.10, 21, 22.1–2; 1 John; 2 Peter 2, 3.5–6; Exod. 10, 13, 24, 25, 27; Judg. 16, 19; 2 Sam. 23; Job 2; Luke 8.22–5; Ezek. 47; Jer. 2.13; 2 Kings 6.18, 25.7; Acts 9; Deut. 28.28–9; Rom. 1.21; Matt. 14, 15.14, 23.16–17, 19.24, 26.

*Exercise 3*
Read Luke 8 and Matthew 14. How is the mastery of nature an imagistic portrayal of the divine? Read selective passages from the Gospels. How do the writers demonstrate the presence of God?

*Exercise 4*
Review the lives of Kings Saul, David, and Solomon. How should they be assessed relative to their advancing Israel's history in relation to keeping and abiding by the covenant relationship? Which covenant most applies?

*Exercise 5*
The Christian Church considers the following to be archetypes: lamb (Gen. 3.21; Exod. 12.3, 5; John 1.29); Noah's ark (Gen. 6, 12, 13, 14); Egypt and Canaan; Mount Sinai and Mount Moriah; Abraham and Isaac (Gen. 30, 37); Eliezer and Rebekah (Gen. 24). Provide rationale for or against this use.

*Exercise 6*
Explain how characters such as Elijah (wildman), Moses (warrior), and Solomon (king) function as archetypes. Are there female equivalents?

*Exercise 7*
To what extent may the Christian New Testament be explained as a reinterpretation of Old Testament traditions?

*Exercise 8*
Describe how the Bible in its entirety exhibits a myth of creation, fall, exodus, migration, the destruction of the human past (deluge), the future (apocalypse), and redemption?

*Exercise 9*
Choose one concrete image, then demonstrate how the Bible uses it as metaphor, motif, symbol, and archetype.

*Exercise 10*
Choose a well-known passage such as Isaiah 53 or Psalm 23 and explain whether it should be read as mostly literal or mostly metaphorical and figurative.

## Questions for Reflection

1  What differences exist between reading the Bible literally and reading it symbolically?
2  How can images become symbols and archetypes?
3  In what ways do human beings come to know God and God's law? Illustrate with examples from both the Old and the New Testament.
4  What is the meaning of the name Jesus?
5  Does the Bible achieve an overall unity and coherence among its multiple texts? Can the conflict between arguments for unity and coherence and for originating traditions be reconciled? How?
6  How do light and water function as master images?
7  What metaphors express the divine–human relationship?
8  How do these metaphors move from the literal image to figurative meaning?
9  What dangers exist when readers interpret metaphors in the Bible literally?
10  What were some of the failures of the three kings during Israel's monarchy?
11  How does adding "new" to the words man, creation, birth, covenant, and Jerusalem change their original meanings?
12  To what degree should the Old Testament be read as a collection of ancient texts that have meaning separate from the Christian tradition?
13  How do Joseph and Boaz emerge as ideal pictures of husbands?
14  How does the kinsman-redeemer motif relate to the Christian concept of salvation?
15  How does fertility become a metaphor for blessing and fulfillment?
16  How does "son" function as a symbol for Israel?
17  How do the Mount Horeb and crucifixion experiences present archetypal encounters with the divine?
18  How can an image contribute to meaning, coherence, and unity in the Bible?
19  What is the symbolic significance of the crucifixion?
20  What essential differences exist between the tree of life in Genesis and the tree of life in Revelation?
21  How does use of the "**literary present**" enhance the experience of the reader?
22  What is the connection between baptism, the wilderness experience, and the crossing of the Jordan?
23  Do you consider the presentations of God as father and God as judge as incompatible?

# 4 Major Genres: A Way of Seeing

## Outline

Preliminary Considerations
    Major Genres and Related Definitions
    Genre Criticism
Narrative
    Stories with Structured Plot
    Linking Episodes
    Episodes in the New Testament Linked to the Old Testament
    Genesis
        Genre
        Stories
        Groups of Stories
        Cycles and the Macro-Plot
Drama and Poetry
Close Reading
Questions for Reflection

*I have been suggesting throughout this introductory text that the basic tools of literary analysis can be used for reading and understanding the Bible. I want us to keep in mind the importance of close reading and the need to focus on the Bible as a whole. The first chapter gives you the background for beginning to read more closely. The second chapter explores several rhetorical devices that, when recognized, become extremely important in helping you to understand what a text is saying and how it says it. The third chapter, on the use of image, metaphor, symbol, and archetype, explores the larger patterns in language that connect Bible texts to the language of literature and to its expression of universal human experience.*

*In this chapter and the one following, I introduce the major genres (the types and categories) into which literary works are grouped according to form, technique/style, or subject matter/content; I explain how a literary genre, once recognized, contributes a set of expectations that shapes a reader's interpretation of a text. Other terms that require a working definition are narrative, prose, poetry, fiction, and nonfiction. As you think about prose and narrative, both probably familiar to you from your introductory courses in literature, you may want to keep in mind the fact that these make up more than half of the Old Testament (about one-third is poetry) and at least half of the New Testament.*

## Preliminary Considerations

*The following definitions create only a "starting point" for understanding genres, and you will need to be careful about applying them rigidly. For example, poetry and prose overlap; the language of prose can be poetic, and poetry will sometimes appear in the form of prose. What has been called "creative or imaginative literature," as opposed to the literature of science, history, and philosophy (more closely related to fact or what has actual existence), can be found in both prose (think of novels and short stories) and poetry. Creative works may be valued to the extent that they accurately interpret the human situation and reveal what is true to life.[1] The definition of literature as creative and imaginative has a more recent history than the written works of the Bible itself, but a case can be made that the Bible uses the universal language of literature that arises from the earliest forms of verse, music, and imitative gesture.[2]*

*The Bible has been regarded as a model for literary genres, its overriding form being that of an anthology made up of diverse genres. Both the Old and the New Testament, beyond being looked at as literature, have some degree of documentary and didactic purpose: to get historical facts before the reader and to impart theological ideas and moral imperatives.[3] In fact, a study of genre in and of itself leaves unaddressed the inner matter and spirit of the books. This text introduces the common tools of literary analysis and, to this end, introduces genre as an interpretive tool belonging to a culture shared by writers and readers. Those unfamiliar with biblical genres will recognize the familiar types – prose, poetry, and drama. Recognizing these conventions or norms helps to guide you in your encounters with text, telling you what to look for and how to organize your experience of it.[4]*

A French term, **genre** means "type," "sort," or "kind" and designates the literary form into which works are classified according to what they have in common, either in their formal structures or in their treatment of subject matter, or both.[5] Genre criticism belongs to the more encompassing "form criticism," which directs attention to four elements: (1) the plot, structure, or shape of the passage in question; (2) the identification of genre or category to which a text will be assigned, such as narrative, prophecy, poetry/psalmody, wisdom, law, proverb, satire, parable, and drama (the New Testament expands the types with the addition of travelogue, oratory, sermon, and courtroom forensics; the Letters mix epistolary conventions, exhortation, and lyric; and Revelation, for example, includes a collage of genres, mixing epistolary, visionary, poetic, narrative, and dramatic); (3) the history of the text being analyzed and its genre, positing a setting in actual life; and, finally, (4) form criticism, which looks at the purpose of the genre in the passage under scrutiny. Form criticism overall, then, addresses structure, genre, setting, and intent.[6]

## Major Genres and Related Definitions

*In classical times (Plato, Aristotle, and, later, Horace), the major genres, from which other genres have proliferated, were known as* **lyric** *(clearly identified as poetry),* **drama** *(relating to performance, with characters speaking for a writer in prose or poetry), and* **epic** *(in its classical form, referring to poetic narrative, but broadened to include poetry and prose). As modes or kinds of communication,* **prose, poetry**, *and* **drama** *vary in different cultures and historical periods, the first characterized by being closer to the language of normal conversation, and the second by literary artifice and the special use of poetic form and devices.*[7] *In literature,* **narrative** *has been applied to prose which presents chronological or sequenced events to tell a* **story** *or stories (what happens) in a particular way.*[8] *Stories can be based on fact or made up imaginatively.*

As genres, prose (narrative), drama, and poetry provide a way of seeing the world and arranging its content; this arrangement creates new forms of reality. Such new forms require readers to understand the relationship between actual life and the life depicted in literature. Stories that have been made up imaginatively belong to the genre called *fiction*, which, too narrowly, has been interpreted as "not true." Fiction, metaphorically, tells the truth of human experience, and should not be classified as false in the sense that it has no correspondence to historical reality. In fact, imagination takes actual events from history and reorders them deliberately into a fiction that often tells profound truths about human beings, the world they inhabit, and the human condition.[9] With regard to the Bible, people over the centuries have traditionally read it as telling the perennial truths about a paradoxical God and the paradoxical nature and situation of human beings.[10]

Story and narrative require that special attention should be paid to the literary elements of plot, characterization, point of view, narrative voice, and closure, these contributing to the overall complex literary structure of narrative. *Plot* refers to the story or succession of events, including conflict, suspense, and conclusion, events linked explicitly or implicitly in a cause-and-effect structure.[11] The arrangement of plot in narrative emphasizes chronological order (sequentiality) and themes (a unifying quality or idea). Characters people the story and generate the actions that make up the plot. Both theme and character will be explored in later chapters. *Setting* includes time, location, and everything in which a story takes place; it can also influence characters. A *narrator* is the entity that tells the story to its readers. *Point of view* refers to the perspective from which the story is told and can exist in first person (I, we) or third person (he, she, it, and they). In first-person point of view, the narrator participates as a character in the story. In third person, the narrator functions as an "all-knowing mind" standing behind the stories. Biblical narrative has its own set of narrative devices: repetition (words, motifs, themes, whole scenes), which provides coherence and composite unity; omission (a tendency to omit information); dialogue (narrating through dialogue, using dialogue to reveal psychological and ideological points of view, often with two-character dialogue dominating); and irony.[12]

Like fiction, drama, through a sequence of interconnected events, tells a story and presents actors confronted by conflicts that they attempt to resolve. Fiction, drama, and poetry all use speech or dialogue to reveal or conceal characters' thoughts, motives, and intentions. Biblical poetry uses rhythm and meter, structure and form, as well as special devices of repetition such as allusion, ambiguity, puns and paradoxes, irony, imagery, comparisons, personification, apostrophe, animism, symbol, and allegory, and generally conforms to the rules of employing quantity, meter, and compact language. Fiction and drama also make use of these poetic devices.

### Genre Criticism

Genre criticism has been plagued by a number of critical attacks over its 2,000 years of use. A first doubt arises from the way one understands reality. Do genres exist objectively, or are they merely constructions? For the most part, genre theory has been concerned with dividing the world of literature into types and naming those types, similar to the scientific process of establishing genus and species. Types, however, may be viewed as timeless essences or ephemeral as opposed to time bound. Is the taxonomy finite or infinite? Culture bound or transcultural? Descriptive or proscriptive?[13] The Renaissance through the eighteenth century tended to view genres as fixed and timeless; with the Romantics, imagination and experimentation were preferred to rules, genres, and decorum, and genre criticism fell into disuse. Complex discussions revolve around whether genres should be viewed as extrinsic or intrinsic to their content or as having both an outer and an inner dimension; most today view them as generic conventions from which authors draw to set up reader expectation. The argument can be made that genre will be affected by the one making the grouping and that types cannot be clearly distinguished one from another, since they may overlap and become mixed.

*You should be aware that a fairly standard approach to the Bible, since the eighteenth century, has looked predominantly at originating sources, usually referred to as source criticism. Because it is commonly applied to studies of the first five books of the Old Testament, I have summarized some of this in supporting tables (www.readingthebibleasliterature.com) and allude to it in my discussions in this chapter of stories and narratives. Generally, source criticism may be said to focus upon texts and textuality and to belong to a view of reality that sees truth as external and discovered by reason and science; against this view, what has been described as a rhetorical approach sees human beings as creating meaning, fashioning and manipulating what is construed as reality.*[14]

At the root of much of the discussion about sources is an ongoing debate about whether the Bible is one book or consists of many books.[15] A product of source theory has been a growing understanding of the Bible as a composite text, evidence for this arising out of repeated accounts of actions or stories, different names for God, variations in political assumptions, diction, and style, incompatible or inconsistent statements, and different viewpoints on religious matters.[16] A focus upon historical study leads to a search for originating sources.[17]

The traditions or sources giving rise to the Bible have a close relationship with the existing forms or genres of biblical literature as they developed out of an oral history. Biblical writing, some suggest, mingles, subverts, renews, and sometimes rejects these traditions.[18] Usually, biblical scholars have argued that the first five books of the Old Testament (known as the Pentateuch and also as the Torah) were not written by one person, Moses, but that multiple strands of traditions were woven together to produce these books (composites). The **Documentary Hypothesis** usually presents them as composed by a series of editors out of four literary traditions known as J (Yahwist or Jerusalem source), E (Elohist or Ephraimitic), P (Priestly), and D (Deuteronomic). The New Interpreter's Study Bible dates the Yahwist and the Elohist traditions to the monarchy (1000–800 BCE) and the Priestly to the exile and restoration (587–500 BCE).[19] The Deuteronomic is usually dated to the era of King Josiah in the 600s BCE. Richard E. Friedman has made attempts to separate the various sources in the Pentateuch, and Harold Bloom and co-author David Rosenberg have attempted to reconstruct the Yahwist writings.[20] Different models of source criticism exist: Classical, Fragmentary, Supplementary, and Mixed.[21]

The majority opinion among biblical scholars today suggests the Gospels were also based upon two sources. The **Two Source Hypothesis**, first proposed in 1855, stresses Markan priority. Mark was written first, and Matthew and Luke used it as a source. Matthew and Luke also used a second source, usually called "Q" for Quelle (the German for "source"), and other unique materials (consisting of sayings not included in Mark).

## Narrative

I turn now to the twofold purpose of this section: I want to introduce you to the key elements of story evidenced in selections from the Bible; I also want to explore with you how the Bible takes individual stories and weaves them together to form an ever greater narrative that has been described as having its own beginning, middle, and end – a unifying plot conflict that begins with the beginning of human history and ends with the consummation of history.[22] In the first chapter, I suggested several ways in which the Bible can be divided into narrative sections, such as the First and Second Temple periods and epic-like past events. The Documentary Hypothesis itself divides biblical narrative into four *separate and independent story lines. This section begins with a discussion of story as a discrete unit that can stand independent of the whole, and then moves to the linkage of episodes into greater wholes.*

Biblical narrative distinctively consists of episodes that link together chains of stories to form an overarching framework with its own story and plot.[23] Defined simply, an **episode** consists of phases and steps grouped into a complete story, and results in some form of problem/resolution that can often be subdivided into rising, turning, and falling action.[24] Most modern translations of the Bible make clear distinctions between prose and poetry, chapters, books, and topical headings. Determining boundaries among units, however, requires careful reading and attention to language, and readers may still disagree about the beginnings and endings of stories and overarching episodes. Discrete stories may be the easiest to identify; biblical scholars, though, point out that even a simple story such as the creation, told in two accounts, poses a problem for identifying where one account ends and another begins.

### Stories with Structured Plot (Luke 19.1–10; 2 Kings 4)

*You will recognize many of the familiar stories of the Bible. In the Old Testament, for example, stories stand out: the flood, Moses, the stories of Isaac and Ishmael, Joseph's revenge, Israel in Egypt, the Red Sea, the Golden Calf, the walls of Jericho, the conquest of Canaan, and the stories of characters such as Samson, Ruth, Samuel, Elijah, Elisha, Naaman, Daniel, and Esther.[25] The New Testament is equally rich: think of the Lost Sheep, the Prodigal Son, the Ten Virgins, the Good Samaritan, the rich man and the beggar Lazarus, Ananias and Sapphira, the stoning of Stephen, Paul's conversion, and the ascension of Jesus.*

An example of a short story in the New Testament that has all the characteristics of story – structured plot, protagonists, and theme – is that of Zacchaeus, a favorite with children (Luke 19.1–10).[26] In this story, the conflict involves the main character (**protagonist**), Zacchaeus, who wants to see Jesus, but is prevented from doing so because he is not tall enough to see over the heads of the crowd. The **exposition** gives the setting, Jericho, and introduces Zacchaeus, who resolves (**resolution)** his conflict by climbing a tree. This decision brings the plot to its crisis or turning point: Jesus talks (**dialogue)** with Zacchaeus and asks him to descend and host him for lunch, a life-changing event for Zacchaeus.

The story of the poor widow in 2 Kings 4 demonstrates the careful structure of a well-written composition.[27] Her husband has left a debt that she can't pay, creating the threat that her children will become slaves. Elisha provides a solution to her problem by giving her vessels that continually replenish themselves with oil. Without saying so, the **omniscient narrator**, who takes the reader behind doors to observe the continually full vessel of oil, allows the prophet to have the last say, telling the widow she can sell the oil and repay her debt, and that she and her children can live on the rest of the proceeds. The story has two characters, the Shunammite woman and Elisha. The woman speaks and formulates the problem and is then instructed by Elisha; the story, though, remains her story: she is the heroine who experiences the miracle.

### *Linking Episodes (1 Kings 17; Jer. 35.8–16; 2 Sam. 1, 12, 18; Job 1)*

Story exists at the level of the simplest unit of narrative, displaying significant independence from the larger context; narratives also have larger structures whereby episodes can be arranged thematically, chronologically, as parallel stories, or as stories in a cluster. The above story of Elisha and the poor widow becomes an episode when placed into the greater whole of both 1 and 2 Kings and of the Old Testament itself. Elisha's story parallels that of Elijah in 1 Kings 17.14–16). In this story, the prophet Elijah is commanded to go to the widow of Zarephath, who will feed him. The widow shares her predicament, having only a handful of meal in a jar and a little oil in a jug. She expresses her desperate state: after she takes this little bit home to eat, she expects that both she and her son will die from starvation. Elijah, like Elisha later, provides a solution – a jar that will not be emptied and a jug that will not fail. The story ends happily: Elijah, she, and her son eat for many days.

Readers will find in Jeremiah (35.8–16) a link to the Elisha story in the practice of reducing to slavery those who cannot pay their debts. By this time, a practice has evolved of setting slaves free every seventh year (35.14). This narrative makes clear, however, that the people have been guilty of granting release only to enslave once more (35.16). The New Testament book of Philemon addresses the issue of slavery and a view of liberation as physical, social, spiritual, and theological, linking this book to the traditions of the past.[28]

The repetition of narrative events hints at an overall shape and purpose in the composition of the Bible.[29] Some scenes and episodes occur so often that they can be called **type-scenes**, a term originated by Robert Alter, with a conventionally predetermined set of motifs or plots.[30] An example of this can be found in 2 Samuel 1. An Amalekite servant brings news to David of the deaths of Saul and his son Jonathan. The servant then tells David that he, at Saul's request, helped him to commit suicide. Mourning follows the news, including the traditional tearing of clothes, weeping, and fasting. The lament then occurs in 1.17–27.

Comparing the above account to other similar passages, 2 Samuel 18 and Job 1.13–21, helps to identify it as a "type-scene." In the first, David mourns for his son Absalom, the passage resonating with the familiar words, "Oh my son, Absalom. My son, my son Absalom. Would that I had died instead of you" (18.33). The second has a messenger reporting to Job that his servants, daughters, and sons have been attacked and killed, and describes Job's response. Taken together, these episodes have essentially the same structure and same sequence of events: arrival of a messenger, listener's response, mourner's verbal response.

Another lament (2 Samuel 12) inverts the conventionally expected behaviors. Instead of expressing sorrow relative to the profound loss of his infant son, David instead asks and answers his own question: "Can I bring him back again? I shall go to him, but he will not return to me" (12.23). This **parody** signals its presence by the behaviors of those in the story: the reluctant, fearful messenger and the servants who question David's lack of grief. The question of why this lament inverts the "type-scene" occurs naturally, and at least one possibility is that it pictures David in the beginning of a downward spiral of psychological well-being and political career.[31] The first two episodes distance David from the acts and seem to garner public approval; in the last, the servants clearly do not approve of his behavior.

*When you come to the New Testament, you will hear consistent echoes (allusions) that remind you of stories in the Old Testament. Without attempting to resolve the controversial question of whether events foreshadow or reinterpret each other, I want to suggest that the literature as it exists must be understood not only in relation to itself, but in relation to the whole. A characteristic of biblical writing is its density of allusion and its remarkableness for activating one text with another.[32]*

### Episodes in the New Testament Linked to the Old Testament (Mark 1.12–13, 21–8, 29–31; 3.21, 4.35–41, 5.21–4, 35–43; 6.1–6, 30–44, 45–52; 7.14–30; 8.1–10; 10.13–16; 1 Kings 19.15–17; Exod. 4.27–8; 8.14–21; 18; Jonah 1; 1 Sam. 10.1–27; 2 Kings 4.42–4)

Once familiar with the Elisha and Elijah stories above, readers will immediately pick up on similarities in stories in the Gospel of Mark.[33] Recall that Elisha solves a poor widow's problem by providing her with vessels that are continually replenished with oil; Elijah provides the widow of Zarephath with a jar of meal and a jug of oil that are also continually replenished. In the latter story, after the advent of Elijah's provision of food, the woman's son becomes ill, so severely so that he nears death, with "no breath left in him." She then comes to Elijah, asking, "What have you against me, O man of God?" In Mark (1.21–8), a man with an unclean spirit cries out to Jesus, "What have you to do with us, Jesus of Nazareth? Have you come to destroy us? I know who you are, the Holy One of God." In a later passage in Mark, a Syro-Phoenician woman (7.24–30) begs Jesus to cast a demon from her daughter. Jesus tells her to let the children be fed first, just as Elijah tests the widow by asking her to take her remaining meal and to feed him first.

Other stories in Mark activate memories of the Elijah and Elisha narratives. In the case of the healing of Peter's mother-in-law (Mark 1.29–31), echoes from both stories can be heard. In this story, Jesus hears that the mother-in-law of Simon (Peter) has a fever; Jesus takes her by the hand and lifts her up; the fever leaves her, and she begins to serve the disciples. The woman of Zarephath, after Elijah provides for her and her son, serves him. The Shunammite woman, after her son has been raised from the dead, serves Elisha. In this case, Mark uses similar ideas but makes the mother herself the recipient of the restorative act. The Shunammite story is also echoed in the raising of Jairus' daughter in Mark 5.21–4 and 35–43. In this account, Jairus comes to Jesus, begging him to heal his daughter, who lies at the point of death. Both the Shunammite prototype and her New Testament counterpart are ecstatic when the children are rescued from death. The writer of Mark clearly expected the audience to recall the account of the Shunammite so that they know what to expect from Jairus, whose name means "he will awaken."

Other familiar New Testament episodes with roots in the Old Testament further suggest the importance of close reading in the context of the whole. Most will recognize in the temptation story (Mark 1.12–13) the link to Moses' years in Midian before he goes back to rescue his people from Egypt, as well as Elijah's forty-day retreat after his contest with the worshippers of Baal (1 Kings 19.15–17). Jesus' recruitment of his disciples (Mark 1.16–20) recalls Moses' recruitment of his brother Aaron (Exod. 4.27–8). Consider the calling of the twelve (Mark 3.21) as being in some ways analogous to Moses' choosing successors (Exod. 18). In both stories families hear of successes and journey to see for themselves what is going on. The stilling of the storm (Mark 4.35–41) has parallels with Jonah and the storm at sea (Jonah 1.4–6). Think of the story of Jesus' family rejecting him (Mark 6.1–6) and then reflect on 1 Samuel (10.1–27), where those who have known Saul ask what has come over him when he begins to speak in tongues. In the story of Jesus, too, the expectation seems to be that prophets must come from out of nowhere, not from a familiar family member. The familiar loaves and fishes story (Mark 6.30–44, 8.1–10) resonates with the story of 1 Kings 19.19–21, where Elisha multiplies twenty barley loaves to feed 100 men. Or, again, the disciples no more understand the feat of Jesus' walking on the sea (Mark 6.45–52) than the children of Israel understand the crossing of the Red Sea or the provision of food in the wilderness (Exod. 8.14–21).

At an overarching level, biblical narrative consists of larger, more comprehensive parts, such as the primary story of the Old Testament consisting of Genesis to the end of 2 Kings, the story being that of a people chosen to realize its vision of land and nationhood and ending in its succumbing to competing nations.[34] A second major narrative consists of Chronicles, Ezra, and Nehemiah, which give an account of Judah from the death of the first king of the monarchy to Judah's restoration from exile. When the New Testament is included, expanding the narrative framework to the Bible as a whole, it can be divided into epic-like stories that take in Moses (the exodus and conquest), the monarchy (kings Saul, David, and Solomon), the divided kingdom (kings, prophets), the exile and restoration, and the advent of Jesus and the establishment of the Church.[35] The story has also been described as paradise, paradise lost, and the redeeming activity in Israel and through Jesus, concluding with paradise restored.[36] In addition, the Bible can be understood through three "macro-stories": the exodus from Egypt, the story of the exile and return from Babylon, and the priestly story of temple, priesthood, and sacrifice – all of these building the foundation for the New Testament.[37]

### Genesis

*If you open Genesis in any version, you will find it, first, printed as a book, suggesting some coherence among its parts that allows it to be thought of as a whole. The next divisions will be into chapters and verses. At yet another level, you will discover headings, either built into the text or appearing as lead-ins to columns. These last will be very useful to you as you attempt to understand literary structure. For example, in the NRSV, you will find the following headings: Six Days of Creation, The Creation of Humankind, The Garden of Eden, The First Sin and its Punishment, Expulsion from Eden, Cain Murders Abel, Adam's Descendants, God Instructs Noah to Make an Ark, The Great Flood, The Flood Subsides, The Covenant of Noah, Nations Descended from Noah, The Tower of Babel, and The Call of Abram (later Abraham); after Abraham, the headings continue but, if you look carefully, you will now find that named people begin to play a role: Isaac, Jacob, Joseph. I want to use Genesis to demonstrate some of the structuring techniques used for biblical narrative.*

### Genre

The opening chapters of Genesis consist of a narration of cosmic and universal events, referred to in literature as myth, a genre embodying a people's perception of its realities: cosmology, cultural values, social structure and customs, internal and external political relationships, and religious rituals and beliefs.[38] As literary genre or type of literature, it has similarities to **ancient, pre-scientific historiography**, a type of writing intended to raise in readers a sense of identity and citizenship – a consciousness of belonging to a great and noble city or race. Like historiography, Genesis interweaves elements of **myth**, **legend**, and historical fact; unlike historiography, though, the Bible presents God as the primary character and human beings as foolish creatures, not always heroes and heroines, who frustrate God's intention toward them. The Bible further differs from Greek and Mesopotamian epics (written in narrative verse) by intermingling prose and poetry.[39]

*Understanding that Genesis resembles historiography should enable you to accept the genres of legend, myth, and tale without concluding that these, in some way, diminish its importance for explaining the Primeval*

*Age or the beginning of the world's civilizations. You will note that, from general beginnings, the Bible moves more specifically into concrete details about the lives of the Patriarchs and to increasingly shorter life spans, making these stories more historical in nature. Understanding that Genesis cannot be described as belonging to the genres of science and history as they have emerged in the modern world will also free you from troubling issues such as assigning an exact chronology to the beginning of the world and to the appearance of the first man and woman. Accepting the Bible's often symbolic use of numbers (seven, for example, signifying completeness and perfection) may give you another tool for understanding the six days of creation and the Sabbath.*

The first chapters of Genesis, known as the primeval history, certainly can be described as bringing together in narrative prose the genres of fable, legend, and myth, using formal rhetorical devices that may echo ancient epic poetry.[40] Early chapters (1–11) contain several stories: the creation of the world and human beings, human beings expelled from the Garden of Eden, Cain and Abel and the first murder, the beginnings of civilization, the generations from Adam to Noah, and the wickedness of humankind.

The next major section of Genesis may be referred to as patriarchal **tales**. Its narrative accounts for the beginnings of the Israelite nation, chapters 12–36 presenting loosely strung together **sagen**, or folktales, of the lives of Abraham, Isaac, and Jacob. It first describes the relationship of God to people through a series of promises to the Patriarch Abraham and his son Isaac (12.21–25.18). The promise of posterity, a land, and people makes Abraham's near sacrifice of Isaac one of the Bible's most poignant and moving stories and raises questions about the character of God.[41] With progressively greater specificity, the Jacob cycle (25.19–36.43) tells the story of the events leading to the people of Israel, the descendants of Jacob's twelve sons. Chapters 37 to 50, a narrative in the form of a **novelette** containing plot and character development, and realizing a more complete closure, tell the story of Joseph with the Israelites settled in Egypt.

The classical Documentary Hypothesis, introduced earlier in this chapter, views these tales as originally independent but eventually built into larger complexes by (a) skillful editor(s).[42] Even given a composite theory of creation with an insistence upon disparate materials, Genesis notably exhibits much of the cohesiveness and unity of a work of literature. It is constructed with two main narratives related in outlook and theme, the first treating origins and the second introducing a chain of fathers concerned with continuity and the future.[43] It frames these stories in "a history of journeys and settlements, conflicts and treaties, and human and divine encounters"[44] and interweaves them (their plots, characters, settings, and narrators/points of view), initially episodic (a succession of episodes), to achieve a degree of unity, coherence, and emphasis when set within the framework of the book as a whole.

### Stories (Gen. 1–2)

*As has already been remarked, the first eleven chapters of Genesis consist of several stories that can be read independently. The first two involve the creation of the world and the creation of human beings. An examination of these stories reveals several differences in tone and scope that have led to the idea that they originated from different original sources, the Priestly (Gen. 1–2.4a) and the Yahwist (2.4b–24).*

*To get the most out of these stories, you need to become an active participant, visualizing, imagining scenes, interpreting, and entering into the spirit of events.[45] You will need to pay attention to the narrator of the story, to the tone used, to the pattern of events as sequenced, and to the relationship suggested as existing between the Creator and the creation.*

The first account provides an omniscient narrator and cosmic view, this contrasted to the limited **third-person** down-to-earth presentation in the second. More pointedly, the **tone** differs: the first emphasizes a perfectly ordered creation (accomplished in seven days), with human beings created in the image of God; the second describes an anthropomorphic God (Yahweh) creating the first human being from the earth and then providing a companion of like nature (created from a rib of the first). In the first, God orchestrates the events of creation, following the same pattern: divine command, result, divine approval, and enumeration of the day.[46] The first story removes any possibility for human beings to be other than God's creation, suggesting a relationship in which the great and almighty God demands respect. The Yahweh of the second account forbids and punishes; themes include alienation and competition between human beings and God. The same God, however, rescues and redeems a human creation evicted into the harsh outer world.[47]

Both of these creation stories embed poetry, the oldest form of biblical literature, into their narrative accounts, in which the poetry functions to articulate the material, offer a lesson, or make a point; it also intensifies meaning or formulates a conclusion.[48] The first creation account uses poetry to make the point that duality or dialogical dimension constitutes the image of God:

> So *God created* **humankind** in his image,
> in the image of *God he created* **them**;
> **male and female** *he created* **them**. (Gen. 1.27)[49]

Here, the narrator places poetry at the climax of the story to emphasize the previous acts of creation and to let the verse make its own point. God creates man and woman in their reciprocity as the seal of creation. The second and third lines repeat the "created" of the first; the "humankind" of line 1 becomes "them" in line 2, then changes to "male and female" and "them" in line 3. The first line makes the point that humankind is created in "his [God's] image," with the second line making "them" the "image of God" and the third repeating that "them" consists of male and female. In the following context, the emphasis upon reciprocity continues with the added suggestion of sexual differentiation.

The Yahwist account (chapter 2) dramatizes the LORD God as a character, the narrator acting in a limited third-person role and recording what God can be seen doing: he forms "Adam," a human being, from the soil and breathes in the breath of life, animating the dust and making a psycho-physical being (2.7). God empathizes with this human being in need of a helper and partner. Sharing language with God, the human being names each animal and bird but finds none suitable as a partner. Not until God makes a second human being out of the flesh of the first will the first declare poetically, using pairs (woman and man) and parallelism (repetition of being):

> This [being] at last is bone of my bones
>    and flesh of my flesh;
> this [being] one shall be called Woman ["isha"],
>    for out of Man["ish"]- this [being] one was taken. (Gen. 2.23)[50]

Through this direct link, this duality of flesh ideally functions as one, serving as the prototype for future generations where "man leaves his father and mother and clings to his wife, and they become one flesh."

A story normally consists of five parts: (1) **exposition**, the beginning section in which the author provides the necessary background information, sets the scene, establishes the situation, and dates the action, and usually introduces the characters and the conflict; (2) **complication**, or rising action, which develops and intensifies the conflict; (3) **crisis**, the moment at which the plot reaches its point of greatest emotional intensity, the turning point that directly leads to resolution; (4) **falling action**, the point at which tension subsides and the plot moves towards its conclusion; and (5) **resolution**, the final section of the plot, recording the outcome of the conflict and establishing some new equilibrium, also referred to as denouement. The second creation story evidences all of these features. An ideal, physical place provides the **setting** for the characters of God, Adam, Eve, and the talking serpent (J), this last bestowing on the story the characteristic of **fable**. The plot and resolution involve a test and choice on the part of Adam and Eve. God creates a perfect world and asks only that Adam and Eve not eat fruit from the tree of knowledge of good and evil; the serpent tells them that God forbids the fruit because it will make them like God, knowing good and evil, thus casting suspicion upon God's motives, causing Adam and Eve to doubt God, and opening them to the possibilities of freedom (note 3.1–7). They yield to the temptation, breaking the innocent, trusting relationship they have had with God, then hide from God in anxiety and guilt. They also engage in an elaborate play of guilt-shifting: Adam blames Eve, who, in turn, blames the serpent. The just Creator must punish disobedience but, already, another side of deity reveals itself in a God providing protective coats of skin for the vulnerable couple. A just God drives them to the harsh external world where they must struggle to exist, a world where immortality exists only in generational succession. Poetry intensifies the three curses (3.14–19). Careful reading observes three chains and two reversals that make up the plot of this story. First, the reader meets (1) serpent, (2) woman, and (3) man; then God questions (3) man, (2) woman, and (1) serpent; then God curses (1) serpent, (2) woman, and (3) man.[51] This arrangement highlights the order of complicity of act. Every other character in the Bible inherits these curses and lives in a hostile environment.

*Groups of Stories (Gen. 1–4, 6–11)*
The primeval history of Genesis includes two groups of stories ("group" usually meaning five to six stories that can be referred to as an **act**): chapters 1–4 and chapters 6–11, each of these ending with a genealogical register (5, 11).[52] In the first, God creates human beings for one purpose: relationship – man and woman, brother and brother, and (by association) man and fellow human beings.[53] The stories consist of the six days of Creation, the creation of humankind, the expulsion from Eden, and Cain murdering Abel, this last act demonstrating a breakdown in relationships that gets so bad that Lamech, a descendant of Cain, can boast to his wives that he avenges himself "seventy-sevenfold." The second group of stories centers on Noah and his family, with other genealogies (chapter 10) detailing the spread of the human race and eventually settling on Abraham. Here, we have the stories of God instructing Noah to make an ark, the Great Flood, the flood subsiding, the covenant with Noah, the nations descended from Noah, and the Tower of Babel. Another way of describing the narrative structure in the first eleven chapters of Genesis is that it consists of concentric circles that narrow: the origins of the world, the origins of the vegetable and animal kingdoms, and the origins of all known people, ending this universal history in chapter 11 with God calling Abraham out of Ur of the Chaldees.[54] The ancestry and heritage motifs continue into the New Testament with the ancestry of Joseph, Mary, and Jesus.

*To this point, I have focused on the single story, a literary unit most accessible to beginning readers, and on groups of stories. I turn now to a discussion of how biblical narrative links multiple stories into a carefully sequenced macro-plot, a larger and overarching plot. This means that readers must learn to read the Bible not as a book containing isolated, self-contained stories, but as a narrative that both encompasses and transcends these simpler units.*

*Moving from individual stories to sequenced stories requires you to pay attention to layers of text: words, sentences, paragraphs, stories, and narrators and characters speaking, then to increasingly larger sections and, ultimately, to books.[55] The style of a piece of writing exists in the way the writer puts together these elements, usually in relation to themes and effective communication. An important principle in literature is that all writers have literary styles and that these styles are reflected in the writing. In the first chapter, I introduced style as an essential characteristic in the study of the Bible as literature. In relation to narrative, the linkage and sequencing of texts means that you need to read with awareness of the overall shape of a text and of the details within a text.*[56] *You should pay attention to words and phrases, their repetition (as motifs, concrete objects, themes, or more abstract ideas), actions (recurrent, parallel), analogies (where stories comment upon each other), dialogue (marking what is deemed essential), and narration (marked by omniscience and unobtrusiveness).*[57]

### Cycles and the Macro-Plot (Gen. 17–22)

Beyond groups of stories, Genesis is structured into four **cycles** that consist of three to five groups of stories: the first consisting of the primeval history (1–11) and the next three found in the patriarchal history (12–50): Abraham (11–25), Jacob (25–35), and Joseph (35–50).[58] The cycle in each of these contains an overriding macro-plot (a plot larger in scale) that helps to unite their several stories. As part of the Abraham cycle, the account of Isaac demonstrates how multiple stories and cycles become intricately linked.[59] The near sacrifice of Isaac becomes a link in the chain of stories that follow, for without Isaac no Jacob or Joseph cycle would exist. More than a link, the emphasis upon continuity of the family line and fulfillment of God's promise becomes an overarching or macro-plot.[60] The story of the near sacrifice of Isaac takes place in the context of more extended narrative.

In earlier narrative, God promises Sarah and Abraham a child, setting up a tension between Sarah's barrenness and the promise of progeny and land; in their old age, God gives them Isaac only to command Abraham to sacrifice him (chapter 22), accentuating a continuing tension between promise and reality. Generally, the Yahwist tradition emphasizes the promise of descendants and land to Abraham and stresses obedience; the Elohist tradition emphasizes Abraham's moral integrity and acknowledges his understanding of the threat to the status of Sarah's son. This tradition involves the repeated motifs of journey, wilderness, and test, including divine messengers and fear of God.

Before God opens Sarah's womb and enables her to give birth to Isaac, she follows a common practice of providing for succession by giving Abraham her slave girl Hagar; Sarah later becomes jealous and drives Hagar away. In the Yahwist account, Abraham takes a hands-off attitude to Hagar's plight, since she can justifiably defend her role as primary wife; the Elohist tradition emphasizes his moral integrity and shows him to be distressed about her condition but accepting what God says. Both traditions use the story of Hagar and Ishmael to account for origins and for two nations and the relationship of Israel to the Ishmaelites. The Elohist tradition emphasizes fear as an appropriate response to God, so Hagar wonders who can see God and remain alive

(16.13). When the angel tells Hagar that God will use Ishmael to make a great nation (21.18), the narrator explains that God opens Hagar's eyes (recognition being an important motif) to see a well (another motif) that will save the boy's life. This story concludes by pointing out that Ishmael grew up in the wilderness and that he took a wife from Egypt.

The command to sacrifice Isaac creates a terrible dilemma for Abraham: to murder his son (not really an act of moral integrity) or to disobey God (again, not the act of a moral man). God prefaces the command to offer Isaac as a burned offering with the motif of **test**: "God tested Abraham" (22.1). Abraham portrays himself obedient in his response, "Here I am" (22.1), an answer he repeats when Isaac, carrying the wood for his own sacrifice, exclaims, "Father!" and is reassured: "Here I am, my son" (22.7), repeated a third time when God commands Abraham not to sacrifice Isaac. Abraham tells his son, "God himself will provide the lamb for a burnt offering, my son" (22.7, 8) even as he takes the knife to kill him. An angel of the LORD calls out to him, and Abraham replies once again, "Here I am." Only after this reconfirmed resolve to carry out the required sacrifice does a ram appear. Abraham names the place "Jehovah Jireh," meaning "God will provide." Christians link this account, in particular, to the provision of the Passover Lamb in the Gospel of John, "Here is the Lamb of God" (1.29, 35), using both typology and allusion.

The macro-plot of the Abraham cycle (chapters 12 to 25) consists of a quest for a son.[61] This quest for continuity through offspring is complicated by the fact that Abraham's wife is barren. The tension grows when God appears to Abraham, aged seventy-five, telling him that he is to leave his native land and journey to a land where he and his offspring will become a great nation (chapter 12). Once he has arrived in Canaan, he is further told that the land will belong to him. As the plot works itself out, Sarah does, in fact, miraculously conceive and give birth to Isaac. The continuity becomes threatened once again when God commands Abraham to sacrifice his only son. The two promises, however, of becoming a people and of possessing a land recur in the cycles of Jacob and Joseph, again with obstacles and threats to continuity. Structurally, the cycle of Abraham begins with 11.27–32 and the genealogy of Terah, Abraham's father; it completes the genealogical frames in 25.1–18 with the descendants of Abraham's sons, Ishmael and Isaac.

## Drama and Poetry (Job 1–42)

One book in the Bible brings readers into contact with all the leading literary forms.[62] Job, composed in its present form sometime between the seventh and second centuries BCE, has the narrative shape of beginning, middle, and end, much of it consisting of poetry, and much of its poetry existing as dialogue. It presents, on one level, **theodicy** or moral issues (exploring the justice of God and the traditional morality of **retribution**) and, on another, legal issues, or duties and rights. It provides a philosophical answer in poetry and prose through the vehicle of drama, sometimes said to be **comedy**, with restoration as the final outcome; it has also been described as **tragedy**. As a literature of contemplation and philosophical discussion, it belongs to the **wisdom tradition** – personal rather than national, existential rather than historical, experiential rather than revealed, reflecting the movers and shakers rather than the marginal and dispossessed.[63] Its prose **prologue** and **epilogue** have been thought to be ancient folktale. It contains speeches (colloquies and soliloquies or monologues), **aphorisms**, parable, hymns, laments, and legal disputation.[64] Structured dramatically into prologue, epilogue, a cycle of speeches and actors, scenic effects, and an ash mound serving as the stage, the book of Job addresses itself purely to the imagination. The sky and atmosphere serve as the dramatic background, and its spectators resemble a chorus. Its omniscient point of view permits approach on two levels: the omniscient divine and the limited view of Job and his friends, with Job presenting God as man sees him and as God sees himself.[65] The prose prologue establishes Job as a blameless and upright man who fears God and turns from evil. The scene shifts to a heavenly council where an enemy or adversary called Satan raises doubt about Job's reason for serving God and suggests that, if he were deprived of prosperity, he might refuse to worship God. The prose section addresses human integrity. The idea of Satan as a personification of evil does not yet exist. The experiment proceeds and, in a few verses, Job finds himself deprived of wealth, posterity, and health (1.13–21). The dramatic movement consists of poetry in which Job and his three friends take different positions and each presents a different theological point of view about human suffering. The poetry, exploring philosophically how God can allow evil to exist, asks about the justice or fairness of God.[66]

In a spectacular **theophany**, dramatically arranged by the approach and crescendo of a storm, God steps into the debate, not to solve the mystery of human suffering as in the divine intervention of the gods in Greek drama, but to justify Job, to show his displeasure with the friends' reliance upon conventional answers, to leave the suffering of the righteous still a mystery, and to point to the great, good, magnificent, and sublime in nature still shrouded in the same mystery that surrounds evil.[67] In the prologue, the councils of heaven review the province of earth and Job, a righteous man who lives a life of prosperity under the conventional understanding that prosperity results from righteous living and that ruin visits the unrighteous (the retributive notion of justice). When the prologue opens, Job's love of good for its own sake, and not as a reward for righteous living, has not been tested; the Adversary suggests that adversity would reveal whether Job would cling to unrewarded goodness. Job, however, responds stoically: "Naked I came from my mother's womb, and naked shall I return there; the LORD gave, and the LORD has taken away; blessed be the name of the LORD" (1.21). The experiment proceeds and Job, afflicted with loathsome sores, removes himself to an ash heap, where he sits scraping off his scabs. His wife accuses him of persisting overlong in his integrity and tells him to curse God and die. Job reprimands his wife, reminding her, "Shall we receive the good at the hand of God, and not receive the bad?" (2.10). Deserted by his wife, Job sits unspeaking among curious friends for seven days and seven nights. At the end of this silence, a poetic debate of three cycles occurs. Structurally, the book proceeds through two series of **colloquies** (chapters 3–14 and 15–22), in which Eliphaz, Zophar, and Bildad speak (in seven speeches), and **monologues** (chapters 23–42), in which Job speaks seven times, followed by Elihu and God in another seven speeches. It should be noted that Eliphaz argues that revelation supports God's goodness; Zophar, from a philosophical stance, argues for the power and wisdom of God, and Bildad upholds the authority of the fathers (tradition) and argues for God's justice.

As narrative and poetry, the book of Job represents a superbly blended poetic drama of the human encounter with God.[68] What makes it drama is the characters (including God), theme, plot, dialogue, setting, scenic effect, spectators, and structured prologue, argument, and epilogue.[69] Job has the classic U-shape of comedy, except, as everyone admits, the ending remains bittersweet: what was taken cannot be restored, and new-found prosperity will itself be subject to the storm and stress of a contradictory universe. What makes Job poetry consists of imaginative vision and a "sheer expressive power" that pushes, soars above the ordinary, and reveals "the panorama of creation . . . with the eyes of God."[70] Much of the book seeks to grasp the ungraspable, to span "the unbridgeable gap between the powerful God and limited creature," to see through poetry into "an immense world of power and beauty and awesome warring forces"[71] – all of this in metrical symmetry.

Attentive readers, listening to God speaking to Job out of the whirlwind (chapter 38), will recall the "formless wind" in creation and the experience of the prophet Elijah, who, afraid for his life, flees the destructive death threat of Jezebel by retreating into the wilderness (1 Kings 19). There God addresses the solitary, despairing Elijah, telling him to get up and eat, to take a journey of forty days and forty nights to Mount Horeb; the New Testament echoes this motif in the experience of Jesus in the wilderness. At Horeb, Elijah encounters a strong wind splitting the mountains and breaking the rocks in pieces, an earthquake, a fire, and then sheer silence (19.12); from this sheer silence, Elijah hears a voice telling him to go back and face Jezebel and Ahab, an encounter in which he will discover, contrary to his sense of being alone in serving God, that 7,000 in Israel have remained faithful. In 2 Kings, God takes Elijah up to heaven in a whirlwind. In Job, as in Elijah's experience, the whirlwind signals a theophany, or divine appearance.

Job has questioned why misfortune happens; God answers by bringing Job into the mystery and heart of creation, of which his suffering forms only a part.

God's response out of the whirlwind (chapter 38) addresses Job's death wish, constituting "a brilliantly pointed reversal, in structure, image, and theme" presented in two modes of poetry, one spoken by the limited creature, with "a relentless drilling inward" on suffering, and one spoken by God, "affirming the splendor and vastness of life."[72] The first concentrates on the external world, only to cancel it, and expresses anguish in seeing and feeling "all too much," until the wish becomes a desire to "see nothing at all."[73] Against this focusing inward, the mode of poetry spoken by God sweeps "over the length and breadth of the created world," each created thing "evoked for its own sake" and its own beauty.[74] Job sets out the oppositions of day and night, with light finally swallowed up in darkness; God reprimands Job's darkening counsel, and leads him gradually to turn his affirmation of death into one of life. Job is led to look beyond the human and to see a dialectical balance of light and darkness belonging to "an unfathomable beauty of creation."[75] In addition to the inward/outward movement and the light/darkness images, generation and birth images expand from Job's birth and entry into the world into cosmic purpose, where God hedges in primeval chaos and keeps it from engulfing the earth.[76] Job wants the dark day of his birth to perish, the "dark" poetically intensified by images of gloom, deep darkness, clouds, and blackness of day claiming it; in this barren night of darkness, no joy will be expressed, only the cursing of the sea. The creature of the deep dark, Leviathan, rouses to a dark dawn that hopes for light where none exists; from this darkness, Job cries, "Why did I not die at birth, come forth from the womb and expire?" (3.11). Job here views death as the great leveler, where the small and great no longer hear the voice of the taskmaster (3.19). He wonders why light is given to the blind and laments his present misery and bitterness (3.23, 20).

Job's view and God's view can best be understood by setting them side by side. In the first part of his lament, Job wishes he had not emerged from the human womb (3.1); God addresses another womb, that of primeval chaos, when he asks "who shut in the sea with doors when it burst out from the womb? – when I made the clouds its garment, and thick darkness its swaddling band, and prescribed bounds for it, and set bars and doors" (38.8, 9). At that creation, the morning stars sang for joy, and heavenly beings shouted; Job, in his present plight, wants no rejoicing. He wants the doors of his mother's womb shut to prevent his birth and Leviathan roused to be cursed (3.8); God, on the other hand, orders and sets bounds to the primeval sea. In the second part of his lament, Job wants to lie down and be quiet (3.13), to sleep with kings and counselors, all alike reduced to ease and rest from the taskmaster (3.13, 18); God wants to know about the expanse of earth, the dwelling place of light and darkness (38.18, 19), the origins of snow and hail, the place of light and scattering of the east wind (28.22–4). God asks about more than birth; he wants to know about the springs of the sea, the recesses of the depths, the gates of death (38.16, 17). Job wants to know why life is given only to end in misery and bitterness of soul (3.20, 21), to which God replies by asking about power:

> Can you bind the chains of the Pleiades, or loose the cords of Orion? Can you lead forth the Mazzaroth in their season, or can you guide the Bear with its children? Do you know the ordinances of the heavens? Can you establish their rule on the earth? Can you lift up your voice to the clouds, so that a flood of waters may cover you? Can you send forth lightnings, so that they may go and say to you, "Here we are"? Who has put wisdom in the inward parts, or given understanding to the mind? Who has the wisdom to number the clouds? (38.31–7)

Job imagines physical birth images; God imagines "cosmic uterine pulsations" and a life-generation process "infinitely larger than human beings that informs nature" as a whole.[77]

The two passages use an operating principle of organization and the formal structure of poetry. Job seeks to be enveloped in the "womb tomb"; God closes the doors on "the gushing womb" of chaos and makes the clouds its clothing and the darkness its swaddling bands.[78] Beyond Job, beyond all human beings, beyond history, generation begins in the place where both light and darkness dwell (Gen. 1). God, through poetry, reveals to Job an "ungraspable creation surging with the power of its Creator," a Creator who cares enough about Job to allow him to see beyond his human plight.[79] No wonder Job exclaims, "But now my eye sees you" (42.5).

The book of Job has long been considered literature that captures the sublime and engages the emotions and imagination, accomplishing this with a dazzling array of poetic techniques that include repetition, allusion, figurative language, imagery, and formal structure. Chapter 28 perfectly illustrates the impossibility of achieving wisdom except through fearing God and shunning evil, both attributes ascribed to Job. The hymn consists of a formal structure of three **strophes** or **stanzas**. The first presents an extended image of the accessibility of ores and gems, setting the stage for the question raised in verse 12, "Where is wisdom to be found?" Strophe 2 describes wisdom as being more precious than gems (simile), and the final strophe (verses 20–8) concludes that wisdom, unlike gold and gems, cannot be found in the physical world; only God knows the source of all things and, thus, the source of wisdom. The aphoristic conclusion states, "See! Fear of the Lord is wisdom; to shun evil is understanding" (28.28). In light of describing poetry as "a way of seeing," the command "See!" in verse 28 captures the essence of the full revelation that humbles Job into declaring, "I have uttered what I did not understand, things too wonderful for me, which I did not know" (42.3).

Job uses the poetic devices of repetitive words, phrases, and clauses to enrich style and meaning – this apparent even within the prose prologue when the Sabeans fall upon Job's servants, killing them with the edge of the sword, followed by the fire of God falling from heaven and burning up the sheep and servants; before this bad news settles, another messenger tells Job that a great wind has destroyed the house where his sons and daughters have been eating and drinking, killing them all. The scene presents escalating violence. Overall, about 1,020 lines in Job exist in poetry (chapters 3 through 42.6), generally divided into two clauses or lines parallel in content; about sixty times, the clauses present themselves in triplets. Controversy exists about the numbering of poetic lines on account of differences in counting – whether by syllable, accent, or stress – a fact that explains different metrical arrangements in different translations based upon the original Hebrew.[80] The speeches arise from strophes (stanzas), usually paired and sometimes separated by intermediate strophes which are not paired.

Job exhibits the prominent binary form of biblical poetry, so much so that it can be described as an example of "extreme parallelism."[81] **Parallelism** refers to lines that use different words to express the same or similar ideas in grammatical form: it can be **synonymous**, expressing similar content in similar grammatical form; **antithetical**, in which a second line expresses the truth of the first in a negative way; climactic, where the second line completes by repeating part of the first and then adds to it; or **synthetic**, where a pair of lines form a unit and the second line expands or completes the first. This form of parallelism, or "seconding," may in fact describe most of the poetry in the Old Testament.[82] Modern readers must shift from viewing poetic verse as made up of a particular number or quality of syllables to viewing it as a parallelism of two or more clauses.[83] These can occur in couplets, triplets, quatrains, sextets, and octets.

Job's cursing his birth (chapter 3) illustrates many of these forms of parallelism. He begins his curse: "Let the day perish in which I was born / and the night that said, 'A man-child is conceived'" followed by "Let that day be darkness [the day of conception]! / May God above not seek it / or light shine on it / Let gloom and deep darkness claim it" (3.1–3). The day progressively becomes darker, and the darkness barren (3.7) to the point that Job cries, "Why did I not die at birth, / come forth from the knees and expire?," intensified in content by "Why was I not buried like a still-born child, / like an infant that never sees the light?" (3.11, 16). Job's perplexity mounts: "Why is light given to one in misery, / and life to the bitter in soul / who long for death, but it does not come" (3.20), content repeated in "Why is light given to one who cannot see the way, / whom God has fenced in" (3.23). The poem concludes with Job realizing what he most fears: "my groanings are poured out like water. / Truly the thing that I fear comes upon me / and what I dread befalls me. / I am not at ease, nor am I quiet; I have no rest; but trouble comes" (2.24–6). What the reader notes as being most characteristic in this poetry will be its parallelism, antistrophic structure, and terseness and an effectively pithy and concise language. To this one would add its use of figurative language and sound devices.

Job further illustrates a form of poetry, the **chiasm**, which, as explained in the chapter on rhetorical devices, takes on an X-shape like the Greek letter chi, representing the crossing of two objects in reverse order. Two short examples illustrate the pattern: "As for me, I would seek God, and to God, I would commit my cause" (5.8) and "he sets on high those who are lowly, and those who mourn are lifted to safety" (5.11). In each, a middle term connects concepts repeated in reverse order:

> As for me, (I would seek) God
> To God, (I would commit my cause).

> He sets on high those who are lowly,
>
> And [he lifts] those who mourn are lifted to safety.

In the first example above, the middle term is "God" and the reverse order concepts are "seek" and "commit"; in the second, the reverse concepts are high–low to mourn–safety. An extended example of this chiasmus technique can be found in Job chapter 5, where verses 12 to 14 form the focal or X point in the chiasmus.

The visual force of poetry can be seen in Job's description of Behemoth and Leviathan, amphibious beasts at once part of the natural world and beyond it, greater than mere hooks, snares, cords, ropes, leashes, and even harpoons; both on earth have no equals and cannot be domesticated.[84] The two beasts have their counterparts in the hippopotamus and the crocodile, but, as described, they become figures of the imagination. Behemoth "eats grass like an ox" (40.15), its strength in its loins, its bones "tubes of bronze," and its "limbs like bars of iron" (40.18). The description moves into mythology: "It is the first of the great acts of God – only its maker can approach it with the sword" (40.19). The Leviathan becomes even more fantastical, described as a fire-eating dragon with a coat of mail (41.13), its back made of shields (41.15), the doors of its face shut to the "terror all around its teeth" (41.14); "its sneezes flash forth light . . . / From its mouth go flaming torches; / sparks of fire leap out. / Out of its nostrils comes smoke . . . / Its breath kindles coals, / and a flame comes out of its mouth" (41.18–21). Only the Creator can tame these beasts of chaos, for only God has "entered into the springs of the sea, / . . . walked in the recesses of the deep / . . . seen the gates of deep darkness / comprehended the expanse of the earth," and, thus, knows the way "to the dwelling of light" (38.16–19). Little wonder that Job, in the end, declares, "See, I am of small account; what shall I answer you? I lay my hand on my mouth" (40.4). Job literally sees himself a small being in the face of majestic vastness and splendor, a place graspable only by poetry.

Source criticism would argue that the time of composition makes all the difference in how readers interpret Job. The actual date of composition cannot be determined, although it is generally agreed that it was composed during the period from the mid-sixth century to the mid-fourth century BCE; the Jewish Study Bible says that four or more overlapping compositions may be found in Job. A relatively late date would point to a reconciliation of the suffering brought upon Judah by the Babylonian captivity. Source critics argue that the book is ambiguous, telling one story in prose and another in poetry, the first presenting a patient Job, who persists in integrity, and the latter an impatient Job, who openly attacks the deity for injustice.[85] Considered as genre, wisdom literature, the book of Job belongs to a tradition of debate and legitimizes the human quest for understanding. Its very form participates in this debate: the book begins by asking about the proper reason for serving God, and Job proves he serves out of a sense of integrity; the second question asks about the reason for suffering, exploring the traditional belief that suffering is punishment for sin and, its flip side, that righteousness is rewarded by prosperity. While the book seems to argue against suffering as punishment and righteousness as rewarded by prosperity, the conclusion reopens the debate by restoring Job's fortunes.[86] As theodicy, a treatise about God's justice and the existence of physical and moral evil in the world, Job takes special pride of place in responding to the mystery and imperfect human knowledge of God.[87]

## Close Reading

*Exercise 1*
Read Psalm 106 and Acts 7. What themes and motifs connect the two pieces?
*Exercise 2*
Read the book of Matthew. Explain how Matthew can be interpreted as presenting Jesus as the new Moses.
*Exercise 3*
How does God manifest himself to human beings?
Gen. 12.6–7; 12.8; 13.18; 14; 16.13; 18.1; 22.2; 24.10–11; 32.30; 33.20; Deut. 5.24–6; 18.16; 33.2; 34.10; Judg. 6.22–3; 13.22; Exod. 15.1–3; 19.2–3; 20.19; Isa. 6.1; 6.5; 34.5–6; 59.17; Num. 12.6–8; 23.3; Pss. 3–4; Joel 3.16; Hab. 3.3, 9–15; Mic. 1.3; 1 Sam. 3.1–15; 1 Kings 3.4–5; 19.8–13; Zeph. 2.12; Zech. 9.13–14; John 1.1, 14–18; Mark 9.2–8; Acts 1.9–12.
*Exercise 4*
How does the Bible present the concept of death?
Gen. 2–3; Hos. 6.2; 13.14; 1 Cor. 15.54, 55–6; Lev. 19.31; 20.27; Deut. 18.11; 30.19; 32.19–22; 1 Sam. 14.14; 28; 31.4; 1 Chron. 10.13; Rom. 5.12–21; 6.3; 8.38–9; Ezek. 18.31; 37; 2 Cor. 4.11; 1 Pet. 2.24; Rev. 12.11; 21.4; Isa. 26.19, 66.24; Dan. 12.2; 2 Sam. 17.23; 1 Kings 16.18;

19.4; Matt. 27.5; Acts 1.18; Job 3.21; 7.15; 10.20–2; 14.1–14; 26.6;
Eccles. 4.2–3; Jonah 4.8; Phil. 1.23.

*Exercise 5*

In literature, initiation introduces an individual into human society and
into the world of spiritual and cultural values. Initiation can describe the
transition from childhood or adolescence to adulthood, entrance into a
secret society, or the revelation of a new religious order. Initiates undergo
a series of tasks and events that test their commitment or development;
the experience is often accompanied by a sense of isolation or physical
withdrawal and instruction. Read Mark. How do the disciples' encounters
with Jesus initiate them into understanding the secret teaching of the
kingdom of God?[88]

*Exercise 6*

What clues suggest that Exodus may be a composite work? **J, E, P** –
chapters 1–24; **E** – 1.15–21, 3.9–15, 6.2–7.13, 12.1–20, 40–51, and,
traditionally, the Decalogue (20.1–17) and the Covenant (20.22–23.33)
are now doubted to have appeared in the original sources; **J, E** – chapters
32–4 (**E** – 32, **J** – 34, 33, from both) but may be all **J**; **P** – chapters 25–31,
35–40.

*Exercise 7*

Read Genesis 22. How does the near sacrifice of Isaac represent the way
in which narrative interweaves stories into progressively larger complexes
of materials that advance macro-plots and overall themes in the work as a
whole?

*Exercise 8*

Explore the contrast between the prose framework of Job (1.1–2.13;
42.7–17) and the poetic body. Who are the characters in each? What are
the major themes? How does the prose story differ from the poetic story?
Where is the climactic point in each? What is the resolution in each?

*Exercise 9*

Read the New Testament book of James. How does the book evidence
itself as wisdom literature? Explore its ethical and moralistic content. Look
at its practical exhortations and advice. What are the social attitudes?

*Exercise 10*

Read Job chapters 36, 37, 38, 39. How does the speech of Elihu prepare
for the divine intervention of God into the debate about suffering? To
what extent can God be said to be the "Soul of external Nature"?[89]

## Questions for Reflection

1  How does the Bible, a collection of books, achieve unity – or does
   it?
2  How do the elements of narrative function in the book of
   Genesis?
3  Is Genesis mostly myth, legend, tale, epic?
4  Can fiction tell truth?

5 What two views of truth influence how one reads and interprets the Bible?

6 What similarities can be found in the four narrative cycles of Genesis?

7 How does Genesis describe primordial history?

8 What main differences exist between the two creation stories? The two flood stories?

9 What is the Documentary Hypothesis?

10 What major genres can be found in the Pentateuch?

11 What does it mean to be made in the image of God? Is the image literal?

12 How does Genesis address what the ideal relationship between human beings and God should be?

13 In what ways do the characters in Genesis function as symbols for all humankind? Does this reduce their historicity?

14 Does it make a difference whether the books of the Bible are ascribed to traditional authorship?

15 Do the characters in Genesis tell the same story? How?

16 Why is the near sacrifice of Isaac one of the Bible's most poignant stories?

17 How does primogeniture function in the Bible?

18 How does the narrowing of generations in Genesis prepare for the covenanted relationship of a people to their God?

19 How does the book of Job overturn traditional explanations for human suffering – or does it?

20 Do you consider the book of Job as largely comedy or tragedy?

21 What primary lesson does Job learn?

22 What are some of the poetic techniques used in the book of Job?

23 How do Behemoth and Leviathan in the book of Job function to move forward the philosophical argument?

24 Does God care about human beings? Their suffering? How does the wisdom tradition counter retributive justice?

25 What relationship exists between Job and the characters in the book of Genesis?

26 What chiefly distinguishes story/narrative, drama, poetry?

27 Explain source theory relative to the synoptics.

28 Why is it important to know both the historical setting for the books of the Bible and their approximate composition dates?

29 What main critical approaches have been taken to interpreting the Bible? To what degree can they inform an introductory course to the Bible as literature?

30 What case can you make for reading parts of the Bible as myth, history, allegory?

# 5 Sub-Genres: A Way of Clarifying and Mapping

## Outline

Preliminary Considerations
  Conventions
  Recognition of Genres
  Metaphorical Function
  Objections to Genre Criticism
Familiar Sub-Genres
  Song
  Allegory
  Parable
  Prayer
Close Reading
Questions for Reflection

*I have introduced genres as a way of seeing the world and arranging its content, addressing, in the last chapter, narrative/story, drama, and poetry as kinds of writing, the result of an **expressive** mode of writing intended to convey the thoughts and feelings of the author(s), as contrasted to two other forms of writing: informative (expository) writing, conveying the truth about something; and **argument** (persuasion), making truth claims and defending them.[1] Biblical writing, however, cannot be strictly defined as expressive: it always mixes faith, what people believe, and fact, what actually existed or happened.[2] Anticipating the multiplicity and intermingled genres in the Bible (over 100 when general and specific forms are included), I have from the beginning defined literature more broadly than merely expressive writing.[3] I have talked about how the Old Testament sets out a universal history of beginnings – how it starts in prehistory, then moves into the historically based ancient world, events, and people's experiences – and how, existing as it does today in multiple languages, it addresses itself to anyone who can read. You will immediately recognize that the New Testament appeals to historical fact in the presentation of Jesus as a person who lived and whose life impacted faith. Its writing, however, is literary, appealing to the imagination and using language in metaphorical and mythical ways.*

*In this chapter, you will be asked to focus on what we have in the existing Bible.*[4] *Beginning with what is before you means you will not need to come equipped with an understanding of ancient languages and cultures or sophisticated exposure to literary criticism; rather, you will begin by asking questions: What kind of thing is this – is it prose or poetry? What is the literary form? Can the text be recognized as a song, an allegory, a parable, a prayer, or another genre? This way of reading restores the commonsensical approach taken by most people throughout the course of the Bible's history – at the basic level, knowing what words mean, seeing how they are used, noticing grammatical connections, and reading words in sequence to reconstruct meaning. Beyond this, you will begin to pay attention to overall form and to ask what kind of literature you are reading.*

*The way in which the Bible has been printed, and traditionally read, encourages you to read apart from context. You are tempted to read verses and chapters; sometimes, if they tell a story – as in the case of Joseph in Genesis 37–50 – you will read several chapters. You will occasionally read a whole book, particularly a short book such as Ruth. These habits of reading piecemeal detract from looking for connectedness and unity among parts of the Bible.*[5] *Further, reading the Bible as it is arranged, even if it has to be the basic approach, contributes to a continuing focus upon the literal word over the figurative and symbolic, significantly impoverishing its rich potentialities.*[6] *Such reading prevents you from recognizing the many examples of multiple and diverse genres, a number of them familiar, that shape and help you to understand what it is you are reading. You need to know, however, that simply looking for genres (forms and types) of literature will sidetrack you from living through the story, a group of stories, a cycle, a book or books. You will find that the Bible, like all literature, embodies human experience which pulls you in and in which you participate vicariously, living through all the imaginative, emotional, and intellectual highs and lows of the experience.*

## Preliminary Considerations

### Conventions

Genres have to do with conventions that guide readers into a text and help them to understand what to look for and how to organize their experience of reading.[7] Knowing about genres – in the case of narrative, about plot, character, setting, point of view, and diction – brings interpretive insight and provides a basic foundation for beginning to appreciate the literature in the Bible.[8] A literary approach emphasizes the familiar genres found in other kinds of literature as well as the universal features present within these that make them similar and recognizable across the centuries.[9]

*Recognition of Genres*

The book of Job becomes more meaningful when readers understand its overall form and the relationship of the speakers to each other. In the larger complex, it can be addressed as a drama and as a philosophical discussion. Readers upon first coming to a text naturally read for a sense of the whole piece as opposed to asking immediately about the authorship, source, dating, and purpose, or even, for that matter, studying rhetorical devices such as "extreme" parallelism.[10] Traditional literature courses encourage this close reading, interpretation, and appreciation of an existing text – "reading it" being preferred to reading "about it."[11]

The emergence of genres occurs almost naturally in a normal reading of the Bible. For example, in Genesis, following the creation stories, other stories trace the history of a family and include a collection about heroes, in which the latters' quests are domestic and spiritual, almost epic in its narrative of national destiny.[12] The rest of the Pentateuch (the first five books) fuses narrative and legislative genres, creating a hybrid form, as well as including poetry and prophecy.[13] Books following the Pentateuch – Joshua and Judges, for example – raise genre questions: should they be considered fiction or history?[14] Other Old Testament books also raise genre challenges: should the book of Ruth be read as a story, a folktale, or a narrative structure paralleling Greek drama?[15] Should 1, 2 Samuel, 1, 2 Kings, and 1, 2 Chronicles be read as single, coherent narratives or as pieces taken from earlier source materials, or can they be meaningfully approached in both ways? Either way, they contain familiar genres: parables, prayers, judgment speeches, and history-like **narrative**. Moreover, the genres cannot always be easily separated; the book of Job, in addition to drama (legal, historical) and philosophical discussion, has been identified as **wisdom literature** in prose, allegory, and poetry. The Psalms include lyrics, laments, praise, worship, nature poems, hymns, songs, psalms of confidence, remembrance, kingship, and wisdom. Proverbs, classified as a collection of sayings, also reveals the overall logic, coherence, and literary plan usually found in wisdom literature.

*Metaphorical Function*

Metaphorically, biblical genres can be described both as mapping divine action in history – God's will for human behavior and the privileges and responsibilities of God's covenant people – and as providing an explanation of how persons fit into God's created order –a question that certainly the wisdom literature addresses in practical and reflective ways.[16] Readers of the Bible become active participants in a story stretching from creation to consummation, the story itself a metaphor for individual life and how it should be lived.

*You should know that the Bible does not set out to present a theory of literature or to classify its texts into a set of recognizable literary genres. Nonetheless, you will need to sample only a few selections to recognize forms such as song and book (the latter including history and chronicle), psalm and proverb in the Old Testament, and, in the New Testament, gospels, history, letters, and **apocalypse**.*[17]

## Objections to Genre Criticism

Recognizing the diverse types of literature in the Bible helps readers make sense of a collection of texts they would otherwise find hard to read, difficult to understand, confusing, esoteric, and ancient.[18] It can even be argued that the external form of biblical text must be settled before readers come to grip with its content.[19] Critics object, though, to regarding genres as ready-made heuristic tools for interpretation.[20] As pointed out in the previous chapter, they argue that genres seem to be reduced to essences derived from a study of other works and that they become the subject of regulations established by critical abstraction.[21] They also object to an approach to literature that looks only at the technicalities of form, using it in deterministic ways rather than understanding it as a covenant made between the author and the reader that helps to shape its composition and reception.[22] The literature of "living text," these critics argue, resists such reductions to classification and types.[23]

## Familiar Sub-Genres

*Once the danger of reductionism and overly simplistic use of heuristic tools has been confronted, genres, identified as being both exclusive and inclusive, with considerable overlap and mixing of modes, become one element among a complex set of elements useful for coming to a fuller reading of the text. I have chosen to focus on song, allegory, parable, and prayer because they are readily accessible as short units of text and because they are familiar and easily recognizable as genres. The context surrounding them will always be important and should be considered.*[24]

### Song

The Bible contains many examples of words meant to be sung: victory hymns and songs, marching songs, and songs of celebration, music apparently being very important to the people of Israel. Their "lived" songs express joy, relief, praise, thanks, and deliverance; in lifting their hearts and voices outward and upward to their God, they provide a cultural inheritance for the generations that follow them. These songs evidence many of the common characteristics of poetry: inset arrangement, genre and mode markers, occasional **antiphonal** arrangement, concrete imagery, parallelisms, **cognates**, and allusion, creating an intricate net of connections to other biblical texts.[25]

Fortunately, translations of the Bible generally now inset poetry recognizably from the surrounding prose. This convention may be traced in Hebrew literature to the First (1006–586 BCE) and Second Temple periods (516 BCE to 70 CE), and may have roots in the much earlier Egyptian period.[26] In addition, the surrounding prose will often provide an explicit marker of the genre poetry and its mode – whether exhortation, praise, song, performance with a musical instrument, spoken by characters, or inviting audience participation. For example, we find such markers in the Song of Moses at the Red Sea (Exod. 15.1–8): "Then Moses and the Israelites sang this song to the LORD . . .: 'I will sing to the LORD, for he has triumphed gloriously! / horse and rider he has thrown into the sea'" (15.1); the Song of Miriam (Exod. 15.20–1); the Song of Jephthah (Judg. 11.29–40), where Jephthah (11.34) comes home victorious from battle to find his daughter coming out to meet him with timbrels and dancing; the Song of Deborah (Judg. 5, dating perhaps to the twelfth century BCE), in which Deborah explicitly identifies her genre: "to the LORD I will sing, I will make melody to the LORD, the God of Israel" (5.3); Hannah's Song (1 Sam. 2): "Hannah prayed and said, 'My heart exults in the LORD'"; Mary's Song (Luke 1.47–55), based largely on Hannah's prayer, beginning, "My soul magnifies the Lord"; and Zechariah's Song (Luke 1.68–9), which praises God: "Blessed be the Lord God of Israel."

The Song of Moses, the Song of Miriam, and the Song of Deborah represent the genre of victory hymn, well known in Egypt and Assyria from the fifteenth to the twelfth century BCE, as well as the device of antiphonal singing or chanting. In the Song of Moses, Moses and the Israelites begin the song (15.1), and Miriam and the women sing the refrain: "Sing to the LORD, for he has triumphed gloriously . . ." (15.21). Although the refrain comes at the end of the poem, the exhortation "sing" suggests the refrain may have been sung first by the women, the men following with a stanza, and the women repeating the refrain, through at least three rounds. By custom, women came out singing and dancing to celebrate the men coming back victoriously from battle; in this poem, men and women sing praise to the victor/deliverer God (Judg. 11.34, 1 Sam. 18.6). Miriam (Exod. 15.21) may have originated Moses' Song and certainly, as strategically placed in the text, echoes the antiphonal (chorused) reply of the Hebrews to Moses' statement "I will sing to the LORD, for he has triumphed gloriously . . ."

The Song of Deborah, like the Song of Moses and the Song of Miriam, is presented as antiphonal, probably with Barak leading the men in the refrain "When locks are long in Israel," and the women replying, "when the people offer themselves willingly," with both groups joining together for "Bless ye the LORD!" In a prelude, the men sing, "Hear, O kings," the women then repeating, "O princes." The men sing "to the LORD I will sing," and the women repeat, "I will make melody to the

LORD, the God of Israel" – the "make melody" repeating the motif of celebration in Miriam's Song (5.3).[27] The victory song celebrates the defeat of Jabin. A long **apostrophe**, a poetic device in which the singers turn aside from the story to address the heavens, in this case, the LORD, provides the historical setting (the desolation of the country under Jabin's rule). An enlarged refrain, continuing the antiphonal alternation of men and women, occurs in verses 9 through 11, ending with "there they repeated the triumphs of the LORD / the triumphs of his peasantry in Israel." The people then rally to the cause: "Then down to the gates / marched the people of the LORD" (5.11b), six tribes responding to the call to battle and the rout. More than likely, men sing the "Most blessed of women be Jael, the wife of Heber the Kenite, / of tent dwelling people most blessed . . ." (5.24–7). Then the women pick up the reply, which depicts an aristocratic mother peering out of a latticed window and awaiting the victorious return of her son (5.28–30).

Stanza, imagery, and parallelism make the poetry of the Bible striking and memorable. **Stanza**, in poetry, refers to the grouping of regular, rhymed, recurrent units; strophe also groups words and lines, but these evidence less regularity, rhyme, and recurrence. Each subsequent strophe in the song of Moses augments or builds upon the first, each presenting a greater fullness.[28] The first strophe presents the event: "Pharaoh's chariots and his army / he cast into the sea" (Exod. 15.4) where they sink like a stone (15.5). The second expands the event with detail and vivid imaginative pictures (imagery): the waters pile up, the floods stand in heaps, the deep congeals in the heart of the sea (15.8). And, finally, the third strophe stretches the event, its details and pictures, into the consequences: the people led, redeemed, and guided through the wilderness, the terror of the people into whose land the Israelites will come, the bringing of the people into the land and the establishment of the sanctuary (Temple) of the LORD, and the conclusion, "The LORD will reign forever and ever" (15.13–17, 18). Finally, the song contains extensive use of parallelism and cognates. "You overthrew your adversaries" (17.7) parallels "Your right hand, O LORD, / shattered the enemy" (15.6), the latter stepping up the devastation. Verse 11 asks a question, "Who is like you, O LORD, among the gods?" then repeats the question and answers with mounting praise for a God "majestic in holiness / awesome in splendor, doing wonders." Consequentially, this majestic, holy, and awesome God wondrously holds back the Canaanites "until the people whom you acquired passed by / You brought them in and planted them on the mountain of your possession" (15.16, 17). The cognates, too, build climactically: "For he has triumphed gloriously" (15.1) becomes "majesty" (15.7); "mighty" (15.10) waters cognates with God's "glorious" right hand (15.6).

Consisting of four stanzas, the Song of Mary evidences the characteristic parallelism of biblical poetry. In the first stanza, "my soul mirrors my spirit" and "magnifies the Lord" parallels "rejoices in God." The next verses present parallel reasons for the ecstasy: "for [because] he has looked with favor on the lowliness of his servant" (Luke 1.48) and "for the Mighty One has done great things for me" (1.49). Attributes of God reveal a God mighty, holy, and merciful (1.49–50). The third stanza inaugurates the future, where the results of the birth of Jesus have been achieved, again in a series of parallelisms: "He has shown strength with his arm"(1.51a); "He has scattered the proud in the thoughts of their hearts" (1.51b); "He has brought down the powerful from their thrones / and lifted up the lowly" (1.52a); "He has filled the hungry with good things / and sent the rich away empty" (1.53a); and "He has helped his servant Israel" (1.54a). Contrasting parallelism with the proud juxtaposes those of low estate, the rich with the hungry. The song concludes with praise for God's faithfulness in keeping covenant, beginning with Abraham, and now fulfilling prophetic promise in the birth of the Son of God.

The Song of Deborah depicts a theophany in a layered imagery of motion (Judg. 5.4–11), with God appearing, the earth trembling, the heavens dripping, and the mountains quaking before him. Likewise, the song has structure and logic: it provides an introduction to the Divine Warrior, an overview of the historical setting, a catalog of the participants, an accounting of their successes or failures, and the tale of Jael.[29] Deborah sings praise for Jael in poetic parallel and describes Sisera's death in an unfolding set of repetitions: "She put her hand to the tent peg / and her right hand to the workmen's mallet; / she struck Sisera a blow, / she crushed his head, / she shattered and pierced his temple" (5.26) until, before her force, he sank, lay outstretched at her feet, lay still, lay – utterly destroyed. The poetry here expresses itself in escalating repetition.

Completely characteristic of the Bible is the use of allusion to connect biblical texts across traditions. Vocabulary in the Song of Moses (Deut. 32.1–43), after he had finished writing the law in a book, for example, alludes to other biblical poems that tell of God's primordial defeat of the sea and assumption of kingship (Pss. 74.12–16, 89.10–14, and 93), these poems alluding back into ancient Near Eastern myths about the storm god's defeat of the sea god followed by the building of his temple. The language and form of the poem suggest it is one of the oldest in the Bible, but reference to Philistia and the Temple imply a later redaction. Its theology connects it to the eighth to fifth centuries BCE: it recounts an exodus and wilderness wanderings in the distant past (7), describes the Israelites settled in Palestine (13, 14), explains that the Israelites are guilty of idolatry and brought to potential ruin because of it by surrounding enemies (15–19), and finally, there is God's promise to rescue them (30, 34–43).[30] As a whole, the poem expresses an unrestrained enthusiasm for God's deliverance of the Hebrew people, a victory culminating in the building of the Temple, redemption, and a people abiding in the presence of God.

The poem, in fact, is one of ten preeminent songs in the history of Israel, alongside the Song on the night of the Exodus (Isa. 30.29), the

Song at the Sea (Exod. 15.1–21), the Song at the Well (Num. 21.17–20), Moses' Song on completing the Torah (Deut. 31.31), Joshua's Song on stopping the sun (Josh. 10.12–13), Deborah's Song (Judg. 5), King David's Song, the Song of the Dedication of the Holy Temple, and Solomon's Song of Songs.[31] These songs, placed in the context of overall narrative, reflect Israel's movement forward to the final song celebrating ultimate redemption, global and absolute, annihilating all suffering, jealousy, and hate – a song capturing all of creation's ultimate striving.

The Song of Mary reveals amazing economy in its use of prophecy in the birth of Jesus, an event initiating, Christians believe, a promise kept until the end of time.[32] The annunciation recalls that to Hannah in the birth of Samuel. The Psalms use "Holy is his name" as traditional Jewish words of praise (Ps. 111.9); "Strength with his arm" echoes "You have a mighty arm; strong is your hand, high your right hand" (Ps. 89.13) and "He has scattered the proud" recalls "You scattered your enemies / with your mighty arm (Ps. 89.10) and also "I will redeem you with an outstretched arm and with mighty acts of judgment" (Exod. 6.6). The promise to Abraham recalls events in Genesis (17.6–8, 18.18, 22.17) and the promise to David in 2 Samuel 7.11–16. Similarities can be found with Habakkuk 3.18: "Yet I will rejoice in the LORD; / I will exult in the God of my salvation"; Malachi 3.12: "Then all nations will count you happy, for you will be a land of delight, says the LORD of hosts"; Job 5.11: "he sets on high those who are lowly"; Isaiah 12.6: "Shout aloud and sing for joy, / O royal Zion, / for great in your midst is the Holy One of Israel"; and Isaiah 49.3: "And he said to me, 'You are my servant, / Israel, in whom I will be glorified.'" This intertextuality invites readers to see biblical texts constantly in relation to each other, and, for many, contributes to unity and connectedness within the Bible as a whole.

Luke, in Zechariah's Song (Luke 1.68–9), makes a theological point by linking the annunciation to Mary with that to Zechariah, the parallelism of the accounts joining the events and making the annunciation to Mary climactic, ending one age and inaugurating the future.[33] Zechariah has been singled out for divine favor, being chosen by lot from among the twenty-four orders of priests officiating at the Temple to enter into the sanctuary and into the divine presence; Mary, Gabriel announces, has been selected for a blessed conception and birth. The angel, appearing to Zechariah, tells him that John, a Nazarite from the womb, will be permanently dedicated to God's work and will perform it "with the spirit and power of Elijah" (Luke 1.17); Jesus will inherit David's throne, rule over the house of Jacob, "and of his kingdom there will be no end"(1.32, 33). Zechariah demands a sign to back up the promise (1.18); Mary questions, "How can this be since I am a virgin?" (1.34), and is reminded that "nothing will be impossible with God" (1.37). John, filled by the Spirit from the womb, follows in the tradition of prophets equipped to perform a particular work; in Luke's account, John recognizes Jesus by leaping in the womb (1.44), this setting the background for Mary's song. Jesus has a greater work than John in bringing about the fulfillment of promise made to the ancestors (1.55). The angel tells Mary that Jesus will be called the Son of God, surpassing David and his royal heirs, who were adopted sons of God (Ps. 2.7). Mary responds with the archetypal "Here am I, the servant of the LORD; let it be with me according to your word" (Luke 1.38).

*Both the Old and the New Testament contain many examples of allegory and parable, allegory being more closely associated with metaphor and parable with simile. Both use analogy (showing resemblance in some particulars between things otherwise unlike) and make comparisons, both direct and indirect, both explicit and implied. Beginning with analogy leads to understanding "allegory as an elaborated set of parallel meanings."[34] Allegory, like songs, ultimately should be understood contextually. In the next section, I use the Song of Solomon and the prophets Jeremiah, Ezekiel, and Hosea, as well as the New Testament, to illustrate the overall importance of allegory to biblical narrative. Allegory generally may be said to represent abstract ideas or principles by characters, figures, or events in narrative, dramatic, or pictorial form. This parallelism extends to parable as well.*

### Allegory (Ps. 23; Judg. 9.7–15, 9.54; Mark 11.20–5; Rom. 9.4–5; John 15; Song of Solomon; Jer. 2; Isa. 54; Ezek. 16, 23; Hosea)

**Allegory** may be defined as a continuation of metaphor, where a term or phrase is applied to something to which it is not literally applicable to suggest a resemblance. Through metaphor and allegory, the Bible often expresses abstract or spiritual meaning in concrete or material forms. Psalm 23 is a continued metaphor or allegory; it mentions two things: the LORD and the Shepherd's care. The LORD, represented as the divine Shepherd-King (a commonly used Near Eastern metaphor for royalty), cares for people, here represented as sheep and needing protection to stay alive, receive nourishment, and find safety. The shepherd leads the sheep to pasture and water and through difficult terrain. Walking through the "darkest valley" (23.4) leads to this psalm's being frequently used to comfort the bereaved. The Jewish Study Bible points out that some scholars interpret it as an exilic or postexilic portrait of a new exodus, leading to the return to the land of Israel.

The Old Testament, in accounting for the early tribal leaders, provides a suggested allegory in the story of Abimelech, who killed his seventy brothers, leaving only Jotham, the youngest, before having himself proclaimed king by the citizens of Shechem (Judg. 9.7–15). No overt similitude exists by which one thing is said to be like another; rather, the story mentions four species of tree (olive, fig, vine, and bramble) – with a reference to Israel and its history only implied.[35] The fig tree suggests Israel's national position, described in the New Testament as withered away and cut down (Mark 11.20–5). The olive tree, by implication, suggests the covenant privileges of Israel, described in Romans 9.4–5 as "Israelites, and to them belong the adoption, the glory, the covenants, the giving of the law, the worship, and the promises; to them belong the Patriarchs, and from them, according to the flesh, comes the Messiah, who is over all, God blessed forever. Amen." The vine brings to mind Israel's spiritual blessings, described in the New Testament as being found only in Christ, the True Vine (John 15). Finally, the bramble brings up the idea of Israel consumed by fire in the day of Jacob's trouble and the Great Tribulation (Revelation). The story criticizes an ambitious Abimelech, who is willing to pay any price to become king. The fact that all the trees wish to anoint a king suggests that care should be used in finding a suitable candidate. Three trees decline their suitability, making Abimelech's acceptance the more questionable. By making the most unsuitable of the trees (the bramble) accept kingship, the story makes the point that, for Israel, the pursuit of kingship is unnecessary and dangerous. Indeed, Abimelech holds the throne for only three short years before the citizens break faith with him. He dies a less than honorable death occasioned when a woman drops a millstone from an upper tower that cracks his skull; he then begs to be stabbed so that he doesn't have to die at a woman's hand (Judg. 9.54).

From the second century onward, church fathers debated whether the Bible should be read as literal, within a historical context, or as symbolic, resulting in one tradition that reads the Bible almost exclusively as allegory and another that argues the dangers of this allegorization. The debate continues into the way people read the Bible today. Reading the Bible literally as fact resists full consideration of the complex nature of language as symbol.[36] For example, concretely and vividly, Eve functions as a possible actual human being, but she also functions metaphorically as the "first woman" and "mother" of humankind. Allegory would extend the comparison of the details of Eve's life to those of the lives of women everywhere and in every time. This analogy moves from seeing Eve as herself to seeing her as "the rest of us" – her relationship with God and her relationship with Adam, her children, and her role in the transition from one generation to another. Without the move into analogy and allegory, much of the meaning of Eve's life would be lost; religion and theology would be reduced to talking about a woman, a garden, and a snake!

One book in the Bible, more than any other, contributes to the ongoing debate about whether to read literally or allegorically.[37] The Song of Solomon – eight chapters, 117 verses – describing itself as a song in its title, can also be referred to as drama (although lacking a developed plot, dialogue, and any clear identity of its speakers); as belonging to the universal genre of love poetry extant from the ancient Near East; and, if not allegorical in itself, as allegory in traditional interpretations. As a love poem, the Song of Solomon celebrates human sexuality and uses the motifs common to love poetry: nature imagery, specific descriptions of physical attractions, perfumes, ornaments, and terms such as prince, king, queen, lover, shepherd, and beloved. Interpreted as religious allegory, the poem celebrates, for Jewish people, "right relationship" between Israel and its God and, for Christians, the relationship of Christ to the Church. "Right relationship" in the Hebrew and Christian sacred texts expresses itself in the idea of love, harmony, and commitment; the contrary image is that of unfaithfulness, rebellion, and rejection.

The fact that the Hebrew prophets viewed the marriage relationship as analogous to God's position toward Israel and regarded apostasy as constituting infidelity may be one reason that the Song of Solomon continues to be read as allegory. Isaiah, Jeremiah, Ezekiel, and Hosea commonly used allegory to address metaphorically the "right relationship" between Israel and its God. Isaiah 54 (dating from 540 BCE, after the destruction of Judah and Jerusalem) portrays Zion/Jerusalem as a woman, childless, forsaken by her husband; she is assured that God remains her husband and protector, that she will have abundant children. The deported community needed to be reassured of the sovereignty of God and of their status as a chosen people. Allegorically, the poem means that the exiles will soon return to Judah, that God remembers his covenant, and that the relationship will endure: God will punish but not abandon Israel. The theme of covenant recalls God's orderly provision for the fulfillment of His promises, and the motif of barrenness the threat to continuity. Isaiah assures Israel that God's love is steadfast, his compassion constant and redeeming – that he will restore the covenant of peace and fulfill the promise of posterity.

Jeremiah, a book that tries to come to terms with the national tragedy and theological disruption of Judah's exile after its defeat by Babylonia (597–582 BCE), uses the common metaphors of marriage and divorce to describe God's relationship with Israel and with Judah, describing both as adulterous and God as showing mercy and appealing for their return.[38] Jeremiah stands against the people and their disobedience, and pictures Israel's eagerness to accept other gods in images of animals in heat. The love and purity of the bride contrasts with the desire and immoral ways of the whore – the latter image referring both to sacred prostitution and cultic fertility rituals practiced within the Temple and to physical infidelity. At the time it was written, Jeremiah captures the idea of Israel as leaving God to pursue other idols or lovers; Judah claims to be God's wife but engages in idolatry. The Ark of God and the return of Israel and Judah reference God's faithfulness and covenant of promise.

The prophet Ezekiel, a priest and spokesperson during the Babylonian exile, explains the defeat of Israel as a nation as the result of unfaithfulness to God. Chapters 16 and 23 describe graphically God's discovery of the foundling Judah/Jerusalem abandoned and exposed in the common practice of infanticide. God rescues the helpless female infant, covers her vulnerability and nakedness (16.8) – the covering itself an image of intent to marry – rears her to adulthood as royalty, and adorns her with the ornaments and rich clothing of a princess. The fully mature woman plays the whore (16.15), lavishing her favors on any passer-by whatsoever. Ezekiel condemns the practices of Judah as worse than that of the whore, who at least receives money in exchange for her favors; Judah bestows favor without receiving anything in return for her gifts. Nonetheless, God says, "I will remember my covenant with you in the days of your youth, and I will establish you with an everlasting covenant . . . I will establish my covenant with you, and you shall know that I am the LORD" (16.60, 61).

The Bible frequently explains its allegories. Ezekiel, for example, explicitly unravels the allegory of the two harlot sisters (chapter 23). He explains that the two women, daughters of the same mother, played the whore in Egypt, that the elder sister's name was Oholah and that of the younger Oholibah; Oholah is Samaria and Oholibah is Jerusalem (23.2–4). The poem recounts how God abandoned Samaria to her lovers, the Assyrians, and Jerusalem, learning nothing, to her lovers from every side – the Babylonians and all the Chaldeans, Pekod and Shoa and Koa, and all the Assyrians. Just as Ezekiel 16.58 emphasizes the necessity for bearing the penalty of lewdness and abomination, Judah must pay for her idolatry by being exiled into Babylonia.

The book of Hosea addresses unfaithfulness relative to Israel's alliance with the Assyrians (786–746 BCE). The entire book deals with an unfaithful wife, Gomer, and her husband, Hosea; it becomes an elaborate allegory (with two parallel meanings, one literal and the other suggestive) for the Lord's dealings with Israel, and, indeed, the divine love that seeks throughout all time to redeem the wayward human being. The prophet took a wife of whoredom, marrying a prostitute, who has children by other men, and leaves Hosea. Hosea brings her back very publicly to himself.

God's ideal state for Israel and for humankind finds expression in chapter 2 of Hosea: "And I will take you for my wife forever; I will take you for my wife in righteousness and in justice, in steadfast love, and in mercy. I will take you for my wife in faithfulness; and you shall know the LORD" (2.19, 20). The prophet envisions the LORD bringing Israel back to himself: "I will make for you covenant on that day with the wild animals, the birds of the air, and the creeping things of the ground; and I will abolish the bow, the sword, and war upon the land; and I will make you lie down in safety" (2.18).

In the meantime, reality provides a harsher picture. Hosea finds himself instructed to "Go, love a woman who has a lover and is an adulteress, just as the LORD loves the people of Israel, though they turn to other gods . . ." (3.1). Hosea responds as instructed by the LORD; he marries Gomer, who has three sons, all named to have prophetic significance: the first will be named Jezreel, "for in a little while I will punish the house of Jehu for the blood of Jezreel, and I will put an end to the kingdom of the house of Israel" (1.4); the second will be named

Lo-ruhamah, "for I will no longer have pity on the house of Israel or for-give them" (1.6); and the third will be named Lo-ammi, "for you are not my people, and I am not your God" (1.8). Despite judgment, a theme begun with Adam and Eve, continued with Noah, carried through the history of Israel, and extending into the New Testament, God will keep faith and save a remnant: "Yet the number of the people of Israel shall be like the sand of the sea, which can neither be measured nor numbered, and in the place where it was said to them, 'you are not my people,' it shall be said to them, 'Children of the living God'" (1.10).

Hosea clearly intends meaning beyond the literal when he addresses the people of Israel: "Hear the word of the LORD, O people of Israel." God judges Israel for its continued rebellion: "There is no faithfulness or loyalty, and no knowledge of God in the land" (4.1). Like Gomer, Israel plays the whore (4.15), and Judah faces the same temptation and succumbs: "O Ephraim [Ephraim is the younger son of Joseph from whom Judah springs], you have played the whore" (4.3). The writer makes the connection to Adam, linking rebellion and transgression as continuing characteristics of humankind: "But at Adam they trans-gressed the covenant" (6.7). Adam here seems to refer to geographical location but also suggests some remote time. What God wants from humankind repeats a theme found in the Pentateuch, particularly in Deuteronomy: "For I desire steadfast love and not sacrifice" (6.6). The word sacrifice points forward to an image that will play itself out in a people who engage in sacrifice and empty ritual; the theme continues into the New Testament. Hosea picks up the tension between a God of judgment and the God of mercy and steadfast love: "How can I give you up, Ephraim? How can I hand you over, O Israel? . . . My heart recoils within me; my compassion grows warm and tender. I will not execute my fierce anger" (11.8, 9). Exactly as Hosea has pleaded to the wayward Gomer to return, God in the end pleads with Israel: "Return O Israel to the LORD your God, for you have stumbled because of your iniquity . . ." (14.2). Ephraim is reminded that God has nothing to do with idols but demands faithfulness and that the upright walk within just precepts (14.8–9).

Hosea addresses God's relationship to the chosen people through the metaphor of marriage. The husband, aggrieved by the wife's unfaithfulness, reaches out in compassion and love to seek out and to redeem the wayward wife – pointing typologically to a gospel of redeeming love: this is completed in the New Testament with Christ as the bridegroom and the Church as the bride he comes to redeem.

In the New Testament, Ephesians, written to effect union between Jews and Gentiles and arguably not authored by Paul, clearly refer-ences marriage as a unifying process where "two become one flesh" (5.31), a great mystery (5.32).[39] Where unity exists, duality ceases: one does not love selfishly but loves in a way that promotes the other and self within the union. Only in that context does the writer introduce the idea of submission. Christian love, and ideal marital love, builds upon the foundation of the purifying sacrifice of Christ: "Christ loved the church and gave himself up for her [sacrificially], in order to make her holy by cleansing her with the washing of water by the word, so as to present the church to himself in splendor, without a spot or wrinkle or anything of the kind – yes, so that she may be holy and without blemish" (5.25–7).

Revelation uses the metaphor of marriage in its magnificent vision of a new heaven and earth. John describes "the holy city, the new Jerusalem, coming down out of heaven from God, prepared as a bride adorned for her husband" (21.2), this followed by a wedding supper and celebration: "Blessed are those who are invited to the marriage supper of the Lamb" (19.9). The last half of Revelation, suitable to a book providing closure for the other sixty-five, emphasizes recurrent motifs from the earlier books: a woman giving birth to a son, a dragon that threatens to devour the child (recall Genesis 4.7, which describes sin lurking at the door, its desire for Cain, who must master it), a whore described as Babylon destroyed, the hero on a white horse who kills the dragon, the marriage of the triumphant hero to his bride, and a consummating wedding supper.[40]

### Parable (Mark 3.3–20; 13.28–31; 1 Sam. 1; Ezek. 17.1–24)

*The Bible evidences many examples of parable, closely related to allegory, which are particularly abundant in the teaching of Jesus in the New Testament (aphorism being the other dominant way of helping audiences come to see differently).[41] Parables make explicit use of analogy to show a similarity between two things, to demonstrate a common denominator between two unlike concepts, characters, events, or objects. In contrast to allegory, parables tend to be brief and realistic. In this section, I introduce parable through examples in the book of Mark, 1 Samuel, and Ezekiel 17. The parable, any more than allegory, should not be decontextualized or interpreted apart from the greater narrative.*

A **parable** continues simile (an explicit comparison characterized by realism, brevity, absence of allegorical names, persuasive strategy, subtle undermining of ordinary patterns of thinking, variability in details calling for corresponding meaning, and artistic excellence).[42] **Analogy**, demonstrating a similarity of features between two things, serves as the common denominator for all parables, often explicit and overt, as in the parable of the fig tree and the sower in Mark 13. 28–31 and Mark 3.3–20.[43] Here the analogy exists in the phrases "as soon as its branch becomes tender and puts forth its leaves" and "you know that summer is near"; "when you see these things taking place" and "you know that he is near, at the very gates."

A similar logic of analogy – "listen," signaling something to be learned – reveals itself in the sower: "as soon as the seed falls, the birds devour it; when some hear the word, Satan comes and takes it away." The parable lends itself to being understood immediately in its familiar meaning; the less familiar meaning emerges from this basis of more familiar use. Furthermore, Jesus explains the parable overtly: the seed is the word sown (4.14); like the birds who eat the seed, Satan comes and takes away the word; rocky ground prevents the seed from yielding much more than sudden growth – no root, and premature death; thorns refer analogously to the cares, lures, and desire that choke the word so that it cannot yield fruit; and, finally, good soil leads to a seed that bears fruit a hundredfold.

In a true parable, two meanings must be constructed in parallel action; often, in the Bible, a set of circumstances in the physical sphere will be compared to a spiritual counterpart, leading to the description of parable as a moving picture. Consider, for example, the shortest parable in the Bible: "Physician, cure yourself!" (Luke 4:23). First, the verb and noun which make a parable must be literal with respect to each other: a physician cures. A parable must contain a figurative object and a figurative action. In the example, "physician" and "cure," though physical, should be interpreted figuratively and spiritually, with the physician attending to himself, not to others. As illustrated by this example, a parable does not have to include a lengthy story, and the Bible contains several of these. In a case such as "put on . . . the old humanity" (Eph. 4.22) no parable exists, though both noun and verb must be understood as figurative: we (literally) strip off clothing, not humanity. The most extensive parable in the Scriptures refers to the tabernacle and its ritual (Heb. 9.9).

Jesus did not create a new literary genre when he used parables; the genre had a long tradition, and was employed throughout the Mediterranean world, and by Greek and Roman philosophers and rhetoricians. Generally, in the Old Testament, parables were used by prophets and wise men and women, a common form being the story parables (2 Samuel 12.1–4; Isaiah 5.1–7). In 1 Samuel, the prophet Nathan tells David, who arranged the death of Bathsheba's husband on the battlefield that he might marry her, the story of the rich man who takes the poor man's pet lamb and prepares it as food for a wayfarer; when David condemns the act, Nathan tells him that he is the man. Other parables, fables, and allegories in the Bible include Judges 9.7–21; 2 Kings 14.8–10; Ezekiel 16, 17.1–24, 19.1–14, 20.45–9, 23, 24.3–14; 1 Kings 20.39–42; and Isaiah 5.1–7, 28.21–9.

*Prayer (Deut. 6.4–9, 11.13–21; Gen. 12, 15.1–6; Exod. 31.13; Neh. 1, 9; Luke 11.2–4; Matt. 6.9–13)*

*Prayer can be described as a life-changing, character-constituting dialogue between the human and the divine.*[44] *As with song, allegory, and parable, you need to resist any tendency to read the prayers as isolated texts and to understand them, instead, as embedded in a traditioning context. Understood in this way, prayers have a historical, traditioning, and faith context.*

Prayer, as genre, should be distinguished from the poetic compositions intended to be sung as a form of worship found in the book of
Psalms. Prayer, rather, exists in a continuum between conversation
and formalized address. In the individual's relationship with God,
prayer expresses the conviction that God can and will respond.[45] Psalm
141.2 refers to prayer as incense, connecting it to the evening sacrifice described in Exodus 30.8. The Psalmist prays "I call upon you, O
LORD; come quickly to me; give ear to my voice when I call to you. Let
my prayer be counted as incense before you, and the lifting up of my
hands as an evening sacrifice." Sacrifice in the Old Testament carries
the idea of offering some commodity to God, expressing itself in the
New Testament in the sacrifice of Christ.[46] In following the example of
Christ, Christians come to understand their lives as "a living sacrifice,
holy and acceptable to God, which is your spiritual worship" (Rom.
12.1). As verse is older than prose, the chant is older than prayer, and
separating songs from prayers comes only with difficulty. The Song
of Moses, for example, and those of Miriam, Hannah, Deborah, and
Mary, have all been identified as being both genres. The Old Testament
contains over ninety prose prayers in which individuals petition God
in times of need,[47] and Jesus, in the New Testament, modeled prayer,
praying twenty-seven times.

Prayer evolved and changed through the patriarchal and Temple
periods, exhibiting both individual and communal expressions.
Individual prayers, voluntary and spontaneous, lack the ritual and
liturgy associated with communal prayer. Abraham (Gen. 15.2) speaks
to God directly, confiding his concern that God has not provided him
with an heir, to which God responds by telling him his own son will
be his heir and that his descendants will be as many as the stars in
the heavens; God appears again to Abraham (Gen. 17), establishing a
covenant with him, this marked by circumcision, reminding him that
he will be father to many nations, that Sarah his wife will bear him
a son, Isaac. Isaac (Gen. 25.21) prayed to the LORD because his wife
Rebekah remained barren, the motif from Abraham repeated, and God
grants his prayer, seemingly immediately, telling him that two nations
struggle within Rebekah's womb, repeating the motif of sibling rivalry
already introduced in the story of Cain and Abel. Source theorists
believe the rivalry of these brothers describes later tensions between
the Israelites and the Edomites.

The oldest fixed prayer in Judaism, the Shema (Deut. 6.4–9, 11.13–
21, and Num. 15.37–41), calls for prayer in the morning and night; the
words must be recited to the children, be talked about at home and
away, and "when you lie down and when you rise" (Deut. 6.4, 11.19).
The people of Israel, in Numbers, recite and remember the commandments for one purpose: to be holy to their God. In the Babylonian
exile, unable to sacrifice at the Temple, the people gathered three
times a day to pray, prayer substituting for the three daily sacrifices,
the prophet Hosea reminding them that God desires steadfast love,

not sacrifice, and knowledge of God rather than burnt-offerings (6.6). In the fifth century BCE, Jews developed the "Shemoneh Esrei," a comprehensive prayer originally in eighteen parts, addressing blessings, requests, and gratitude; a final part was added in the second century CE addressing the threat of Christianity.[48]

The prayers of Abraham, Moses, and Nehemiah address concerns for God's provision and preservation of a people of God. Abraham presents himself as childless (Gen. 15.1–6) and without an heir (Yahwist motifs), even though God has promised to make of him a great nation (Gen. 12); he is told that he will have an heir of his own house, a promise Abraham believes, with God counting his faith as righteousness. God appears to Abraham again, reminding him that he will be the ancestor of many people; the only stumbling block is his age, ninety-nine. Finally, the much delayed miraculous conception occurs, and Sarah bears a son, Isaac, to Abraham in his advanced years.

Moses prays for the deliverance of his people from Egypt and, in the sojourn to Canaan, asks that God preserve and not destroy the people: "Remember Abraham, Isaac, and Israel, your servants, how you swore to them by your own self, saying to them, 'I will multiply your descendants like the stars of heaven, and all this land that I have promised I will give to your descendants, and they shall inherit it forever'" (Exod. 31.13). Moses continues to intercede for the people and for his brother Aaron when it looked as if God would destroy them (Deut. 9, Exod. 32).

At a postexilic date, Nehemiah (chapter 1) reminds the people of God's promise and provision, acknowledging God as steadfast in love, keeping covenant with his people, attentive to prayers and forgiving their offenses. In Nehemiah 9, Ezra recites the history of the people of Israel, calling them back to God and to return from exile: he reminds them that God had seen the distress of the ancestors in Egypt and had delivered them; at Mount Sinai, God had spoken and given them ordinances, statutes, laws, and commandments. He points out that God had sustained them in the wilderness, and that he had given them kingdoms and a people. They had gone in and possessed the land but then had disobeyed and had been given into the hands of their enemies to suffer; they had cried to God, who delivered them from suffering, only to have them become again rebellious and stubborn. But the merciful God had not made an end of them; in Babylonia, Ezra reminds them, they had again become slaves, but the just and faithful God had heard their reading of the Law and had given them a firm agreement in writing (8.38).

While no prayer rivals the Shema for Jewish people, the Lord's Prayer in the New Testament, existing in 1,395 languages and dialects, has influenced people worldwide; in fact, the Convent of the Pater Noster, built over the site where traditionally Jesus is believed to have prayed with his disciples, is decorated with 140 tiles that record the prayer in different languages. Simple, natural, and spontaneous, the prayer has been regarded as a compendium and synthesis of the Old and New Testaments. It begins with an invocation, "Our Father in heaven," a recognition of divine paternity and the roles of God in creating Israel as the first-born child of God: electing, establishing covenant, remaining steadfast and merciful, asking for holiness and faithfulness, forgiving and restoring right relationship. Yahweh as Father in the Old Testament enters a new phase in the New Testament: Jesus now describes his sonship relative to the Father: he declares himself to have been sent by the Father, his word to have been affirmed by the Father, his works fulfilling those of the Father. Jesus becomes the fount and foundation of love, fusing the Old Testament commandments to love God and neighbor. "In heaven" locates a new homeland for God's people, a place of blessing, reward, hope, inheritance, and divine reality. The prayer then presents six petitions, the first three with regard to God – sanctification of name; the coming of the Kingdom of God; and the actualization of the will of God – and the final three concerning the messianic people – the bread of life; the remission of sins, and the preservation from temptation and liberation from evil. The Lord's Prayer has been interpreted as an invitation to participate in a new exodus into the new world of God's kingdom, involving the salvation of Israel, the defeat of evil, and the return of YHWH.[49]

*In addition to songs, allegories, parables, and prayers, the Bible provides many other sub-genres, including genealogies, tribal lists, legal codes, legends, fables, speeches, sermons, theophanies, gospels, epistles, epigrams, acrostics, wisdom, and apocalypse, to name a few. You may want to look at the website (www.readingthebibleasliterature.com) for biblical references to these genres. You are invited to use these to gain a more complete sense of the common forms of literature found within the Bible as well as to understand some of the genres that are unique to biblical traditions themselves. If you keep in mind the purpose of this text – to provide a basic introduction to studying the Bible as literature – it should become clear at once that any one chapter, or any one tool presented, belongs to a much more encompassing and complex set of discussions.*

## Close Reading

*Exercise 1*
After reviewing the section on poetry, find two or three other examples in the Bible and explain the features that make them recognizable as poetry.
*Exercise 2*
What are the characteristics of parable found in the tares (Matt. 13.24–30), the seed (Matt. 13.31–2; Mark 4.31–2; Luke 13.19), and the grain of mustard seed (Matt. 13.33; Luke 13.21) and the sower (Matt. 13.3–8; Mark 4.3–8; Luke 8.5–8)?

*Exercise 3*
What do you learn by reading several of the twenty-seven prayers of Jesus?
(Heb. 2.12, 13, 7.25, 9.24, 10.5, 7; Luke 3.21, 22; Mark 1.35–9, 7.32–7,
8.6, 10.13–16, 14.32–42; Luke 5.12–16, 6.12, 13, 9.18, 28–35, 10.17–19,
19.41–4, 20, 21, 11.1, 22.31–4, 23.34, 46, 24.13–35, 50–3; Matt. 6.9–13,
11.25, 14.22, 23, 16.14–17, 23.37–9, 26.26–8, 39–46, 27.46; John 6.11,
11.41, 12.20–8,17, 19.30, 20.17; Rom. 8.34; 1 John 2.1)

*Exercise 4*
Read Psalms 118 and 116. In what ways are the poems alike in thought
and situation? How does Psalm 118 demonstrate an antiphonal structure
in contrast to the solo suggested by Psalm 116?

*Exercise 5*
Many Psalms can be described as laments: 10, 35, 38, 51, 54, 64, 74,
and 77. Find in each of these the characteristics of lament: invocation,
complaint, petition or supplication, statement of confidence in God, and
the vow to praise God.

*Exercise 6*
Read the Song of Solomon. This book was incorporated into the Jewish
canon over objections that its subject matter was unsuitable for sacred
literature. It has been described as a literary unity, a systematic collection
of love poems, and a random collection of lyrics. Additionally, it has been
interpreted allegorically, dramatically, typologically (parabolically). What
rationale exists for each of these approaches?

*Exercise 7*
Read Hebrews 9. Explain how it may be interpreted as a parable.

*Exercise 8*
Locate the "Shemoneh Esrei" and discuss it in terms of its three genres:
praise, petition, and thanks.

*Exercise 9*
Review several birth stories of important people (Isaac, Samuel, Joseph,
John, Jesus) in the Old and New Testaments. What features do they share?

## Questions for Reflection

1 How does defining genre as seeing and arranging, mapping and
   following, require readers to become active participants in a
   story stretching from creation to consummation, the story itself a
   metaphor for individual life and how life should be lived?
2 How do songs in the Bible evidence concrete imagery, parallelisms, metaphors, and symbols?
3 What was the Hebrew idea of immortality? How does this idea of
   immortality express itself in song?
4 In what ways should allegory and parable be understood as genres
   using analogy or making comparisons, both direct and indirect?
   What then distinguishes allegory and parable?
5 What dangers exist in reading the Bible allegorically? Literally?

6 What is the relation of parable and allegory to simile and metaphor?

7 What primary differences exist between reading the Song of Songs as allegory and as love poetry?

8 What is the allegorical meaning of Isaiah 54 and Jeremiah 2?

9 In what ways is the book of Hosea allegorical?

10 What primary differences exist between prayers in the Old Testament and those in the New Testament?

11 What distinguishes prayer as a genre?

12 How does recognizing genres in the Bible contribute to an overall unity or disunity among its books?

13 How does reading the Bible without recognizing its various genres diminish or impoverish its overall impact?

14 How do the apocryphal texts contribute to new ways of looking at the Old and New Testaments?

15 How is the literal reading of the Bible a direct reflection of religious interpretation?

16 How do the Hebrew Prophets use metaphor to express their criticism of apostasy?

# 6 Character: A Way of Identifying

## Outline

Preliminary Considerations
    Definitions
    Traditional Approach to Reading the Bible
    Unique Characteristics
Identifying Characters
    Context – King Saul and the Witch of Endor
    Actions – King Solomon and Two Women Prostitutes
    Other Characters' Responses – King Josiah and Huldah
    Words – Stephen
    Symbolic Actions – Ezekiel's Wife
    Requests – Salome
    Impact – Eunice
    Description – The Elect Lady
    Structure – Mark
Close Reading
Questions for Reflection

*Perhaps the easiest way to begin appreciating a piece of literature is through its characters. Characters, after all, are people – human beings – they must seem like real people, even if they represent a stereotype such as a good or bad person. You get to know people by becoming careful observers of them: this takes time and effort. What do they say about themselves? What do others say? In the case of a story, what does the narrator say about them? How do they act? Do they reveal habits or patterns within what they say and do? What are their abilities and preferences? What do they look like? What do we know about their past? What do we know about their friendships or the people they admit into their inner circles? As we learn about characters, we learn about ourselves – coming to understand our own motives, attitudes, and moral natures.*

## Preliminary Considerations

### Definitions

The Bible has a cast of thousands of multifaceted, lively, and complicated characters representing a wide range of human activity, appearing as both **one-dimensional** and **multidimensional**. Narrators present them by what they do and say, through their actions, words, and thoughts. **Characterization** refers to the revelation or display of a character's habits, emotions, desires, and instincts. Motives, attitudes, and moral nature must be figured out through direct speech, reported speech, quoted interior dialogues, statements and facts presented by the **narrator**, what other characters say, actions and reports of actions, and physical appearance.[1] What the narrator says provides the greatest certainty, followed by inner speech (and lesser certainty), then direct speech by the character or others, and, most indirectly, actions about which readers must draw inferences.[2] In the end, like people, the Bible's characters will remain fragmented, contradictory, mysterious – eluding any attempt to say who they are concisely.[3]

## Traditional Approach to Reading the Bible

Traditionally, readers have come to the Bible expecting to discover religious truth, believing its storytellers worked with a didactic purpose: through setting, action, and characters, their stories address the great issues of life.[4] Omniscient narrators presume to know what God knows and imagine their characters as collectively revealing God's work in history, permitting readers to know these characters momentarily and imperfectly, to observe them as they learn of self, others, and God.[5] God, in fact, becomes the central character, revealing himself through acts in history, through the stories of the early ancestors of Israel, the Patriarchs, and subsequent generations.[6] Characters in the Bible live lives filled with urgency, reacting to the possibilities of human freedom in relation to God and to each other.[7] In light of divine purpose, they carry a burden of meaning larger than themselves.[8] The Christian New Testament resonates with the same urgency in light of the question "Who do you say I am?" (Mark 8.29). It advances a belief that the human and the divine come together in one specific person, Jesus, who becomes the central way of interpreting divine presence.[9]

## Unique Characteristics

The Bible presents its material, including characters, with a "cryptic conciseness," describing everything in sparse detail – but with every detail important to the plot – and without embellishment; at the same time, it presents its information progressively, even systematically, revealing and enriching data by the addition of subsequent detail, setting stories and characters within an interconnected background of events and meaning.[10] Characters must be interpreted: it becomes important to ask questions about why the narrator presents material in particular ways, ascribing motives and designating feelings, remaining quiet on these points, introducing dialogue, and noting particular identifications to characters; it becomes critical to understand how the narrator uses one part of a text to provide oblique commentary on another, and why one syntax is chosen over another.[11]

Instead of giving abstract propositions about virtue or vice, the Bible presents stories of characters in action.[12] It embodies its meaning experientially through characters who change, grow, and develop; almost always they face choices that contribute to their development. Stories focus on what leads up to choice, what actually happens, and what consequences emerge.[13] Tests – physical, mental, spiritual, and moral – become a common motif. Taken together, their struggles provide a glimpse into the universal human condition.[14] The Song of Songs, for example, presents the arousal, commitment, contentment, and communion of lovers; Job and Jonah both reveal dilemma, choice, and catastrophe; the story of Ruth describes a woman who makes the difficult choice to leave her own land and people to join another people; the books of Joshua and Judges introduce characters who experience life as enigmatic, unpredictable, and paradoxical, where characters achieve resolution in a choice to serve God.[15]

Not all characters, of course, represent human beings: things and animals may be personified. For example, Zion/Jerusalem is embodied and known as a lady, and two animals functioning most notably as characters are the serpent and Balaam's ass, both of which actually speak. Another creature, Leviathan, functions in counterpart to God, warring against creation; Psalm 74.13–14 describes Leviathan as having many heads, which are ultimately crushed by the Creator. Canaanite myth knows this same Leviathan as an enemy of Baal, who finally slays him. Generally, animals provide the backdrop for human beings. The Bible, in fact, makes over 300 references to sheep and lambs.[16] In addition to Leviathan, Job introduces another mythological creature, Behemoth; in Jonah there is the great fish; and 2 Kings 2.23 records the story of Elisha being taunted by small boys who call him "old baldhead," Elisha's cursing them, and two she-bears coming out of the woods and mauling forty-two boys. Both Ezekiel (chapter 1) and Revelation (chapter 5) present four living creatures in the form of the human, the lion, the ox, and the eagle; Revelation continues to use an eagle to signal symbolically the movement of time. Among the non-human characters, angels play a significant role, appearing from Genesis to Revelation – Michael (Dan. 10), Raphael (Apocryphal Tobit 12), and Gabriel (Dan. 8) being among those named. Angels are connected with the birth of Christ (Matt. 1, Luke 1) and appear to Paul (Acts 27.23), Peter (Acts 12.7–11), and Cornelius (Acts 10.3–6); and four books address the fall of angels (Deut. 32.17; 2 Peter 2.4; Jude 1.6, and Rev. 12.7–9).

## Identifying Characters

*Some principle of selection must be used to introduce characters in a textbook on the Bible as literature.[17] I've chosen characters to illustrate*

*processes you can use to examine the immediate and extended framework*
*in which they are found: context, actions, responses, words, symbolic*
*actions, requests, impact, description, and structure. Examining these,*
*you will begin to appreciate the complexity and ambiguity that arise*
*within situations. I have chosen characters who are less well known or,*
*in some cases, familiar characters who deserve reassessment.*

*As you read the following selections, you will want to keep in mind*
*some guidelines. First and foremost, you are looking at events and char-*
*acters presented by narrators. A critical distinction must be kept between*
*the narrator's and the characters' points of view.[18] This will mean that*
*you will need to ask several questions about what you read: for example,*
*What is the conflict between prophet and king? In relation to the mon-*
*archy (an important issue examined from many angles throughout the*
*Old Testament), does the narrator consider the desire for a king by the*
*people an act of disobedience? What is the prophet Samuel's view? Does*
*it represent Yahweh's view?*

## *Identifying Character through Context: King Saul and the Witch of Endor (1 Sam. 28.3–25)*

Joshua, Judges, Samuel, and Kings have been described as belonging
to a single Deuteronomistic tradition or to an original Deuteronomistic
and a later exilic tradition, with one tradition emphasizing hope and
approval of the monarchy and another emphasizing punishment
and disapproval of the monarchy.[19] Tracing the evidence for the two
traditions may be less helpful than understanding them generally
as together providing the context in which characters participate
in a national life and set of events being worked out in a theology of
absolutes: justice and injustice, faithfulness and unfaithfulness, and
righteousness versus unrighteousness. It is a theology that emphasizes obedience to the covenant and the laws of Yahweh and in light of
which moral character must be understood.

Saul functions against the backdrop of an Israel seeking to end
tribal confederacy and rule by judges (1 Sam. 8.4, 5) by choosing a
king in order to be "like other nations." The narrator reveals that
Samuel is old at this point, that his sons have behaved corruptly, and
that this prompts the request. Told by God to listen to the voice of the
people, Samuel warns them that having a king will lead to oppression
(8.10–18).[20] The possibility exists that Samuel may be more bothered
about the possibility of being rejected than about the new form of gov-
ernment, this revealed in the narrator's explicit statement to him that
they have rejected not him, but Yahweh. When later God expresses
regret for making Saul king (15.11), Samuel insists ironically that God
does not change his mind (15.29) – revealing, perhaps, his commitment to the project of monarchy once he has been entrusted with it.[21]
The narrator states explicitly that Samuel is angry about God's change
of mind (15.11).

1 Chronicles, a later redaction, explicitly links Saul's own fate (and certainly that of Israel) to retributive justice and deserved punishment: "So Saul dies for his unfaithfulness; he was unfaithful to the LORD . . . he had consulted with a medium, and did not seek guidance from the LORD" (10.13–14). This formulaic reading – punishment for unfaithfulness and divination – tells, however, only part of the reason for Saul's fate. In counseling Saul, Samuel explains to him the kinds of personal characteristics that can contribute to the downfall of a person and nation: "For rebellion is no less a sin than divination, / and stubbornness is like iniquity and idolatry" (1 Sam. 15.23). The intricate, interconnected accounts in 1 Samuel reveal yet other personal characteristics – ambition, impulsiveness, confusion about where to seek advice, failure to heed advice, hypocrisy about internal motivations – that help to develop Saul as a complicated, conflicted, and tragic human being who, after Samuel's death, afraid and despairing on the eve of his own death, consults with the Witch of Endor (28.3, 9).

Early in the narrative, Samuel introduces an irony between what Saul says about himself and what the reader knows about him through context and actions. When selected by Samuel as the man God has identified to be king of Israel, Saul presents himself over-humbly: "I am only a Benjamite, from the least of the tribes of Israel, and my family is the humblest of all the families of the tribe of Benjamin. Why then have you spoken to me in this way?" (9.21). The context reveals that Saul comes from a wealthy family; physically, he is superior in degree to others, being unusually handsome and tall, standing "head and shoulder above everyone else" (9.1, 2). Apparently, the Israelites not only want to be like other nations, they also choose a king based on his outward appearance. The Benjamite tribe, far from being least among tribes, built a reputation as warriors, defeating the other tribes in a civil war.[22] Saul's emergence as a leader may have much to do with this background.

Saul soon reveals personal flaws; he acts speedily, for example, to take on responsibilities without preparing fully for the consequences; he behaves impulsively. The writer ironically subverts the early positive description of Saul by describing him as ready quickly to abandon his quest for straying donkeys.[23] The servant who accompanies Saul then takes charge, knowing where to go for information. The context reveals that Saul considers Samuel a seer or clairvoyant, a prophet, someone who can help him with his present circumstances – someone, in this case, who can help him find his donkeys. This is exactly what Samuel does: "When you depart from me today, you will meet two men . . . they will say to you, 'The donkeys . . . are found, and now your father has stopped worrying' (10.2). This early event foreshadows Saul's later willingness to consult with the Witch of Endor, revealing also his confusion about the role of a prophet and the role of a sorcerer. In yet another impulsive act, Saul lays an oath on his troops, swearing that anyone who eats food before he avenges the enemy will be cursed.

This unfortunately turns out to be Saul's own son, returning from victorious battle with the Philistines (14.24–46).

In still another impulsive act, one with lasting consequences, Saul, suspecting a conspiracy, slaughters his own priests at Nob, just east of Jerusalem. This results in a complicated set of consequences connected to the future of the monarchy and the later divided nation. While eighty-five priests die, Abiathar flees to David, becoming one of the latter's high priests. David, attempting to forge a united kingdom, appoints Abiathar (north) and Zadok (south) as priests. Solomon banishes Abiathar for supporting his rival to the kingship. With the accession of Jereboam (north) and Reheboam (south) as rival kings in a divided kingdom, a rival priesthood also comes into existence. Deuteronomistic history, it has been suggested, originated in the north, carrying with it anti-king and anti-city sentiments, then shifted to Jerusalem after the collapse of the northern kingdom in 722 BCE. While Deuteronomy generally advances a theology of restorative justice (where repentance leads to restoration), redactors after the Babylonian captivity reinterpreted the exile and destruction of the Temple as just punishment for transgression.[24]

In an early scene, Saul fails to follow advice, demonstrating a willful and conscious deviation from the instruction of Samuel to wait for seven days for him as priest to come to offer sacrifices (10.8), irony being evident in Saul's feeble protest, "I forced myself and offered the burnt offering" (13.12). Readers know the real motivation by the simple fact that the narrator has revealed that the people have begun to slip away from Saul (13.8); this is confirmed in Saul's own words (13.11).

In yet another example of disregarding advice, Saul spares the choice sheep and cattle of the Amalekites, taking what is most valuable, even though he has been instructed to spare nothing, and then lies to Samuel, telling him, "I have carried out the command of the LORD" (15.13).[25] In Exodus (17.8–16), God had said to Moses that Amalek, a descendant of Esau, would be blotted out through war from generation to generation. After his battle with the Amalekites, Saul reveals his own ambition when he goes to Carmel to set up a monument for himself (15.12). Once again confronted by Samuel, Saul tries to minimize his behavior, insisting, "I have obeyed . . . I have gone on the mission . . . I have brought Agag the king of Amalek, and I have utterly destroyed the Amalekites. But from the spoil the people took . . . the best of things . . . to sacrifice to the LORD your God in Gilgal" (15.20, 21). Samuel tells Saul that, because he has rejected the word of the Lord, he will be rejected as king (15.23). In the Old Testament, following battle, the Israelites would often destroy the city or country, along with its people, animals, and possessions – a practice known as "the ban." The spoils of war were to be put aside for God, with the Israelites forbidden to take anything. Anyone who did so would be severely punished (Num. 21.2, Deut. 20.16–18, Josh. 6.17). The Samuel text interprets Saul's disobedience theologically: he plunders, an act God will punish.

Deuteronomy (18.9–14) provides the broader context for the Witch of Endor story by explicitly forbidding the pagan practices of divination, consultation with the soothsayer, auger, or sorcerer; the casting of spells or consultations with ghosts or spirits. The disguise (1 Sam. 28.8) and deception, beyond the theology, suggest a character fully and consciously involved in wrongdoing. When the witch reminds Saul that he himself has cut off the mediums and wizards from the land (28.9), the dramatic irony further accentuates the wrongdoing and Saul's hypocrisy. Deuteronomy 18.11 specifically forbids consulting with ghosts, but Saul under pressure relapses into necromancy and consults with the dead Samuel, who reproaches him: "Why have you disturbed me by bringing me up?" (28.15). Samuel tells Saul that both he and his sons will die because he did not utterly destroy the Amalekites; he also tells Saul that his kingdom will not continue, that God has sought out another in his neighbor David (28.17), a man Samuel has earlier described as "after his [God's] own heart" (13.14).[26]

The witch, who asks Saul, "Why have you deceived me?," demonstrates remarkable compassion for Saul, who falls "full length on the ground filled with fear because of the words of Samuel" (28.20). Having first feared him, the witch now sets bread before him and urges him to eat to regain his strength. She also slaughters a fatted calf and serves that to Saul, who has not eaten for over twenty-four hours. In the New Testament, the parable of the Prodigal Son, told in the Gospel of Luke, picks up the motif of "killing a fatted calf" in celebration of a son returned safe and sound, perhaps making a conscious allusion to the kind of compassion demonstrated for the now repentant Saul; unfortunately, Saul's momentary replenishment will not provide him the spiritual and physical strength he needs for the next day's battle. After eating, Saul and his servant take leave of the witch – their leaving that very night indicating that Saul will, unwisely, not have slept very much.[27] The Philistines kill three of Saul's sons in battle, and Saul takes his own life, fulfilling Samuel's prophecy (31.4).

Ambiguity surrounds the different accounts of Saul's death: the narrator of 1 Samuel reports that he killed himself by falling upon his own sword (31.4); in 2 Samuel, an Amalekite claims to have killed him (1.10); 1 Chronicles also reports that Saul killed himself (10.4). Following the principle that the narrator provides the greatest degree of credibility for the truth of an account, Saul would seem to have died tragically, both accepting and initiating his own fate. Yet another means of sorting out what happened exists within the larger context of Exodus 17, where Moses, Aaron, and Hur have fought against the Amalekites, and Moses has said, "The LORD will have war with Amalek from generation to generation" (17.16). In short, the context undercuts the likelihood that an enemy can be believed.[28] Ironically, the Amalekite, unlike the armor-bearer, dares both to kill a sacred king and to be mercenary about it. 1 Samuel reports that Saul's head was cut off and carried by messengers throughout the land of the Philistines, that they put his body in the temple of Astarte and hung it on the wall of Beth-shan; and, finally, that the bodies of Saul and his sons were taken to Jabesh, burned, and their bones buried (31.8–13). 1 Chronicles reports a more dignified outcome: "all the valiant warriors got up and took away the body of Saul and the bodies of his sons [which have been on display in the temple of Dagon], and brought them to Jabesh. Then they buried their bones under the oak in Jabesh, and fasted seven days" (10.12). Although both accounts consider exposure disgraceful and unworthy of a king of Israel, the latter account still firmly affixes the cause of Saul's death as the result of his unfaithfulness and, specifically, his consulting a medium rather than seeking guidance from the Lord (10.13–14).

*The account of Saul above introduces a multidimensional or **round character** understood against the background of a growing tension between prophet and king as well as a moral compass gauged by loyalty to Yahweh. The actions of King Solomon, the third king of the monarchy, must be weighed using these same scales. If you review the actions recorded of King Solomon in 1 and 2 Kings and then compare these with the stories presented in 1 Chronicles 2.1–9.39, you will discover two things: the first account introduces an assessment of his actions as both good and bad (multidimensional); in the second account, gauged by his actions, Solomon emerges as essentially a **flat character** or a good king.*

### Identifying Character through Actions: King Solomon and Two Women Prostitutes (1 Kings 11; 3)

The reign of Solomon in 1 Kings consists of actions that give this character tragic overtones: his rise to power, his tainted glory, and his downfall.[29] There emerges in his early rise to power a clear blood agenda initiated by David's deathbed charge to Solomon to kill Joab (1 Kings 2.6) and Shimei (1 Kings 2.9; 2 Sam. 16.1–8), the former for retaliating the wartime death of his brother Asahel, and the latter for cursing David "as a man of blood," deeply implicated in the deaths of Abner (Saul's commander) and Ishbaal, Saul's son (2 Sam. 3). Solomon capably carries out his father's charges and then aggressively secures the throne by having his brother Adonijah, a threat to his accession, killed. Through this early struggle and bloodshed, Solomon emerges largely as a positive figure, doing what he has to do: a secure throne represents a fulfillment of prophecy, a united Judah and Israel "as numerous as the sand by the sea" (1 Kings 4.20), and results in a Temple built and dedicated to "a God who keeps covenant and steadfast love" (8.23). Pre-exilic theology identifies as "good" kings those who support the Temple and centralized worship. It is at this stage of character development that the writer (1, 2 Kings) emphasizes the positive aspects of Solomon's character, including his prayer for wisdom and an early story of its practical application.

The memorable story of two prostitutes laying claim to the same child advances Solomon's reputation for wisdom and demonstrates his ability to execute justice. The less than admirable roles for these women can be explained, in part, relative to local customs: women sometimes resorted to prostitution for commercial reasons. The Bible presents the details of this story through the point of view of one woman, who reports that the two live together, that they gave birth at about the same time, that the son of other woman died when she rolled over on him in the night, and that, discovering this, she substituted her dead son for the other woman's live son. The seemingly insignificant detail, "there was no stranger in the house," makes clear that only the women know what has happened, and the narrator seems to have all the advantage in recounting the story. Solomon, by proposing to cut the child in half to resolve the dispute, appeals to the strong maternal ties that exist between the real mother and son, and she responds, "O my lord, give her the living child, and in no wise slay it," this in contrast to the callous reply of the other to "divide it" (1 Kings 3.26). Ironically, Solomon's practical and surpassing wisdom in the discernment of a mother's protectiveness (4.30) holds little sway over his own personal actions and his choices between right and wrong.

At the apex of his power, Solomon's successes begin to be undercut: he has acquired wealth and wives, tolerating pagan cults and marrying outside his own people, and has indulged himself with 700 princesses and 300 concubines (1 Kings 11.3). He has also created adversaries by raising a levy out of Israel to build his own palace (1 Kings 5.13–14), a project on which he apparently spent more time and money than on the Temple. Exilic theology identifies those who permit **syncretism** as "bad" kings, and Solomon here takes on decidedly negative overtones. The narrator of 1 Kings reports, "For it came to pass . . . his wives turned away his heart after other gods . . . And Solomon did evil." As a result, Solomon is judged for not keeping God's covenant, and the kingdom is torn from him (11.11).

While Kings portrays a multidimensional Solomon, the narrator of 1 Chronicles presents a largely idealized and flat character, a wise, political leader who succeeds in gaining the support of his nation and who rules as a religious leader.[30] Instead of a balanced portrait of a king with both good and not so good traits, the narrator of 1 Chronicles simply omits events: the warning by Nathan that wrongdoing would be punished (2 Sam. 7.14; 1 Chron. 17.13); the struggle for power (1 Kings 1.12.46); the Egyptian wife (1 Kings 3.13); and Solomon's downfall (1 Kings 11.14). In short, a king of Israel could do no wrong.

*In reading and reconsidering the stories of two kings of the monarchy, you have been encouraged to reassess their characters and behaviors against the full context in which their actions are presented. At the same, I have wanted you to become aware of how you make decisions about them: what is being inferred, claimed, what is certain, and what information is reliable. You probably have discovered that, just about*

*the time when you think you have these characters figured out or know*
*what they mean, a full grasp of their motives or the narrators' intentions*
*for them eludes you. They cannot be reduced to a simple statement of*
*meaning but must remain characters within the story or episode within*
*which they are found.*[31]

### Identifying Character through Other Characters' Responses: King Josiah and Huldah (2 Kings 22; 2 Chron. 34)

After Solomon, national calamity resulted from kings' failing in their religious duties, with the expected retribution: disobedient kings and nations are punished. Individuals familiar with the Bible recognize the role King Josiah plays in bringing a short-lived reform to Judah (622 BCE); the formulaic account in Kings makes his positive role clear: "he did what was right in the sight of the LORD" (22.2). Josiah loves God with all his heart, overseeing the destruction of idol shrines, reinstating priests in the Temple, and celebrating the Passover. Readers often overlook the role of the prophetess Huldah in bringing about this religious reform. The narrator presents her through brief introductory facts and then through her reported words, beginning with a prophetic formula: "Thus says the LORD." She is most known by the immediate response of the priest in seeking her out within the "house of the LORD."

The Bible, with typical economy, reveals little about Huldah, the wife of Shallum, keeper of the wardrobe for either the priests or the king, other than the fact that Hilkiah, when commanded by Josiah "Go, inquire of the Lord for me, the people, and for all Judah" (2 Kings 22.13), goes immediately to her; she apparently was well known in Jerusalem.[32] Huldah declares uncompromisingly the message to be taken back to Josiah, declaring, "Thus says the LORD, the God of Israel: Tell the man you sent to me, Thus says the LORD" (22.15–16). She sends back a message of judgment: that disaster comes upon Jerusalem because its inhabitants have forsaken God and gone after other gods (22.17). That Josiah immediately carries out reform upon hearing the report demonstrates the high regard he must have held for the prophetess.

Josiah, unlike King Saul, seeks out God's direction through a prophet; and to Huldah's "Thus says the LORD" responds by renewing the covenant with God and "taking away all the abominations from all the people that belonged to the people of Israel" (2 Chron. 34.33). Josiah is rewarded for repentance:

> Because [Huldah says] your heart was penitent and you humbled yourself before God when you heard his words against this place and its inhabitants, and you have humbled yourself before me, and have torn your clothes, and have wept before me . . . I will gather you to your ancestors, and you shall be gathered to your grave in peace. (34.27–8)

Huldah's character may be interpreted in view of her role in pronouncing upon the authority of the book of the law that Hilkiah found.[33] Whatever the source of that book, and some scholars insist it was less than a century old, Huldah gives it prophetic authority by verifying it as the words of God, making it prescriptive, and thus establishing it as an early canon. In the scroll canonized by Huldah, God sets before Moses a choice between life and death, a choice followed by blessing or curse. This juxtaposition of life and death, with the imperative to choose, gives responsibility to human beings to exercise discernment and to choose responsibly; it poses the theodicy of divine justice. In the New Testament, the confrontation of Jesus by his adversary Satan in the wilderness provides another example of right discernment: given a choice to affirm a quotation of Satan (Ps. 91.11–12), Jesus chooses a different text (Deut. 6.13). The choices are clear: Satan urges Jesus to throw himself off the cliff, actively to choose death, believing God would protect him; Jesus, on the other hand, chooses a text that offers him life. Huldah's choice becomes human choice: what to say, prescriptively or descriptively, about the Bible's collection of ancient texts, how to choose responsibly, and what the consequences of that choice will be – blessing or curse. Jesus sets before readers an even more critical choice: how to interpret texts in light of the death/life juxtaposition.

Huldah's importance as prophetess most reveals itself in Josiah's legacy: the scroll occasioning religious reform during this era has commonly been identified with Deuteronomy. The religious reform and national restoration that follow emphasize religious centralization and an attempt to reunite Israel and Judah. Josiah becomes pivotal to discussions of the interpretation of Israel and Judah's history and the overall composition of the Bible. Much of the prophetic literature, in fact, interprets Josiah as a Davidic monarch who helps to bring about the ancient promise of a land, a people, and a nation; Huldah plays a key role in this renewed hope.

### Identifying Characters through their Words: Stephen (Acts 7, 8; 1 Sam. 4)

The New Testament recognizes Stephen in the familiar role as the first Christian martyr; in reality, he plays a role close to that of the prophet, a person raised up by God to deal with the problems of day-to-day life.[34] In a memorable speech rehearsing history (Acts 7.12–50, summarizing Genesis), Stephen calls the people into account for their resistance and absolute rejection of God.

Stephen's remarkable speech summarizes the events of Hebrew history (viewed through a Deuteronomistic lens) that, for him, culminate in Jesus of Nazareth.[35] Stephen recounts God's appearing to Abraham in Mesopotamia and telling him to go to a land that God would show him, the generations of the twelve Patriarchs, the 400 years his descendants spent in Egypt, the story of Joseph, Moses, and the emancipation, the story of the giving of the law, the history of disobedience in God's people, David's resolve to build a Temple for God, and Solomon's accomplishment of this. He then makes the transition into current day: "You stiff-necked people, uncircumcised in heart and ears, you are forever opposing the Holy Spirit, just as your ancestors used to do" (7.51). He goes on to tell them that their ancestors "killed those who foretold the coming of the Righteous One and have become his betrayers and murderers" (7.52).

Stephen's speech has five parts, these interlinking with Old Testament history and making the Old indispensable for understanding the New: Israel's rejection of Abraham, Joseph, and Moses, their idolatry, and their disobedience in building the Temple.[36] To understand the disobedience in building the Temple, readers must read within the context of the fuller story in which the people rejected theocratic rule, wanting, rather, to be ruled, like other nations, by a king; with the monarchy and the building of the Temple, they rejected the earlier abode for God's presence in a portable tent. The tent housed Israel's most holy ark of the covenant which they carried into battle with them (1 Sam. 4.4). The tent had been housed at Shiloh, and Eli and his sons served as priests; the prophet Samuel had ministered in Shiloh. Because Eli's sons dishonored God, they died in battle with the Philistines at the same time that the enemies captured the ark; when Eli hears the news, he falls off his seat and breaks his neck (1 Sam. 4). The Philistines place the ark in the temple of Dagon, and a strange story follows: they find Dagon the next day fallen on his face before the ark and put him back in place only to find him the next morning again fallen on his face, head and hands cut off. Following these two incidents, God strikes the Philistines with tumors, the result being that they return the ark to Beth-she-mesh, where it stays until King David takes it to Jerusalem (2 Sam. 6). There, finally, under Solomon, it is installed in the holiest chamber of the Temple. The ark is thought to have been captured when Jerusalem fell in 587/586 BCE.

Stephen rehearses the history of the ark, explaining that the ancestors had the tent of testimony in the wilderness, that they brought it with Joshua when they disposed the nations, that it was there until David inquired about building a dwelling for it, and that Solomon completed the Temple where it finally rested.[37] Stephen makes clear, by quoting Isaiah 66.1–2, that God does not dwell in houses made by human hand: "Heaven is my throne, / and the earth is my footstool. / What kind of house will you build for me, says the Lord, / or what is the place of my rest? / Did not my hand make all these things?" (7.49–50).

Stephen uses the literary tools of foreshadowing and allusion to connect his speech with the Old Testament and to make a theological point: after talking about Israel's rejection of Abraham, he reminds his audience of Joseph, who, like Jesus, is rejected by his own family, suggesting that Joseph foreshadows Jesus; he alludes to Joshua, knowing his audience will understand that both names derive from the Hebrew, meaning "YHWH, help." Stephen makes the theological point that Israel has had a history of rejection, continuing into their current rejection of Jesus and of him. He also makes the point that God continues to fulfill promises: God brings back Jacob and his sons from Egypt for burial in Shechem; God enables Moses to rescue the Israelites from Egypt, appearing to him at Sinai and reminding him that God is God of Abraham, Isaac, and Jacob; and, even though the Israelites have rejected the tent and the ark in favor of a Temple, the prophets have still told them of the Righteous One that they are now rejecting. Hope reemerges in Stephen's final prayer that God will not hold the people's sins against them. His speech reveals the retributive formula, God's justice, but emphasizes also the mercy of God which continues to work among the rebellion.

On a scale of certainty, the narrator leaves little doubt about Stephen's moral integrity, comparing him with Christ: both were filled with grace and power and performed signs and wonders. The narrator introduces Stephen as one of "seven men of good standing, full of the Spirit and of wisdom . . . full of faith and the Holy Spirit" (Acts 6.3, 5) and continues to declare him "full of grace and power . . . [a man who] did great wonders and signs among the people" (6.8). Stephen's death as martyr has overtones of Christ's crucifixion and death, described as a sacrifice. It connotatively picks up the language related to the cross: Stephen, gazing into heaven sees the heavens opened "and the Son of Man standing at the right hand of God" (7.55–7); he prays "Lord Jesus, receive my spirit" (7.59) and "cries out in a loud voice, 'Lord, do not hold this sin against them'" (7.60). Anti-climactically, the story ends in a quiet statement, "he died" (7.60).

*You may be more comfortable thinking of a symbol as a word or an image that stands for something in addition to its literal meaning, but in the next section you will be looking at a character who, apart from her role as wife, functions in a purely symbolic way. You are told very little about Ezekiel's wife, but when she is put into the context of Israel's and Judah's history you learn a great deal more. Ezekiel's grief for his "beloved" wife must have been inexpressible and numbing, a grief experienced by an individual that the narrator extends to a people and nation whose hopes have been dashed by defeat, captivity, and extended exile.*

### Identifying Character through Symbolic Actions: Ezekiel's Wife (Ezek. 24.15–27)

Almost everyone recognizes Ezekiel as a major prophet in the Old Testament, but few know that he was married to an unnamed and unmourned wife. Because Israel practiced demonstrative mourning (Jer. 16.5–9; Mic. 1.8), the people were surprised by the priest's behavior, asking, "Will you not tell us what these things mean for us, that you are acting this way?" (Ezek. 24.19). In biblical tradition, the dead received care and respect (Gen. 23; 50.26); in fact, mourning usually continued for seven days. Readers learn, too, scant but important details about the character of Ezekiel's wife: that she is the "delight of his eyes" and, no less than the analogy reveals, his "heart's desire" and source of sons and daughters (24.21). With the usual economy, the Bible tells the story: the unnamed wife dies in the evening, and the next morning, the prophet goes about his customary tasks. The people do not know that God has forewarned Ezekiel of his wife's imminent death and instructed him not to mourn (24.16).

Ezekiel responds as requested: "I spoke to the people in the morning, and at evening my wife died. And on the next morning I did as I was commanded" (24.18). The sequence of events echoes the formulaic morning, night, and next day, with obedience as Ezekiel's single motive and no explanation regarding his emotions. When the people press him to explain his behavior, Ezekiel prefaces his answer with, "Thus says the Lord GOD" (24.21). Ezekiel tells the people that, just as God has taken away the delight of his eyes, God will also take away the Temple, the people's pride, delight, and desire (24.21). In an extended analogy, Ezekiel explains that the exiles, like himself, will put their turbans on their heads and sandals upon their feet and "shall not mourn or weep" in the face of a more numbing, irrepressible grief: "you shall pine away in your iniquities and groan to one another" (24.23). Those who escape will come to Ezekiel, in exile, to report the news. God tells Ezekiel, "On that day your mouth shall be opened to the one who has escaped, and you shall speak and no longer be silent. So you shall be a sign to them; and they shall know that I am the LORD" (24.27). Even though Ezekiel explains his actions as a sign to his people, they will not recognize the sign until they repeat his behaviors and remember what he has said to them.

Possibly more than in any other book, except perhaps Job, questions arise in Ezekiel about God's justice. God simply tells Ezekiel that he will judge him, that with one blow he will take away his wife; God will show no mercy. More than at any other time in history, a people of God experience a loss of hope. Why are they in exile? Why did God not keep his promise to their ancestors? The answer fits the retributive justice formula: the people have turned away from God, become like other people, have violated God's holy presence.[38] The Temple, their pride, delight, and desire, is taken away and they pine away in their iniquities and groan to one another, all the result of their turning away from God. No such explanation, however, accounts for the death of Ezekiel's wife, just that she serves as a sign to the people; and Ezekiel, unlike the people, does what he is commanded.

### Identifying Character through Requests: Salome (Matt. 20.20–8; Mark 10.35–45)

Among several women who followed Jesus and were present at his crucifixion and resurrection, Salome (Matt. 27.56; Mark 15.40), the mother of James and John, achieves special significance simply through making one request: "Declare that these two sons of mine will sit, one at your right hand and one at your left, in your kingdom" (Matt. 20.21). The request contrasts a mother's ambition for her sons to the kind of greatness modeled by Jesus and expected of his followers: "It will not be so among you; but whoever wishes to be great among you must be your servant, and whoever wishes to be first among you must be your slave; just as the Son of Man came not to be served but to serve, and to give his life a ransom for many" (20.26–8). Salome can be compared with Mary, the mother of Jesus, who never expressed ambition for her son, only pondering what others speak about Him.[39] The request immediately provokes the other disciples' anger at James and John. In Mark (10.35–45), it is James and John, not Salome, who make the request, perhaps helping to explain the displaced anger described in Matthew; the disciples compete with each other, being afraid of losing something themselves.

Christians interpret Jesus as modeling true greatness by making Himself subservient to the Father, who prepares the places of honor and determines who will sit in them; he achieves greatness by assuming the role of servant and surrendering his life in supreme sacrifice for others. He practices the commandment to love others: "This is my commandment, that you love one another as I have loved you. No one has greater love than this, to lay down one's life for one's friends" (John 15.12, 13). Matthew 19 and 20 address the nature of human ambition when Peter tells Jesus that the disciples have left everything and asks, "What then shall we have?" (19.27). Jesus replies that they will sit on twelve thrones judging the tribes of Israel, but follows this suggestion of power with a reminder that "many that are first will be last, and the last first" (19.30). The parable immediately following further overturns the human ambition of seeking to be first. After relating a story about laborers hired at different hours throughout the day but paid the same wage at the end of the day, Jesus asks the disciples, "'Am I not allowed to do what I choose with what belongs to me? Or do you begrudge my generosity?' So the last will be first, and the first last" (20.15, 16).

### Identifying Character through Impact: Eunice (1 Tim. 1; Acts 16)

Nearly everyone recognizes Timothy but may not know the name of his mother or the role she played in the establishment of the Church.[40] The pseudonymous 2 Timothy 1.5 tells Timothy, "I am reminded of your sincere faith, a faith that lived first in your grandmother Lois and your mother Eunice and now, I am sure, lives in you," the linkage between generations echoing the ancient instruction to keep the decrees and commandments and to pass them on by actively reciting them (Deut. 6.7). Acts 16 describes Timothy's mother as a Jewish believer and his father as a Greek.

Although the Bible says very little about Timothy's mother, it makes clear that Eunice was instrumental in shaping her son's sincere faith in the same way that hers was nurtured by his grandmother; Timothy, in turn, contributed to the establishment of the early Church. Paul's concession to circumcision, the Hebrew sign marking a child of the covenant, may have resulted from opposition by the Jews to Timothy's ministry: "Paul wanted Timothy to accompany him; and he took and had him circumcised because of the Jews who were in those places, for they all knew that his father was a Greek" (Acts 16.3). The circumcision has been explained as inconsistent based on his mother's being Jewish, but this understanding is a third-century rabbinic tradition.[41]

Readers learn much about Eunice by considering the many positive traits demonstrated in the son she has taught, earning her distinction alongside other influential mothers in the Bible: although young, Timothy leaves home (2 Tim. 2.22); he submits to circumcision; he is affectionate (2 Tim. 1.4); he is a beloved spiritual son to Paul (1 Tim. 1.2; 2 Tim.1.2; 1 Cor. 4.17); he is not overly assertive (1 Tim. 4.12); and, in spite of being delicate and often ill, he persists in the work of Christ (1 Tim. 5.23).

### Identifying Character through Description: the Elect Lady (2 John)

An epistle in the New Testament accentuates the significant role women play within the Church; the author of 2 John addresses one local church as the "elect lady." After the greeting, the writer commends the woman and her children for walking in the truth and admonishes them to keep the commandment of love for one another:

> But now, dear lady, I ask you, not as though I were writing you a new commandment, but one we have had from the beginning, let us love one another. And this is love, that we walk according to his commandments; this is the commandment just as you have heard it from the beginning – you must walk in it. (1.5, 6)

The elect lady, like Eunice above, has the responsibility for teaching the generations to follow to walk in love and truth. The author then admonishes the elect lady to guard against those who deny that Jesus came in the flesh (1.7) and suggests that hospitality to these would mean to participate in their deeds.

### Identifying Character through Structure (Mark)

The structure and genre of the Gospel of Mark have been much debated. Most have settled for a literary structure in the opening that sets forth a prologue, a parallel account of John and Jesus, and a unity of beginning and end established in the *euangelion* or good news of 1.1 and 1.15.[42] The debate has been over whether Mark belongs to the genre of biography or "lives" familiar in Roman and Hellenistic litera-ture, centering on praising and presenting this concrete character in actions and virtues through a formula looking at ancestry, birth, and education. The opening of Mark does not address these key character-istics, and the question becomes "Why?"

Mark has been acknowledged non-traditionally as the earliest Gospel and as different from the other two Synoptic Gospels that contain an introductory infancy account of Jesus, thus emphasizing ancestry. Mark clearly understands the ambiguity present in Jesus' human ancestry, this evidenced in remarks made about his origin. In Mark 4.33, Jesus denies his biological family in contradistinction to the crowd to whom he ministers; in Mark 6.3, Jesus is identified as the son of Mary, leaving unaddressed the question of his father. Attitudes prevalent in the other Gospels suggest that Mark had to overcome the challenge of Jesus' humble origin and marginal family in order to present the true source of his honor as his intimate relationship with God.[43] Since Jewish people viewed Galileans with suspicion, the town of Nazareth can be seen as insignificant (John 1.46), and Matthew allows it to be asked of Jesus pejoratively whether or not he is the son of a simple carpenter. Structurally, Mark must emphasize Jesus' cre-dentials through other means: he introduces him as "Jesus Christ, the Son of God" (1.1), through the words of the prophet Isaiah (1.2), and through the holy man John the Baptist (1.4–8; John 7.19).

Additionally, Jesus undergoes an initiation that qualifies him as a sage or, perhaps, a holy man: he leaves his home town of Nazareth, undergoes an educational experience with the help of John and the Spirit, and returns as God's messenger. In the shorter ending of Mark, Jesus sends out those whom he has taught to proclaim, from east to west, eternal salvation. The longer ending (16.9–19) moves well beyond the sage teaching his disciples through question and answer into an account of the resurrected Jesus as a further credentialing of his honor and authority as originating from God (16.19).

*Other characters in the Bible evidence a great deal of complexity in their humanity and deserve careful, attentive scrutiny for their contri-butions to the history of Judaism and Christianity.*

## Close Reading

*Exercise 1*

The Bible records several examples of women prophets. What characteristics do they share? How does the narrator reveal their personal characteristics?

Judg. 4; Exod. 15; Isa. 8

*Exercise 2*

Compare the early prophets and the seventh- and eighth-century prophets. Think about the context – who the prophets address and what they say.

What main features of the messages can you identify, and how do the messages change?

Read the following: 1 Kings 17, 18, 21, 22; 2 Kings 3.13–20, 4.38–41; 6.1–7; 9.1–13; 22; 1 Sam. 2; 9.9; 10.10–13; and sample passages from Hosea, Amos, Isaiah, Micah, Jeremiah, and Ezekiel.

*Exercise 3*

Read the following passages. How do prophets react to being summoned to prophesy? What do their actions reveal about them?

Isa. 6; Ezek. 1.1–3.15; Amos 7.15; Jer. 1; Jonah

*Exercise 4*

Compare Stephen's speech in Acts 7 to Samuel's farewell address in 1 Sam. 12. What features do they share? What characteristics of "reported speech" do the accounts share?

*Exercise 5*

During the reign of King David, Abiathar and Zadok functioned as priests. Read 1 Chronicles 12.27–9 and 1 Chronicles 24.1–6. Compare these passages with 1 Kings 2.35; 4.2. Read Ezekiel 40–8; Judges 17.5; 1 Samuel 7.1; 2 Samuel 8.18, 20.26; 1 Kings 12.31; and Judges 17–18. Why does the postexilic writer of Chronicles give Zadok an Aaronite genealogy?

*Exercise 6*

Review the lives of Saul, David, and Solomon in 1, 2 Samuel and 1 Kings 1–11. Assess the strengths and weaknesses of each king and the role they played in the monarchy. To what degree can their acts be evaluated relative to being true to God? Do they come over as being complex or simple characters in relation to the extended, unfolding plot?

*Exercise 7*

The concept of holy war has sometimes been interpreted to justify war and genocide, a literal reading that suggests God sanctions such acts. Read the following: Josh. 6.17, 8.2, 26, 11.12–14, 22.8; Deut. 5.17, 20.1–20, 23.9–14; Exod. 15.1–3; 2 Kings 3.4. Can the above interpretation be justified?

*Exercise 8*

Read 2 Kings 22–3. What is the role Huldah the prophetess plays in King Josiah's reform? To what degree is Huldah a fully developed character?

*Exercise 9*

What authority do women play in deciding the authority of the Bible? Read Gen. 2–3; Exod. 15.20–1; Deut. 34.10, 24.9; Num. 12.5–9; Mic. 6.4; 2 Kings 22.3–20, 23.1–30.

## Questions for Reflection

1 In what ways can God be said to be the Bible's protagonist?
2 What are the functions of the many characters described in the Bible?
3 What is meant by the omniscient narrator within selected texts of the Bible?
4 In what ways do characters reveal themselves to readers?

5 How do characters in the Bible illustrate choice between life and death?

6 Why is context important to understanding the behaviors of characters in the Bible?

7 How do characters define themselves through their actions?

8 How do characters reveal themselves through what they say?

9 In what sense can a complex character's behavior ultimately be summarized as good or bad?

10 How does Stephen interpret Hebrew history in light of the life of Jesus?

11 In what ways can characters function as "signs" or symbols?

12 How do words, actions, context, and description reveal the motives of characters?

13 What is the Christian standard for "true greatness"?

14 How does Stephen's speech address tensions between God's justice and mercy in light of Old Testament narrative?

15 Explain how the characters in the Bible represent complex human beings.

16 How do characters in the Bible reflect mythology and the monomyth?

17 In what ways does the non-human function as characters in the Bible?

18 What distinguishes a "round" from a "flat" character in the Bible? Provide examples.

# 7 Themes and Motifs: A Way of Unifying

## Outline

Preliminary Considerations
    Definitions
    Objections to Thematic Analysis
    How the Bible Traditionally Has Been Read
Major Themes in the Bible
    Relationship to God and with Other Human Beings: the Decalogue
    The Shema: "Hear, O Israel, the LORD your God is One"
    "He Declared to You His Covenant": Relationship Based upon Promise
    and Obligation
        The Noahic Covenant
        The Abrahamic Covenant
        The Mosaic Covenant
        The Davidic Covenant
    God's Mercy: "I have loved you with an everlasting love"
    God's Justice
    The Heroic Quest
Close Reading
Questions for Reflection

## Preliminary Considerations

*Introductory literature classes often make use of an anthology of writings grouped by several possible principles, theme being one of these. While I have alluded to theme throughout this text, I have delayed a focused discussion on it until now on account of the difficulty, if not impossibility, of separating theological from literary ideas in the Bible and also because of a continuing suspicion against reading the Bible as a unified, coherent whole. I am not suggesting that you reduce your understanding of the Bible to a set of themes; I am, however, making the point that literary and theological themes contribute continuities among the texts and between the two collections and offer a framework for examining the Bible as a whole. It may be helpful to know that the current distrust of the theology of the Bible comes largely from the eighteenth-century counter-culture that largely replaced the much older Judean-Christian world view.[1]*

*Definitions*

Literature has been organized in anthologies about theme, period, genre, nation, region, gender, social class, ethnic group, literary tradition, school, episteme, and discursive system.[2] **Theme**, an organizing idea (abstraction), holds together a work and can be embedded in images, actions, and emotions; it is the main emotional, analytic, and perceptive core of a text. Rather than simply holding together a text or unifying its meanings, theme actually emerges from the genre or "kind of thing the composition is."[3] **Thematic analysis** refers to the approach that systematizes the work of identifying, analyzing, and reporting patterns (themes) in a text, paying attention to how theme affects the text and shapes social and psychological reality.[4]

Closely related to themes, a **motif** (introduced in chapter 1) consists of recurrent patterns – themes, characters, events, situations, verbal patterns, and associational clusters of concepts or objects, generally symbolic. The distinction between theme and motif becomes one of degree, with motif commonly understood as more concrete, and theme more abstract.[5] The line between them blurs such that theme can become concrete and motif abstract.[6] Motif consists of recurring situations that set expectations in the minds of writers and readers. For example, the Bible refers often to the motif of "entering into the land" (Gen. 12.1; Josh. 1.13). The New Testament continues this in a generalized way, with "land" becoming the "earth" or "world." Revelation ends with a "new heaven" and "new earth" yet to be realized. Paying attention to motifs enables readers to read the Bible as a complex of parts in which reiterations multiply and enhance meaning as well as create coherence.[7]

An example of a set of unfolding motifs that helps to unite and hold together a story (in this case, called a **plot motif**) can be seen in the story of Jacob: in the journey of a man to a foreign country seeking a wife, the arrival, the meeting at the well, dialogue, the woman's running home, the man's meeting the parents, and the betrothal.[8] Plot motif holds together a number of stories of founding ancestors, advancing the narrative of reaching a promised land and eventually becoming a nation.[9]

The notion of motif can be extended into a set of **type-scenes** that recur in the Bible: annunciation, the birth of the hero to his barren mother, the encounter with the future betrothed at a well, the epiphany in a field, the initiatory trial, danger in the desert, and the discovery of a well.[10] A **leitmotif** refers to less dominant patterns and images such as the way of the righteous and the way of the ungodly. Another would be the "wanderers through life" that accompany Israel's destiny.[11]

Archetype, discussed in the chapter on figurative language, relates closely to theme, and usually is defined as universal images or patterns that recur in literature generally and in life universally: experiences such as hunger and thirst, water, gardens, deserts, the wilderness, sacrifices, and creation–birth–death. Together, themes, motifs, and archetypes provide an intricate network of ideas and patterns that function critically to provide unity and coherence to a piece of literature.[12]

## Objections to Thematic Analysis

Once a traditional and familiar way of approaching and understanding a text, thematic analysis has undergone a decline since the 1970s – explained, in part, by changes in literary critical approaches.[13] Traditionally, literary criticism has been concerned with how the text, the author, the audience, and the world relate. Literary critics have argued about whether a theme exists in the text, the reader, or the culture of the moment.[14] The debate involves whether focus should be upon the text itself or upon its historical and social connections.[15] Earlier twentieth-century criticism stressed heavily the formal relationship between the parts of a text, including themes and motifs; recently attention has shifted, once again, to a renewed interest in the author, the audience, and the world.[16]

Looking for meaning and asking what the text says leads to the possibility of settling too quickly upon a theme or point.[17] Other dangers inherent in identifying themes within any piece of literature include reader bias and social and cultural shortsightedness.[18] The search for a central or main theme also encourages sweeping and holistic reading that misses or ignores significant details.[19] In the end, an identified theme always represents a guess about the text and leads to an ongoing debate between the author's meaning and the reader's interpretation.[20]

## How the Bible Traditionally Has Been Read

Most readers traditionally have read the Bible through its religious and theological themes – the character of God, the acts of God, the nature of people, the nature of the visible world, the existence of two worlds, the divine–human relationship, and salvation. People have read the Bible, particularly the Old Testament, as a manual of moral instruction; they regard it as sacred and resist a merely aesthetic approach.[21]

Both the Jewish people and Christians understand the Old Testament as advancing the idea that God acted and will continue to act in human history; the New Testament adds to these acts the advent of Jesus Christ and the Church.[22] In both traditions, God recognizably performs as protagonist, or main character, in a story that begins with creation, tells of a developing spiritual and moral battle between good and evil, and describes choice and the result of choice in a culminating history.

*Much biblical criticism considers the Bible as a composite text made up of a complicated set of authors and redactors, this discussed in chapter 4. A literary approach, while informed by these discussions, emphasizes a close reading of the texts as they now exist in light of organizing themes, patterns, techniques, conventions, and uses of language that belong to literature universally. The approach generally acknowledges the challenge of origins and authorship without dwelling on them. A literary approach focuses more on entering into and reliving the experiences of the many characters in the Bible, considering them as representatives of the universal human quest to understand its nature, destiny, and place in the universe.*

## Major Themes in the Bible

*In the rest of this chapter, you will explore several major themes important to the Bible. The divine–human relationship functions as a dominant and central theme, developing two perspectives: the relationship of human beings to God and the relationship of human beings with each other.[23] Associated motifs include the "old" and "new" Israel and a people united, having a language, a religion, a land, and past and future goals.[24] Related themes consist of the "oneness" of God and the four covenant relationships (these remarkably absent in the wisdom genre); other themes, among them mercy and justice, emerge early in the Bible, especially in the Mosaic Covenant or Ten Commandments. All of these themes are tied closely to the common literary theme of the archetypal heroic quest, bringing with it alienation, initiation, suffering, and transformation.*

### Relationship to God and with Other Human Beings: the Decalogue (Exod. 20, Deut. 5, 10)

*While everyone agrees that the Old Testament consists of extensive narrative collections, they do not agree on where these narratives begin and end. One view proposes a six-book literary unit that begins with Genesis and ends with Joshua, a view questioned for at least three reasons. First, it ignores differences between two canons – the Torah and the Former Prophets; second, it obscures "the radical divide" between the death of Moses in Deuteronomy and the entering into the land in Joshua; and, finally, it disregards traditions that assign Genesis to Numbers to the Priestly source and Deuteronomy through Kings to a Deuteronomic tradition.[25] Another view identifies continuity from Genesis to the end of 2 Kings, with two main stories: from the beginning of the world to the establishment in the land of Canaan; and the entry into Canaan up until the Babylonian captivity.[26] The books of Chronicles, Ezra, and Nehemiah, along with the prophetical books and the short narratives of Ruth and Jonah, fit the temporal scheme of the first and primary story; Esther and Daniel reveal themselves as narratives of displacement.[27] Interestingly, God's desire for relationship and human desire for place and identity initiate the plot and conflict for all these narratives.*

The Bible lists the Decalogue or Ten Commandments twice (Exod. 20 and Deut. 5). The Elohist (E) writer makes Moses and law a turning point in history; it uses Elohim to refer to God up until the theophany of the burning bush, the place where God reveals his name to Moses as Yahweh (Exod. 3.15).[28] The Priestly writers, active in the exilic or postexilic years (sixth or fifth century BCE), also make Sinai a pivotal turning point relative to the covenants of Noah and Abraham, using the laws to stress holiness and purity.[29] The Deuteronomic tradition (Deuteronomy through Kings) reaffirms the laws disclosed on Sinai, but broadens them to include the covenant made in Moab, and then uses these to tell the history of the people of Israel from Moses to the exile in Babylon.[30] Deuteronomy prepares the people to enter into the land of Canaan and to become one people serving one God at one Temple. With the people in exile, the Deuteronomic tradition ends without the fulfillment of promises made to the ancestors. It develops two themes: infidelity and covenant.[31] The former has been used to explain the fall of the northern kingdom and the destruction of Samaria, while the latter has emphasized covenant faithfulness, particularly in David, Hezekiah, and Josiah (kings of Judah).

**Decalogue**, derived from *deka* ("ten") and *logos* ("word"), is a name given to the Ten Commandments or divine imperatives given to Moses on Mount Sinai (Horeb in Elohist and Deuteronomistic traditions).[32] Characterized by **apodictic** or unconditional laws, these commandments establish for ancient Israel its duties toward God and neighbor. Exodus presents the laws inscribed on two tablets; Deuteronomy repeats these with only minor variations. The Priestly Exodus links the Sabbath to creation and God's resting on the seventh day; the Deuteronomistic links the Sabbath to God's covenant.[33] Moses, in Deuteronomy (5.1–2), convenes all Israel, addressing them, "Hear, O Israel, the statutes and ordinances . . . learn them and observe them diligently. . . . The LORD our God made a covenant with us at Horeb . . . not with our ancestors only, but with us . . ."

The Decalogue commands the worship of God alone, and decries image-making and the vain use of God's name; Catholics regard "I am the LORD your God" and "You shall worship no other gods beside me" as one commandment; and they view "You shall not covet your neighbor's house" and "You shall not covet your neighbor's wife" as two commandments. "You shall worship no other gods beside me" represents not **monotheism** – that there is only one God in the world – but **monolatry** – other gods exist but only one is to be worshipped.[34] It probably also should be noted that the Decalogue does not include the Shema, the topic of the next section, declaring that God is one.

Most scholars identify the Ten Commandments as prohibitions in two categories: crimes against God – apostasy, idolatry, and blasphemy – and exhortation to keep the Sabbath (with honoring parents serving as a bridge) and crimes against society – murder, adultery, stealing, and bearing false witness (with coveting closing off the set).[35] Together, these serve as the core requirements for guiding relationship to God and human beings. **Ethical monotheism**, with its emphasis upon one God who created human beings and declared how they should behave, has been described as Judaism's "major intellectual and spiritual contribution to the world."[36] Biblical Israel's stress upon legal and moral traditions was not, though, unique in the ancient world; the Babylonian Laws of Hammurabi, for example, dating to the eighteenth century BCE, included over 300 laws. These share similarities and contrasts with biblical laws: they prescribe, for example, the death penalty for offenses against the person, such as kidnapping; they also lay out conditions for offenses of retaliation, such as putting out an eye and having an eye put out. The ethical commandments of the Hebrew tradition, while sharing many of the same goals as other ethical codes, have endured and been described as eternal and universal laws.[37]

*In order to appreciate fully the New Testament's understanding of the Mosaic Law, you will need to remember that the Apocrypha consists of fourteen or fifteen (depending on numeration) texts composed between 200 BCE and 100 CE. These texts form an indispensable link between the Old and New Testaments. They include the history of these centuries and the growth of later Judaism. Furthermore, the establishment of the New Testament canon intentionally excluded many of the religious texts written during the first centuries of the Common Era. These texts emphasize salvation, eternity, and other-worldly topics and may actually have led to the establishment of the canon. Taken together with the apocryphal texts, they bring a new perspective to how one reads the New Testament: they raise questions about the divinity of Jesus, present visionary journeys to a graphically pictured Heaven and Hell, introduce mystical theology and ascension through multiple heavens, and describe knowledge and inner illumination as a means of escaping from the human body.[38]*

*Suppressed as they have been, these texts rightly deserve their own place between Jewish and Christian faith and are worthy of study in courses treating more broadly ancient biblical texts, a scope far too wide to be undertaken here.[39]*

Law figures prominently in the New Testament, especially in Matthew, the most Jewish book of the Gospels. Jesus, for example, describes his purpose as fulfilling the law: "Do not think that I have come to abolish the law or the prophets; I have come not to abolish but to fulfill" (5.17, 18). Jesus, in fact, interprets the Ten Commandments relative to motivational intent, advocating obedience from the heart. In addition to not murdering, one must not even be angry (5.22); not committing adultery becomes one must not look at a woman with lust (5.28); the one forced to walk a mile must go also the second mile (5.41); people must refrain from swearing in any form (5.34); the Sabbath and worship of God provide the context for honoring parents (15.4). For Jesus, fundamental principles outweigh the mere keeping of traditions.

*In the days of Jesus, the Pharisees and Sadducees were much preoccupied with instruction explaining Mosaic laws and how these were to be carried out; these oral traditions begin as early as the fourth century*

*BCE and proliferate after the destruction of the Temple in 70 CE into a growing and complex body of materials known as the oral Torah. In 200 CE, the teachings of the oral Law were written down so that they would not be forgotten. The Talmud (actually there are two: the Jerusalem Talmud, compiled around 400 CE, and the Babylonian, put together around the sixth century CE) is a compendium of Mishnah (a collection of early rabbinic instruction developed and transmitted orally down to the beginning of the third century CE) and Gemara (interpretation and commentary covering materials up to the fifth century CE). The **Mitzvot** is a list of 613 commandments found in the Torah.*

The Bible opens up a catalog of human characters living out their choices in relation to the commandments and suffering the inevitable consequences of those choices. King Solomon, who loves many foreign women and their gods, violates the commandment to have no other gods. When Moses delays his return from Mount Sinai, Aaron shapes a golden calf for Israel to worship, violating the commandment to have no idols or images, breaking the covenant entered into by Abraham (Exod. 32). King Zedekiah swears by God's name, failing to keep the covenant and oath, and, as a result, has to endure seeing his sons murdered, while he himself is blinded and carried to Babylon (2 Kings 25; 2 Chron. 36.11–14; Ezek. 17.15–21). Chronicles makes the theological point that Zedekiah's faithlessness, including the pollution of the Temple, results in Judah's destruction and exile and also the destruction of the Temple and city. The Deuteronomistic source – emphasizing the themes of infidelity–defeat–repentance–forgiveness – presents Hophni and Phinehas, sons of the priest Eli, as rebelling against Eli's authority and refusing to listen to him or honor his words, with the consequence that they are killed (1 Sam. 2).[40]

The Bible provides many examples of individuals violating the laws guiding human behavior and suffering the inevitable punishment of retributive justice. In Joshua, Achan covets, and then takes, booty placed under a ban (thus endangering all of his people). For his deeds, Achan and his family are stoned to death by Joshua and Israel (chapter 7). Samuel presents a King Saul who disobeys God and is rejected as king of the monarchy (1 Sam. 15). King David commits adultery with Bathsheba, wife of Uriah; he then schemes to have Uriah killed. The child that results from the adultery dies (2 Sam. 11, 12). King Ahab of Israel steals Naboth's vineyard but dies in battle; his body is then returned to Samaria, where dogs lick up his blood, as prophesied by the prophet Elijah (1 Kings 21, 22). However, 1 Kings (21.19) also says that Ahab humbles himself such that he does not have to witness the destruction of his own family; his act, though, becomes the single reason for the destruction of an entire Omri dynasty.

The first four books of the Torah end with the people of God poised to enter into the land promised to them, but here the action stops. Deuteronomy instructs concerning the conditions for entering the land, reiterates the Ten Commandments, and then provides commentary on them; it separates the generations of Moses from the generations of Joshua.[41] It mediates between a strictly retributive justice and a distributive one that involves a just distribution of material goods and a God equally available to all.[42] It does this by addressing the enactment of Torah and the practice of covenant once the people enter into the land, making provisions, for example, for debt release, and by placing limitation upon debt acquisition.[43] The Priestly tradition, more than Deuteronomy, uses a series of command infractions to pull together the Torah, Joshua, Judges, and 1 and 2 Kings, with an emphasis on "keeping the commandments" and the requirements of a "just" God.[44]

*In the next section, I explore two other themes that build closely upon the theme of relationship to God and to people found in the Commandments. The first expresses a theological concept: that God is one; the second exists in the nature of Israel's relationship to God: that of covenant. The themes serve the literary purpose of holding the parts of the narrative together.*

### The Shema: "Hear, O Israel, the LORD your God is One" (Deut. 6)

Deuteronomy, as noted before, prepares Israel as a nation to live under one law, to settle on one land, and to worship at one Temple, and it advances the theological belief that there is only one God (4.5–8). Deuteronomy 6.4 commands, "Hear, O Israel: The LORD is our God, the LORD alone," and exhorts, "love the LORD your God with all your heart, and with all your soul, and with all your might" (6.5). The **Shema**, named for the first word, "Hear," calls attention to a sovereign and unique God to whom Israel must be loyal, to whom it must devote mind, will, and vital being. The Shema serves as a confession of faith in God for Israel, and most of Deuteronomy concerns itself with the admonitions not to forget God (6.12).

Who is this one God? The Old Testament perceived God in two very different ways: an early model, in which God functions concretely as having a body and behaving in ways similar to other finite beings, and the model that has passed down through Judaism and Christianity, which attributes the abstract qualities of omniscience, omnipresence, and omnipotence to an invisible and abstract God.[45] The New Testament picks up this theme of the "oneness of God," heavily influenced by **Gnosticism** and a belief in the supreme source of the world as being One. Likewise, Gnosticism advances a trinity of being: a Father of all, a Sophia or suffering mother and wife of Jesus, and Spirit.

According to *The Oxford Companion to the Bible*, YHWH refers to a plural of majesty with a singular meaning. The God revealed by combining the Shema and Ten Commandments possesses "oneness" and demands ethical behavior from the people. Why? He is the Creator (Gen. 1.1; P source), and He has delivered them from bondage in Egypt (Exod. 20.2; E source).[46] This YHWH, in Priestly traditions, reveals himself as part of the Sinai covenants; the Yahwist tradition emphasizes an earlier revelation in the promissory covenant with Abraham.

Judaism assumes the existence of God and subsequently asks who God is, what God does, and what the relationship between God and human beings can be. The first three commandments state:

1   I am the LORD your God. (20.2a)
2   You shall have no other gods before me. (20.3)
3   You shall not make for yourself a sculptured image. (20.4)

The Hebrew root word from which YHWH derives means "to be" and theologically, according to **rabbinic tradition**, describes a God who presents Himself in three conditions of time: was, is, and will always be. That YHWH is our God, the LORD alone, signifies a personal relationship and states that God is one and not many. One, in Hebrew, means unique, singular, and refers to a mathematical formula – one, not many; one, not zero – and two negatives equal a positive.[47] Much of the Bible's narrative builds upon the plot motif that presents Israel's founding fathers becoming established upon the land promised to them by their deity, the deity identified in Deuteronomy as Yahweh.[48] The Pentateuchal tradition develops this notion of one God for Israel into an inclusive monotheism.[49] **Inclusive monotheism** belongs to a tradition of Torah that accepts human limitation in the face of the transcendent and evidences a degree of tolerance for plurality.[50] **Exclusive monotheism**, developing after the Babylonian exile, attempts to define and separate ancient tradition from that of surrounding communities; it rejects syncretism or blended traditions and evidences intolerance for them. It also pits itself against the ungodly, sometimes forcing conversions. In the Post-Exile, it recognized only the exiles who had returned as legitimate guardians of the older tradition.

While a religious/theological theme, the Shema works structurally to bring together what has come before, the Decalogue, and what comes afterwards: the responsibility to teach future generations. It follows the structure of the vassal treaty.[51] Because Yahweh has delivered Israel from Egypt (E source), Israel must keep His commandments. The reciprocity extends from what God has done to what Israel should do; what parents should do and what children should do (honor parents); and what responsible parents should teach their children (Deut. 6.6–9; D source).[52] It should not be surprising that the New Testament echoes the command to love God, thus effectively bringing together the two traditions (Mark 12.28–34).

*Along with the Decalogue and Shema, another organizing principle found in much of the Bible consists of several kinds of covenants based on promise and obedience, notably the development of a "new" covenant in the Christian New Testament. In the next section, I introduce several of these important covenants. I point out, however, that many later books of the Old Testament omit this theme – particularly the wisdom literature, a genre that includes Job, Proverbs, Ecclesiastes, and*

*parts of Psalms. These emphasize a deliberate and rational commit-
ment to God that can also be found in the texts of the intertestamental
period (400 BC to 100 CE).*

### "He Declared to You His Covenant": Relationship Based upon Promise and Obligation

The revelation of the Ten Commandments at Mount Sinai completes the
second part of Moses' demand of Pharaoh on behalf of God to "Let my
people go so that they may worship me" (Exod. 10.3). Assembled at Mount
Horeb (in E and D sources), the people come together "out of the camp to
meet God" (20.17). The commandments, together with a number of statutes and ordinances, form a covenant or compact established between
God and a people. Two kinds of covenant existed in the Near East at
this time: a covenant of grant and the suzerain treaty version.[53] Some
Israelites, apparently, understood the covenant to be an unconditional
promise of protection; the suzerain treaty type, however, establishes a
condition such as observing the treaty stipulations. Genesis through 2
Kings develops the idea that the people have been exiled because they
abandoned God.[54] If this narrative is divided into two stories, one focuses
on divine promise to Abraham and fulfillment in the monarchy under
David and Solomon; the other builds upon covenant obligation with
Moses and ends in the destruction of the Temple of Yahweh.[55] The Old
Testament itself contains four important covenants between God and
humankind, mediated through Noah (Gen. 9.1–17), Abraham (Gen.
17.7–8), Moses (Exod. 20.22–23.33), and David (2 Sam. 7).[56]

Genesis establishes covenant as a prototype for God's relationship
with human beings. The first man and woman function as prototypes
for all humankind and tell a story of how people behave and what consequences result from that behavior. Adam and Eve clearly were created
for a twofold relationship, to God and with each other. According to
the Priestly account, God created humankind (male and female) in his
image (Gen. 1.27). Up until this point, God has created and found his
creation good, declaring his creation on the sixth day as very good. Yet,
Genesis describes human beings, much like God, exercising volition
– choosing, resolving, willing, and, ultimately, disobeying (chapter 3).
Though created and placed in idyllic surroundings, asked only not to
eat of the tree of knowledge of good and evil, having been told clearly
that the consequences for disobeying will mean death (1.16, 17), Eve
and Adam choose the forbidden. These first stories in Genesis present
a difference between what God sees and what humans see as good,
creating an unbridgeable gap between them.[57] Against an eternal conflict of will between God and human beings, humanity lives out a fate
determined by its nature – with history reiterating what has been.[58] Out
of this struggle come the two previously mentioned understandings
of God: as transcendent and beyond human understanding (P) and
present and involved in the history of Israel (J, E, and D sources).[59]

*The Noahic Covenant (Gen. 9–11)*

God's covenant with Noah marks the beginning of a new creation. Proponents of multiple sources find Yahwist (J) and Priestly (P) sources intermixed in the flood story.[60] In the Yahwist narrative, a generation of descendants of Cain become progressively violent until, five generations removed from Cain, Lamech can boast, "I have killed a man for wounding me, a young man for striking me. If Cain is avenged sevenfold, truly Lamech, seventy-sevenfold" (Gen. 4.23, 24). In direct consequence to the growing violence and bloodshed of humankind, God determines to make an end of all flesh (6.13). The pre-flood narrative also contains the origins of several occupations and the first city. Later in Genesis, in a Priestly writing, God prohibits bloodshed (9.4–6); at the same time, God lifts the prohibition against eating animal flesh, insisting only that it should not be eaten with the blood in it (9.4). Clearly, blood functions as the repository of life, and ritual demands it be drained from every animal required for food. The book of 1 Samuel describes the people as transgressing this commandment (14.31–2).

The Priestly account of generations (Gen. 5) describes ten generations from Adam to Noah, these coming through the line of Seth as opposed to the murderer Cain, and ten generations from Noah to Abraham. God who brought order from chaos now allows chaos to return. In the Yahwist (J) account, God recognizes Noah's righteousness, a characteristic demonstrated by no one before but shared by his descendant Abraham, and spares him, his wife potentially, his sons, and his sons' wives (6.18). God's relationship with human beings now enters a new phase based on the covenant and a binding promise or oath that sets conditions for a continuing relationship. Because Noah "did all that God commanded him" (6.22), God promises that "the waters shall never again become a flood to destroy all flesh" (P: 9.8–17; J: 8.20–2), this extending the covenant to "every living creature of all flesh" (9.15), a promise sealed with the sign of a bow – perhaps signaling that the instrument of war and death used before the flood should be laid aside for the peace and life assured in the covenant.

*The Abrahamic Covenant (Gen. 17–26)*

The Priestly account of the Abrahamic covenant (Gen. 17.7–8) asks Abraham to walk before God and be blameless like Noah and Enoch; the Yahwist (15.1–21) draws attention to descendants and emphasizes, as does the Davidic covenant, the unconditional, everlasting promise of God.[61] It involves two sets of people: the Hebrews (through Sarah, Isaac) and the Ishmaelites (through Hagar, the Egyptian, and her son). Hagar's Egyptian connection, according to the Yahwist account, serves importantly to connect Sarah's oppression of Hagar, following the birth of Ishmael, with the Egyptians' oppression of the Hebrews; in Yahwist narratives, God punishes rebellion, illustrated by Adam and Eve, Cain and Abel, the flood, and Sodom and Gomorrah (15.17).

In Sarah and Hagar, the motif of the "barren" wife emerges and will be seen again in Isaac's wife, Rebekah, and Jacob's wife, Rachel, as well as in the mother of the prophet Samuel, Hannah, and, in the New Testament, the mother of John the Baptist, Elizabeth. God carries his promises through generations and life cycles by providing children, opening wombs and allowing the miracle of life to continue. The birth story, an identifiable narrative genre, follows a general pattern: a barren wife or a couple who desire a child; the appearance of a heavenly mediator and the promise of a child; a miraculous birth event; hostile forces that threaten the child's maturity; and an eventual development of the child into a hero. A secondary theme marks the cycles of life: the importance of the first-born child, that child's rights and position (primogeniture), and the counterpart emergent theme of sibling rivalry. As with the barren woman, the waywardness, disobedience, or lost birthright of a first son threatens God's orderly provision for the fulfillment of His promises through the four covenants. Much of Abraham's life builds movingly upon the promise of posterity, a land, and a people. The near sacrifice of Isaac (Gen. 22) threatens continuity and the fulfillment of God's promise; the strife between Abraham and his nephew Lot threatens the promise of land.

The covenant with Abraham points to ritual and to convention, introducing circumcision (a Priestly concern; Gen. 17.10–14) as an external sign of the covenant. This ritual of puberty, also practiced by Israel's neighbors and elsewhere, takes on covenant significance with Abraham. Abraham circumcises Isaac when he is eight days old (21.4) and Ishmael at thirteen (17.25). Baptism for Christians in the New Testament takes on the same ritualistic and symbolic meaning of marking or being a sign of the "New Covenant." Some see baptism as foreshadowed in the motif of delivery by water found in the infant Moses and the surviving Noah and family in the flood account. The convention of Hebrew names and name changes also emerges clearly as a part of the covenant theme. Abram will now be called Abraham, and Sarai will be called Sarah; Jacob, father of the twelve tribes of Israel, will receive the name Israel.

### The Mosaic Covenant (Deut. 4–11)

All God's covenants with the Israelites emphasize divine favor or grace, life, and continuity in the life cycles. God rescues, for example, the righteous Noah and his family and brings into being a new creation. The story of Moses begins with divine favor. Sparing Moses from certain death, Pharaoh's daughter takes pity upon him, rescues him from the papyrus basket in which his mother has hidden him in the reeds of the Nile, and gives him back to his mother to nourish. To divine favor, the Mosaic covenant adds obligatory overtones and warns of dire consequences for disobedience.

Deuteronomy presents Moses as the hero of the Old Testament and the Mosaic Covenant (Deut. 4.5–14) as critical: it commits the people of Israel to observe God's statutes (royal announcements), ordinances (civil, social, and sanitation laws), and commandments (religious and ethical demands required by God).[62] These laws, extending beyond those given at Horeb/Sinai to the laws given to Moses in the plains of Moab, prepare the people to enter into the land that has been promised to Abraham; they involve ethical and ritual laws that regulate human conduct.[63] They express at their core the requirements for existence within a community of people: they regulate worship, justice, and family life.

The Mosaic Covenant recognizably has the characteristics of a suzerain treaty: a summary of benevolent deeds of an overlord, stipulations binding on the vassal, sanctions of blessings, and curses in the case of disobedience.[64] Moses tells the people, "the LORD set his heart on you," and "a faithful God . . . maintains covenant loyalty with those who love him and keep his commandments" (Deut. 7.9). He reminds them of their rescue from bondage in Egypt (Deut. 6) and of God's care and protection of them as they wandered in the wilderness; "keeping the laws" becomes obligatory as well as a condition for occupying the land (4.1). He further instructs them, "Take care and watch yourselves closely, so as [not] to forget the things your eyes have seen . . . [and to] make them known to your children and your children's children" (4.9). He then warns them that, if they become complacent, make an idol, do evil, or provoke God to anger, they will not live long in the land, but will be scattered and perish (4.25–6).

A charged tension exists in the Old Testament's presentation of a compassionate, loving and merciful God and a just God punishing command infractions. This leads to interpretive possibilities for explaining the history of Israel as a cycle of deliverances – from Egyptian, Assyrian, Babylonian, Persian, Greek, and Roman dominations – or as a cycle of punishments – a people perishing in the wilderness, enduring long periods of exile, and being scattered. Moses encourages Israel to remember its past as a way of learning not to make the same mistakes. He reminds them, though, "a merciful God will neither abandon . . . destroy . . . [nor] forget the covenant," and will rescue from distress those who return to the Lord and heed him (4.30, 31). This long-term view suggests that Deuteronomy, traditionally explained as the book found in Josiah's reign (600s BCE), may be a later redaction inserted to bring together the themes of promise and commandment.

### The Davidic Covenant (2 Sam. 7.22–4)
God's covenant with David establishes a promise of an unbroken succession of kings upon the throne of Israel, continuing and fulfilling the promise made to Abraham: "I will establish my covenant between me and you and your offspring after you throughout their generations, for an everlasting covenant, to be God to you and to your offspring after you" (Gen. 17.7); God promises David, "Your house and your kingdom

shall be made sure forever before me; your throne shall be established forever" (1 Chron. 17.24; 2 Sam. 7; 2 Chron. 6.16). Yet, as already pointed out, other passages suggest that the people's destiny depends upon how carefully they observe the Torah. The Deuteronomistic editor, many believe, worked out a resolution using "an infidelity–defeat–repentance–forgiveness" motif.[65] Another means of resolving the tension between the eternal throne and crushing defeats makes the conditional apply to the northern kings of Israel, who largely follow a pattern of "doing evil," and the unconditional to the kings holding the throne of Judah.[66] The promise that the throne itself will be eternally available to David's family eventually leads to the idea of a messiah yet to come.[67]

The history of rule under one king (1000 BCE) – first, Saul, then David, and, finally, Solomon – is far from ideal and results in a divided kingdom (Israel and Judah, 922 BCE to 586/7 BCE) in which a long list of kings often behave badly. Through these successive reigns, God remains faithful and steadfast, always saving a remnant and thus fulfilling God's promise to David: "But I will not take my steadfast love from him, as I took it from Saul, whom I put away from before you" (2 Sam. 7.15).

The New Testament interprets the Davidic covenant as fulfilled in Jesus Christ. Matthew traces the origins of the Messiah from Abraham to David through fourteen generations, and from David to Jesus through yet another fourteen, mentioning five women in the genealogy: Tamar, Rahab, Ruth, Uriah's wife Bathsheba, and Mary, perhaps demonstrating through such irregularity the sovereign control of God over creation and destiny.[68] Luke references the many events of the Old Testament as "orderly fulfilled" in the Messiah, tracing origins back to Adam. These two books list genealogies rich in their differences: Matthew traces the genealogy from Solomon to Joseph, including the fated line of King Jeconiah (Jer. 22.30); Luke begins with Nathan, the brother of Solomon, through Mary, avoiding Jeconiah, and conventionally lists names as male up until Mary. The important point is that Luke gives Jesus Davidic descent through his mother, who also has direct priestly descent through Aaron, the brother of Moses, and the Levi tribe.[69]

As a whole, the Old and New Testaments are structured around six covenants – if one counts the Adamic prototype and the New Covenant. Christianity explains Jeremiah's "New Covenant" as a mediation between the covenants of early Israel and the Covenant of the Gospels – these in addition to the Mosaic, Abrahamic, Noahic, and Davidic covenants.[70]

*In the next two sections, I address the character of God and the apparent paradox between a God executing plan, promise, and obligation and a God exercising pity, compassion, and love. Scholarship has struggled with ways to reduce the paradox: the use of multiple sources as the origin of the paradox; God as a complex character evidencing human characteristics; the short- and long-term actions of God; the equation of charity to responsible behavior; and the emergence of a wisdom tradition that emphasizes the unknowable.*

*The New Testament picks up a similar tension between the observance of the core requirements of the law and the rituals of traditional practice. Jesus generally keeps the Hebrew traditions, perhaps seeking to influence but not to overturn them; on the other hand, his greater concern is love and distributive justice, and he condemns any preoccupation with ritual that outweighs this greater concern.*

### God's Mercy: "I have loved you with an everlasting love" (Jer. 31.3; Deut. 1, 30, 7, 4, 13, 18, 23)

While divine–human relationship forms the bedrock and foundation for all other themes in the Bible, love remains the connecting power for achieving this. Both Yahwist and Elohist sources emphasize God's love/mercy in contrast to a primary emphasis in the Priestly account upon justice.[71] As previously remarked, the Decalogue and the Great Commandment require exactly the same behaviors from human beings: love God and love each other. The New Testament unveils a tension between how love manifests itself, with Paul arguing for the new universal law of Christ, as opposed to the legalistic and ritualistic performance of Mosaic law; James,[72] the most Jewish of accounts, emphasizes a love actualizing itself in works. Christianity, building upon the foundation of Judaic literature, describes God's unexplained love for Israel and Israel's reciprocal love of God as the basis for society, reinterpreting Israel as Christ's Church. Critics caution that Christianity risks marginalizing the Jewish family of Jesus and Jesus' own Jewishness, emphasizing, instead, a universalist view that advances the Fatherhood of God and the brotherhood of humankind.

Deuteronomy speaks often about loving God (10.12; 11.1, 13, 22; 30.19–20), but love, as already remarked, has more to do with serving God than it does with emotion. Both Deuteronomy and Exodus (5.10; 20.6), in fact, suggest the treaty-like tradition of keeping the commandments. Love then becomes synonymous with fearing, obeying, and serving God.

Many would regard any interpretation of the Shema and the Great Commandment as devotional, in contrast to obligatory, as simply wrong (Deut. 11.13).[73]

Deuteronomy, called the "second law," reinterprets the Decalogue or covenant in terms of a binding relationship between Israel and its God. It also reinterprets the ritual of circumcision, making the external, physical act into an internal, spiritual act: God will circumcise the heart so that the people will love God and live (Deut. 30.6). Deuteronomy presents a God choosing Israel because he loves them (7.7), loving like a parent (1.31), bringing the Israelites out of Egypt and extending deliverance forward to Israel's descendants (4.39). Keeping God's commandments carries the promise of well-being and the possession of a land for an inheritance (4.40), and the commandments extend to the children who should be taught to keep them (6.6, 7). God commands Israel and its descendants to keep the statutes, ordinances and commandments (11.1), testing individuals to determine their love, loyalty, and steadfastness in keeping promises (13.3; 18.13; 23.21). Finally, life, prosperity, death, and adversity result from choices to keep or not keep the commandments (30.15).

Deuteronomy eulogizes Moses as a prophet without equal (34.7–12). Traditionalists continue to argue for Mosaic authorship. In addition to finding strands of J, E, P, and D, scholars now suggest that interpreters in the third, second, and first centuries BCE changed the character of the Pentateuch, making it into a great book of legal and ethical instruction. The search for origins seems to have left readers wondering how they should read the Torah or Pentateuch and the Bible itself.[74] A "great gap" has opened between how Judaism and Christianity traditionally view the Bible and how modern scholarship interprets it.

### God's Justice (Exod. 34; 2 Kings. 8; 2 Sam. 12, 15)

Source theory explains that a later redactor attempted to create a balance between the paradoxical themes of mercy and justice in the Old Testament.[75] Although one tradition (D) presents God as merciful, gracious, slow to anger, and abounding in steadfast love and faithfulness, forgiving sin, another (P) makes clear to Moses at Mount Sinai (Exod. 34.6–8) that God will by no means clear the guilty but will visit iniquity upon people through the fourth generation.

A merciful and forgiving but, ultimately, just God creates a tension that has been a part of Judaism and Christianity for two and a half millennia.[76] Source theorists argue that the P tradition never mentions mercy while other traditions (J, E, and D) use the word about seventy times. The Bible, in fact, presents Hebrew history as an intensification of suffering, leading to the fall of the nation and the exile of the people. Covenantal theology explains suffering as the deserved consequence of human failure; the prophets of the eighth century BCE explain the destruction of entire nations as a punishment for sins. The contents of the Jewish Bible shift the focus from covenant obedience and punishment to the wisdom hidden in creation and beyond human grasp; later apocalyptic writings go further to focus on a universal drama in which God ultimately will triumph over evil.

Exodus seeks to explain the paradox through the idea of the short term and the long term: the iniquity will be visited until the fourth generation, but the steadfast love of God will endure until the thousandth (Exod. 34.6–7). Part of the challenge of the Bible exists in being able to accept or not accept the sovereignty (and freedom) of God and to recognize that whatever the Creator does ultimately must be right and just, even when human beings cannot see or understand the ultimate purpose. The entire book of Job devotes itself to presenting this paradox:

why a just and loving God allows a righteous man to suffer, with Job far from comforted by friends who advance the retributive justice view that God rewards righteousness and punishes unrighteousness. Some suggest that the Bible reveals God as the standard for justice, using his own power according to his own moral perfection; human beings, less than the Creator, continually fall short of this perfected moral standard and can only hope for steadfast love and mercy. The Mosaic covenant, and some of the minor prophets, in particular, emphasize retributive justice and argue that God judges and fiercely punishes disobedience in his people.

Another way taken out of the paradox has been the Jewish rabbinic explanation that *tzedakah*, meaning "justice" or "righteousness," equates to charity, and charity to responsible behaviors.[77] It includes the idea of taking care of other human beings through personal service, kindness and love to the sick, hospitality, working for freedom, care of the elderly, children, and orphans, and following proper processes for the deceased, and extends even to the care of God's creation and natural resources.

The book of 1 Corinthians argues lyrically that love is the greatest gift among spiritual gifts. This extraordinary love addressed by Paul refers to love not in the usual sense of emotion, but as a command exhibited in action. Much like its Jewish counterpart, the love Corinthians describes expresses itself in behaviors: it does not rejoice in wrongdoing but in truth (13.6); it bears, believes, hopes, and endures (13.7). It also points to the mystery of God and limited, finite human understanding. Paul, in fact, demonstrates the dualism of his age that denigrates the earthly in favor of the heavenly.[78]

**Remnant theology** suggests that God keeps his side of the Davidic covenant. Even when the kings of Judah rebel, "the LORD would not destroy Judah, for the sake of his servant David, since he had promised to give a lamp to him and to his descendants forever" (2 Kings 8.19; D tradition). More than any other king, David demonstrates justice, mercy, and fairness, and thus becomes, on the human level, a model for God's standard of justice, particularly in the later tradition provided in Chronicles (a revisionist work usually described as belonging to the fourth century BCE that advances the dominant role of Jacob's son Judah). "So David reigned over all Israel; and he administered justice and equity to all his people" (1 Chron. 18.14). Whatever his human weaknesses – and he has many – David submits to God and recognizes his dependence upon him: "Who am I, O Lord GOD, and what is my house, that you have brought me thus far?" (2 Sam. 7.18). In addition to ruling with equity and justice, David confesses his own shortcomings, admitting, "I have sinned against the LORD" (12.12). When David's son Absalom rebels against his own father's rule, David distinguishes himself by caring about a foreigner and telling him to go back from battle and almost certain death: "And take your kinsfolk with you; and may the LORD show steadfast love and faithfulness to you" (15.20). David weeps for his rebellious son Absalom in a grief familiar to the bereaved: "O my son Absalom, my son, my son Absalom! Would I had died instead of you, O Absalom, my son, my son! . . . O my son Absalom, O Absalom, my son, my son!" (18.33, 19.4). David not only spares Mephibosheth, the son of Saul who sought to kill him, but brings up the bones of Saul and his son Jonathan for proper burial in the land of Benjamin (21.12–14). In another familiar story, David sets Uriah, the husband of Bathsheba, in the foremost of fighting to be killed in order that he can take Bathsheba as his own wife. Confronted by the prophet Nathan, David confesses, "I have sinned" (12.13). The baby, however, dies, suggesting that human shortcomings often create tragedy within an individual's life as well as the lives of others. In Psalm 2 – the Psalms composed and collected across six centuries, and understood traditionally as authored by David – the speaker pleads for justice and declares his righteousness, an inner state based upon integrity, trusting the Lord, and loving the house of the Lord, attributes that characterize David.

The character of God evidences a tension between mastery and control – plan, promise, and obligation – and pity, compassion, and love.[79] Although often presented as a flat character (a God of mercy, justice, or steadfast love), in the context of multiple stories and characters God takes on the ambiguities revealed in complex human characters. Against this flat character, God often plays out in the Old Testament as a punisher and as a God often indifferent to the individual. This can be seen, for example, in God's bringing evil upon Absalom (2. Sam. 17.14), the death of Uriah and the death of Bathsheba's baby (2 Sam. 11–12), the fate of David's concubines (2 Sam. 12.11), the great account of the Exodus and death in the wilderness (Exod. 1–15), the use of Pharaoh (Exod. 5), and, of course, in the near sacrifice of Isaac. Sometimes presented as a character evidencing human characteristics – such as anger, jealousy, pity, compassion, violence, and favoritism – God in the Old Testament is also depicted at work implicitly and unseen; this God gradually takes on the attributes of omniscience, omnipotence, and omnipresence.

*Beginning courses in literature often spend significant time in the discussion of heroic characters. The Bible, with its cast of thousands, typifies the full scale of heroic literary characters: characters questing for some good and encountering obstacles; anti-heroes determined to overturn the heroic stereotype; superheroes with exaggerated powers; courageous leaders, founders, martyrs, saviors, adventurers, dreamers and visionaries, warriors, prophets, priests, and kings, to mention only a few. They all evidence the archetypal and universal human quest. I introduce this idea in the next section only in an extremely preliminary way simply to call attention to its importance.*

## The Heroic Quest

The Bible throughout evidences the archetypal heroic quest common to literature, with its themes of alienation and sense of not belonging, initiation, exile and suffering, and transformation and rebirth.[80] Exile, in fact, functions as a metaphor for the launching of new beginnings.[81] The quest envisions an end of social effort, a world of fulfilled desires, and a free human society. Together, the Old and New Testaments comprise just such an archetypal story of loss and recovery.

Genesis to 2 Kings pulls together a series of heroic quests emphasizing the exilic themes of expulsion from an ideal home, wandering, journeys, and the dissolution of homogeneity.[82] In literature, the archetypal heroic quest involves separation, initiation, and return. The first three sets of heroes in the Bible – Abraham and Lot, Isaac and Ishmael, Jacob and Esau – realize identities and destinies associated with attaining the land that has been promised to them by God. Against the backdrop of the beginnings of the human race and yet another new beginning after the flood, the Patriarchs play the role of beginning a chosen nation. Each takes on, in a way, as Adam did, the nature of every mortal in its human struggle and destiny. Each of the pair evidences individual quests linked to the beginnings of a nation chosen against all expectation. Abraham's narrated life illustrates an extended quest along the trajectory of progeny and land.[83] Abraham and Lot exist in a simple polar relationship – Abraham, superior in generosity and patronage, becomes the father of many nations; Lot, choosing the land of the Dead Sea, becomes the ancestor to the people of Amnon and Moab. With the introduction of Isaac and Ishmael and Jacob (Israel) and Esau (Edom), other motifs play an important role: family struggle and preference for a child; and the efforts of the first-born to retain birthright. A pattern of rejecting the first-born continues, from Ishmael–Isaac and Esau–Jacob, to Joseph and the choice of Ephraim over Manasseh. As the pattern develops, Judah as a nation lasts longer than its counterpart, northern Israel and its ten tribes.

The macro-plot of Genesis carefully links the beginnings of humankind to the lives of the Patriarchs and the quest for a nation. Careful readers note that Genesis presents the genealogies of Adam and Shem in a pattern of father and first-born son up until the summary statements of 5.32 and 11.26, where a meaningful deviation presents sets of three or a widening search for dynasty: "Noah became the father of Shem, Ham, and Japheth," and "Terah . . . became the father of Abram, Nahor, and Haran."[84] For Abraham, the quest becomes one for continuity, with the ironic presentation of a barren Sarah and a 75-year-old Abraham when God first promises him progeny. God adds the promise that Canaan will belong to Abraham and his descendants (Gen. 12.7; 13.14–17). This becomes the focus of the entire Old Testament, presenting its narrative as a connected whole.[85]

Read as a whole, I have suggested that the Bible achieves a degree of unity and coherence through its themes and motifs. We have explored a core of themes that help to pull together the Bible's diverse collection of ancient literature: the divine–human and the human–human relationship, illustrated in the Decalogue and in the Great Commandment;

the one sovereign God and Creator; the contractual nature of a series of covenants between God and people; the steadfast love of a God who intervenes in history to rescue, restore, and deliver his people; and, finally, the theme of justice, with its moral demands for fair rule and intervention on behalf of the helpless. With the exception of covenant in the books of Job, Proverbs, and Ecclesiastes, these themes help to unify all sixty-six books.

## Close Reading

*Exercise 1*

What common themes and motifs can be found in the stories of characters in the Bible?

Isaac (Gen. 21.1–7); Jacob (Gen. 25.21–6); Joseph (Gen. 29: 22–4); Samson (Judg. 13); Samuel (1 Sam. 1); John (Luke 1.5–25, 57–80); Jesus (Luke 1.26–56, 2)

*Exercise 2*

What are the themes and motifs associated with the following individuals? Cain and Abel (Gen. 4.1–16); Isaac and Ishmael (Gen. 16, 17, 21, 22, 25.12–18); Joseph and his brothers (Gen. 37–46); Perez and Zerah (Gen. 38); Rachel and Leah (Gen. 30.1–24); Jesus and his brothers and sister (John 7.3–10; Matt. 13.5 and 6; Mark 6.3); the Prodigal Son (Luke 15); Martha and Mary (Luke 10.39–40)

*Exercise 3*

Read Abraham's covenant in Genesis 15.1–21 and 17.1–27. Use the hypothesis that they belong to two different traditions – J and P, respectively. What important differences do you find between the two accounts?

*Exercise 4*

Carefully read the story of Joseph and his brothers, assuming two different traditions:

J (Gen. 37.2b, 3b, 5–11, 19–20, 23, 25b–27, 28b, and 31–5) and E (Gen. 37.3a, 4, 12–18, 21–2, 24, 25a, 28a, 29, 30, 36). Account for the differences between the two.

*Exercise 5*

Read the theophany of Moses, assuming the first account comes from J (Exod. 34.1a, 2–13) and the second from E (Exod. 33.12–23). What differences support the possibility of their coming from two distinct traditions?

*Exercise 6*

How do historical passages, such as Nehemiah 9.6–38 and Acts 7.1–51, shape continuity in the Bible?

*Exercise 7*

New Testament writers intentionally quote from the Old Testament for what reasons?

1 Cor. 10.26, 14.21, 15.55; Rom. 1.2, 9–11, 13.8–10, 15.8–12; 2 Cor. 13.1; Matt. 4.14, 12.17–21, 21.4–5.

*Exercise 8*

The New Testament makes frequent use of allusions, these appearing without a formula of introduction, or indirect discourse; what are the allusions in the following passages?

Mark 12.19; Luke 2.33; Acts 3.23; Matt. 2.23, 4.15–16, 8.17, 23; John 8.17; Rom. 2.24; Gal. 3.10; Hebrews 4.4.

*Exercise 9*[86]

Scholars have noted that the Decalogue (Exod. 20) has many of the characteristics of the suzerain treaty or vassal treaty. Re-read the commandments carefully, looking for (1) self-identification of the speaker, (2) historical prologue, (3) treaty stipulations, (4) provisions for placing the treaty in a public place, (5) mention of the gods who acted as witnesses, and (6) blessings and curses invoked on those who did, or did not, uphold the treaty's provision.

*Exercise 10*

Read Genesis 37–50. Explain how the life of Joseph illustrates the heroic quest.

## Questions for Reflection

1 How does the divine–human relationship function as a central, unifying theme in the Bible? What difficulties do you see in using such an overarching theme to talk about the Bible as a whole?

2 What common themes does the Bible share with other literature?

3 What major objections can be raised to thematic analysis?

4 How does macro-plot function to bring together the lives of the Patriarchs and the nation of Israel?

5 Should the Bible be regarded largely as literal, historical, allegorical, mythical, or a mixture of all these?

6 Do the law of the Old Testament and the law of the New Testament express the same basic principles?

7 How does Jesus interpret the Old Testament law?

8 How does the law in Exodus both compare and contrast to the interpretation of the law found in Deuteronomy?

9 Do you find the documentary source theory a useful means of explaining the tensions between a transcendent and a present God, and a God of both mercy and justice? Develop this fully.

10 How do you explain the use of "the LORD your God" and "gods" in the commandments in Exodus and Deuteronomy?

11 What dangers does an exclusive monotheism introduce into intellectual history?

12 What is the twofold nature of relationship and responsibility found in the "Old" and "New" Covenants?

13  What is supersessionism, and what are the dangers inherent in it?

14  What is the function of typology in the Bible?

15  What is the rabbinic explanation for the Ten Commandments being written upon two tablets?

16  Do Protestant, Jewish, and Catholic versions of the order of the Ten Commandments recognize essentially the same moral imperatives shaping the divine–human and human–human relationships?

17  In what ways does the New Testament reinterpret and build upon the foundation of the Old Testament?

18  Do you consider the New Testament as essentially presenting a distorted and censored interpretation of the Old Testament?

19  How is covenant related to law?

20  How do people's moral and spiritual choices affect their lives and destinies in the traditions of J, E, D, and P sources?

21  How does the Bible define ways in which people "ought" to behave in contrast to the ways they actually behave?

22  What are some of the identifying characteristics or attributes of the four main covenants in the Bible?

23  What differences exist among the four main covenants?

24  In what ways do the covenants advance the dual relationship of human beings to God and to each other?

25  How do you explain the absences of covenant in the wisdom tradition?

26  What characteristics in King David's life set him apart from others of Judah's kings?

27  How do the themes of barren women and the significance of first-born sons support the notion of divine sovereignty over life and death?

28  How do the themes of God's steadfast mercy and love contrast with the theme of God's justice? How can the tension be resolved – or can it?

29  What is Judaism's major intellectual and spiritual contribution to the world?

30  In Judaism and Christianity, what are the external signs of "a people set apart for God"?

31  What is the symbolic importance of blood in the Bible?

32  In what ways can Christianity be said to be the child of Judaism?

33  How might the use of literary tools help one to understand the Bible better?

34  How do its themes function to provide a degree of coherence and unity to the Bible?

35  Is it possible to understand source theory apart from finding unity and coherence in parts of the Bible?

36  What are some of the limitations to source theory?

37  How appropriate is it to interpret the Old Testament in light of the New and the New relative to the Old?

38 What is the Shema and its importance in the Bible?
39 What is meant by intertextuality in the Bible?
40 What important differences exist among the ways in which people read the Bible?
41 Does regarding the Bible as a composite creation affect how readers read?
42 What is the documentary source theory hypothesis?
43 In what ways does a literary approach to reading the Bible enhance understanding and appreciation?

# Conclusion

Now that you have reached the end of *Reading the Bible as Literature: an Introduction*, you will have achieved several important goals.

1  You have acquired a familiarity with several of the tools used for reading and understanding literature generally: language and style, the formal structures of genre (narrative, drama, and poetry), character study, and thematic analysis.
2  You have learned that the Bible shares the mythological, metaphorical, and symbolic language that belongs to literature across the centuries.
3  You have been introduced to significant passages and have learned something about the Bible as a whole, which includes the Jewish and Christian canons.
4  You have learned to read the Bible more closely and to appreciate its nuanced and layered levels of meaning and its broad appeal to the interpretive imagination.
5  And, finally, you have discovered a library that invites you to engage at deeper levels of study and to greater depths of insight; you have realized why the Bible continues to appeal to and attract more scholarship than any other collection of literature.

I want to invite you now to focus on the content of the bibliographical notes; they point you to a wide array of resources for further study and enhanced appreciation of the many secondary texts that have addressed the ideas included here. Additionally, I have created a supporting web page, www.readingthebibleasliterature.com, that expands these notes and includes a significant number of tables. Like the Bible itself, this text offers itself for further reading and study, and it has been designed such that it can be used in a more advanced and continuing study of the Bible.

# Glossary

*Abstract* A term in literature that refers to the nonrepresentational and the nonobjective, usually ideas.

*Abstraction* An umbrella term for the process that draws readers away from complicated details and complex readings into generalized and premature summary statements.

*Acrostic* In the old Testament, poetry written such that verses or strophes begin with successive letters of the Hebrew alphabet.

*Act* A group of stories set off in some way structurally, such as by genealogies or parallelism.

*Aetiology* Stories explaining origins or beginnings (*aitios* means "cause," "reason," or "origin"). In cultures which have an aetiological world view, the beginnings or origins of things are seen as providing the meaning for all that follows.

*Allegory* An elaborate analogy in which the narrative intends elements and events to be interpreted in a corresponding other meaning.

*Alliteration* Repetition of an initial consonant sound or any vowel sounds in successive or closely associated syllables.

*Allusion* A direct or an indirect reference to a person, a place, a thing, an event, or an idea in history. In literature, allusion is the practice of echoing or referring to other works.

*Amplification* A rhetorical device that uses more words than the grammar requires.

*Analogy* A relation of similarity between two or more things such that an inference (reasoning from premise to conclusion) is drawn on the basis of the similarities.

*Antagonist* A rival or opponent to the protagonist. Antagonists, who may be internal or external, align against the central character.

*Anthropomorphism* Ascribing human passions, actions, or attributes to non-human things, e.g. deities in mythology and animals in children's stories, and to God.

*Antiphon* Anything composed for responsive chanting or singing (chorused reply).

*Antistrophe* An answering stanza within a poem.

*Antithetical parallelism* A second line expresses an antithesis to the thought of the first line, or the first line is counterbalanced by a contrast in the second.

*Aphorism* Compact crystallization of insight; a short, pithy sentence used to define, make a distinction, or describe a principle in a few telling words that can be easily remembered.

*Apocalypse* Visionary literature that reverses ordinary reality, is cosmic in scope, and has a kaleidoscopic structure. Its structure is more dream than narrative, and its purpose is revelation.

*Apocrypha* Catholicism recognizes, and includes in its Bible, fourteen or fifteen apocryphal (Greek for "things hidden away") or deuterocanonical (meaning "at second level") books. The apocryphal works, written after the canonical books of the Hebrew Bible and before the canonical books of the Christian Bible (200 BCE and 150 CE), provide important historical connections between the two accepted canons and help to provide political, religious, and cultural background important to the study of the Christian New Testament.

*Apocryphal New Testament* Works written during the early centuries of Christianity that augment or seek to supplant the twenty-seven books of the New Testament. Almost two dozen apocryphal gospels as well as apocryphal acts draw up narratives of apostles' acts in early Christianity. Among other apocrypha are letters and apocalypses, written in the second to ninth centuries CE in Greek, Syriac, and other languages, that provide an important supplement to the accepted canon and shed light on practices and ideas condemned by the early Church. They contribute to a fuller picture of Christian thought, life, and piety.

*Apodictic* Describes unconditional and binding laws, such as the Ten Commandments, expressing the nature of necessary truth or absolute certainty.

*Apostasy* Abandonment of religion or faith; a falling away or rebellion against truth.

*Apostrophe* A poetic device in which someone turns aside from the story to address an external audience.

*Appellation* Use of a quality, office, or attribute for a proper noun.

*Archetype* A recurring image or pattern representing the universal elements of human experience.

*Argument (persuasion)* Makes truth claims and defends them.

*Background* The setting or the tradition and point of view from which an author presents his story or ideas.

*BCE* "Before the Common Era." A religiously neutral calendar notation that is numerically equivalent to the "BC" notation.

*Bible* The commonly anthologized thirty-nine books of the Jewish Bible and the twenty-seven books of the New Testament.

*Biblical criticism* Umbrella term for the study and investigation of biblical writings.

*Biography* A genre of literature accounting for a person's life or life history. Christianity often refers to the Gospels as biographies of Christ. They fall within the Greco-Roman concept of biography, which includes subdivisions and borrowing from other genres, such as political propaganda, encomium, moralistic encouragement, and travelogue.

*Canon* Official or authorized list of books accepted as Scripture by a religious community and used by the group as the basis for its religious beliefs, moral precepts, and communal practices. "Canon" comes from a Greek word meaning "measuring rod."

*Canonical criticism* Emphasizes the final form of the text and its place in the communities of faith.

*Catechism* Summary or exposition of theological doctrine (basic beliefs and principles).

CE "Common Era." A religiously neutral calendar notation that is numerically equivalent to the "AD" notation.

*Character development* The multitude of traits and behaviors that give a literary character the complexity of a human being and generate the actions that make up the plot of a story.

*Characterization* Refers to the display of habits, emotions, desires, and instincts. Characters are presented as *one-dimensional,* lacking depth and neither growing nor changing, or *multidimensional,* complex and changing, evolving through emotional, mental, sociological, and metaphysical states of being. The latter have a past, present, and future, and they develop in relationship to plot.

*Chiasm* A Semitic poetic form, sometimes used also in prose arrangements, that juxtaposes, reverses, or contrasts words, dialogues, episodes, scenes, and events.

*Christianity* Designates the religion based on the life and teachings of Jesus Christ.

*Christology* The branch of theology concerned with the study of the nature, character, and actions of Jesus Christ. It includes the doctrine that Jesus is God incarnate.

*Chronicle* A historical record according to date.

*Church order* Ritual and practice within the institutionalized Church.

*Circumcision* The ritualistic removal of a male's foreskin, usually associated with puberty.

*Circumlocution (periphrasis)* A roundabout or indirect way of speaking; the use of a descriptive phrase in place of a name in order to emphasize an association.

*Cliché* A word or expression that has lost much of its force and become trite through overuse.

*Climactic parallelism* A form of poetry in which a line, word, or phrase is repeated in the second and following lines, contributing to progressive movement in a theme or away from a central point (see Ps. 29.1; Prov. 31.4).

*Climax/turning point* Recognizably the point in a narrative at which the protagonist either decides how to resolve a conflict or faces those conflicts. At this point the story moves from building to resolving conflict.

*Cognate* Closely related word.

*Colloquy* Formal conversation or written dialogue.

*Comedy* A story with a U-shaped plot; a comic plot includes progression from problem to solution, from bondage to freedom, or the overcoming of a series of obstacles en route to a happy ending.

*Composite quotation* Combined quoted materials taken from one or more sources.

*Concrete* Describes graphic, visual literature rich in sights, sounds, touch, taste, and feel.

*Condescension* An attitude or act of patronizing behavior.

*Conflict* The opposition between or among characters or forces that shapes or motivates the action of the plot.

*Connotation* Usually contrasted to denotation, refers to the emotional implications and associated or secondary meaning that a word may carry.

*Cosmogony* The name given to any theory or story of the origin and development of the universe, the solar system, or the earth–moon system.

*Covenant* A binding relationship based on commitment that includes promise and obligation, which can be relied on and which endures. It takes on the connotation of an obligation with legal aspects.

*Covenantal theology* A conceptual and interpretive framework for understanding the overall flow of the Bible. It includes the Noahic, Abrahamic, Mosaic, and Davidic covenants. When applied to the New Testament, it emphasizes the New Covenant of Jeremiah and its anticipation of a Davidic Messiah. Strictly, covenant theology in Christianity argues that God has only one covenant with human beings, the covenant of grace. It suggests that Israel was the Church in the Old Testament and that the Church is Israel in the New Testament.

*Cycle* A chain of stories (acts), usually three to five, and has an overriding macro-plot.

*Dead Sea Scrolls* Roughly 1,000 documents found in eleven caves in and around the Wadi Qumran at the northwest corner of the Dead Sea between 1947 and 1979.

*Decalogue* The name given by the Greek fathers to the Ten Commandments – "ten words," as the original is more literally rendered – that comprise a short list of religious and ethical demands required by God. These commandments were at first written on two stone slabs (Exod. 31.18), which were broken by Moses' throwing them down on the ground (32.19). They were then written by God a second time (34.1). The Decalogue is alluded to in the New Testament five times (Matt. 5.17, 18, 19; Mark 10.19; Luke 18.20; Rom. 7.7, 8; 13.9; 1 Tim. 1.9, 10).

*Denotation* The literal meaning of a word.

*Denouement* The final unraveling of the main dramatic complication (plot) in a literary work; the outcome of a complex sequence of events.

*Deuterocanonical* Used, especially in Roman Catholic works, of those books in the Septuagint LXX (sometimes abbreviated as LXX for the seventy to seventy-two Jewish scholars who carried out the translation) not recognized by Protestant Christians or Orthodox Jews as canonical, also designated as Apocrypha.

*Deuteronomic (D) history* The material found in the Hebrew Bible, primarily Deuteronomy (but includes Joshua, Judges, 1, 2 Samuel and 1, 2 Kings), is characterized by its hortatory or preaching style and theology that insists God cannot be seen, does not physically dwell in the Temple or Tabernacle, and must be worshipped in one place only, Jerusalem. D is generally associated with Josiah (and the reform of 622 BCE). The usual date for the book of Deuteronomy is during the reign of Manasseh (696–642 BCE) and Josiah (639–609 BCE).

*Dialogue* Verbal exchanges between characters. Dialogue brings the characters alive to the reader or audience by revealing their thoughts, responses, and emotional states. It advances the action and is consistent with the characters of the speakers.

*Divided kingdom* The reign of several kings in Israel (the northern ten tribes) and Judah (the remaining tribes).

*Documentary Hypothesis* A theory that suggests a redactor composed the Torah by combining four independent source documents: the Yahwist (J), a source active in Judah and responsible for most of Genesis; the Elohist (E), which emphasizes northern Israel and the Shiloh priesthood; the Priestly (P), which is responsible for the first chapter of Genesis, Leviticus, and other sections with genealogical information and a focus on the priesthood and worship; and the Deuteronomic (D), which consists of Deuteronomy, Joshua, Judges, 1, 2 Samuel, and 1, 2 Kings.

*Double meaning* A figure of speech in which a phrase may be understood in either of two ways.

*Dramatic irony* A contrast between a character's self-understanding at a particular point in an unfolding plot and what the reader understands to be the actual case.

*Dynamic character* A character who grows and undergoes significant change as a plot progresses.

*Elohim* "God" or "Lord."

*Elohist (E)* The second oldest source (800 BCE) proposed by documentary source theory is associated with the northern kingdom and takes its name from Elohim, the generic term for "God" or "gods." It begins with the story of Abraham and provides somewhat different versions of the patriarchal tales as well as a different version of Moses' calling and the revelation of the Mosaic Law. God is more distant (spiritualized, transcendent), communicating by dreams and intermediaries, such as heavenly messengers and prophets (not kings). The source mentions Mount Horeb and refers to people in the land as Amorites. The divine covenant through Moses is emphasized, and the stress is on obedience and fear of the Lord.

*Emblematic parallelism* A line uses a figure of speech to illuminate the point conveyed by the following line (see Ps. 42.1; Prov. 11.22, 25.25, 27.17).

*Encomium* A lyric form addressing a person, usually in praise. Examples can be found in Psalms 1, 15, 112, and 128; Proverbs 3.1.10–13; 1 Corinthians 13; and Hebrews 11.

*Epic* A long narrative poem about the deeds of a traditional or historic hero. More specifically, epic uses rhythm and poetic parallelism and is meant to be sung or chanted; it usually treats the mythic stories of the interactions of gods and mortals in early times. Epic literature is expansive, sums up an age, has nationalistic interest, presents a hero whose destiny is tied up with that of a nation, and structures itself about a central feat, usually the winning of a battle and the establishment of a kingdom. The Pentateuch, Joshua, the story of David, and the book of Revelation are full-fledged epics.

*Epigram* A short powerful (pithy) saying marked by compression, balance, and polish.

*Epilogue* The concluding statement of a play.

*Epiphany* An event or happening that manifests or shows forth the essential nature of a person, situation, or object, usually with divine overtones. Biblically, it means a manifestation or "revelation" and is similar to "theophany," as in, for example, God's revelation to Moses at the burning bush (Exod. 3.2).

*Episode* Consists of scenes grouped into a complete story and consisting of some form of problem/resolution that can be subdivided into rising, turning, and falling action.

*Epistle* Used in the New Testament to refer to the genre of letter.

*Eponymy* The way a person's name gives rise to the name of a particular place, tribe, or era.

*Eschatology* A theology concerned with the final events (last times) in the history of the world or of humankind, a belief concerning death, the end of the world, or the ultimate destiny of humankind; theologically, it invokes any of various Christian doctrines concerning the Second Coming, the resurrection of the dead, or the Last Judgment. Eschatology is regarded as synonymous with "end times" discourse.

*Ethical monotheism* Standards of human behavior derived from human reason, emotion, and social norms. Its emphasis is upon one God who created human beings and declared how they should behave, and it has been described as Judaism's "major intellectual and spiritual contribution to the world."

*Etiological tales* Folk traditions that set out to explain puzzling realities, such as the rainbow, why Jewish people refrain from eating the sinew of an animal's thigh (Gen. 32.24–32), and the custom of the daughters of Israel going up into the mountains to lament for four days (Judg. 11).

*Euphemism* A word or phrase chosen to make something unpleasant appear pleasant; a device that uses indirectness to replace a direct statement in order to avoid giving offense.

*Exhortation* Utterance, discourse, or address conveying urgent advice or recommendations.

*Experiential* Relating to or deriving from bodily experience, including the imagination and emotions.

*Exposition* Conveys initial information crucial to developing a plot, giving the setting, introducing the characters, and supplying other facts necessary to its being understood.

*Expository writing (informative)* A kind of writing that has as its purpose explanation.

*Expressive writing* Conveys the thoughts and feelings of the writer and objectifies inner experience.

*Fable* A short narrative tale that points to a moral. Such tales frequently include animals as characters. One of the most remembered fables in the Hebrew Bible is found in the account of Balaam's talking donkey (Num. 22.22–39).

*Figurative language* Appeals to the imagination and should not be interpreted in a literal sense; the figurative departs from the literal and introduces diversity and variability in meaning.

*First man* Adam, the first man, created by God on the sixth day of creation, and placed in the Garden of Eden (Gen. 2.19–23; 3.8–9, 17, 20–1; 4.1, 25; 5.1–5); regarded as the ancestor of all people now living on the earth.

*First-person narrative* An account in which the story is told by one or more of the characters, who refers explicitly to him- or herself as "I". The narrator is thus personally involved in the story.

*First Temple period* The period from 1006 to 586 BCE that includes the building of the Temple by King Solomon and the exile of the Hebrews in the Babylonian captivity.

*Flat character* A minor character who embodies or represents a single or dominant characteristic, trait, or idea, or at most a very limited number of such qualities. A flat character undergoes little change, in contrast to a *round character*.

*Focus* The central point to which all elements or parts point.

*Foil* A character who, through contrast, underscores the distinctive characteristics of another.

*Folk or fairy-tale* A narrative handed down through oral tradition, modified through retellings, and gaining cumulative authorship. Fairy-tales include spirits who manifest as pranksters and adventurers in the form of diminutive human beings.

*Foreshadow* To provide hints or clues for something that will happen in the future; to show, indicate, or suggest in advance; to presage.

*Form criticism* Looks at the history of a particular biblical text or portion of text and both reconstructs its process of development (tradition criticism) and identifies its literary forms or genres.

*Formal parallelism* Poetry in which lines balance clause for clause but contain neither synonymy nor direct antithesis (see Ps. 14.2). Parallelism is found not only in couplets (two lines), but also in triplets and quatrains (three and four lines), and sometimes in whole stanzas.

*Formulaic quotation* Material taken from another source and introduced by a formula such as "the Scripture has said . . ."

*Genealogy* The most important information about the successive members of a family's lineage, including birth, marriage, offspring, age achieved, and death; it serves to preserve the continuity of a family in its progression through time.

*Genre* A French term derived from the Latin *genus, generis,* meaning "type," "sort," or "kind." It designates the literary form or type into which works are classified according to what they have in common, either in their formal structures or in their treatment of subject matter, or both. Genre can also be said to form a narrative covenant between author and reader, creating a framework of norms and expectations that shapes both the composition and the reception of the text.

*Gnosticism* Advances a salvation based on an intuitive knowledge of the mysteries of the universe, as opposed to a Jewish or Christian belief in works and faith.

*Gospel* "Good news," understood in the Christian tradition as telling the story of Jesus. Mark announces that his book is "the gospel of Jesus Christ." The antecedents to the Gospel(s) include biographies about great men.

*Hebrew Bible* The books common to the Jewish canon and the Christian Old Testament. Scholars have used "Hebrew Bible" to avoid connotations associated with "Old Testament," which includes dual covenant theology and the suggestion that the New Covenant supersedes, and is superior to, the Old Covenant. More exactly, the term refers to a set of texts written originally in Hebrew. The Hebrew Bible, it should be noted, contains a number of covenants in addition to the Mosaic (associated with Law) – for example, those associated with Noah, Abraham, and David. The New Testament expands covenant to embrace universal salvation and the inclusion of non-Jewish people.

*Hermeneutics* A science involved with constructing and discovering the rules of interpretation of texts. In biblical studies, it relates closely to *exegesis* – the act of interpreting or understanding meaning in Scripture.

*Hero* Refers in a work of literature to someone with great courage and strength (although that is not always the case) who may risk or sacrifice his or her life for the greater good; in mythology, a hero may come from divine ancestry.

*Higher criticism* Also known as *biblical, historical,* and *literary criticism,* investigates the date, place and circumstances of a composition together with its author's or authors' purpose or intended meaning (including editors, this known as *redaction criticism*), and reconstructs the historical situation out of which a piece of writing arose. It is contrasted with *lower criticism.*

*Historical criticism* Emphasizes the Bible's evolution, the underlying sources that contributed to the existing text, its composite nature, and the social, cultural, and historical setting.

*Historical itinerary* A plan or design leading to destinations.

*Historiography* Writing that aims to raise in readers a sense of identity and citizenship, a consciousness of belonging to a great and noble city or race; typically it interweaves mythology, legend, and historical fact.

*Homiletics* The branch of theology that deals with sermons and homilies; the art of preaching.

*Hymn and ode* Poetry expressing religious emotion and usually intended to be sung. The ode, which is formal, elaborate, dignified, and imaginative, is meant to be accompanied by music and performed by a chorus.

*Hypotaxis* Linkage of ideas through the use of subordinate clauses and complex sentences.

*Idiom* Use of language that native speakers find natural.

*Illusion* Based on an impression of the senses rather than fact.

*Imagery* Figurative or descriptive language.

*Imagination* Refers to the image-making and image-perceiving capacity within human beings.

*Immanence* The transcendent God becomes present in creation and, in Christianity, incarnate in Jesus Christ.

*Implication* The state of something being suggested which offers neither the explicit statement of likeness (as in simile) nor the implied comparison of the metaphor, simply taking the likeness for granted.

*Inclusio* Uses repetition to mark the beginning and ending of a section, framing or bracketing an episode it contains.

*Incongruity* Self-contradictory statements or contrasting words and ideas.

*Interpretation* The reader's act of understanding the ideas or values (meaning) which a text advances. It is not always a simple task, because the ideas of a literary text are almost always presented in indirect or "symbolic" form.

*Intertextuality* The use and reference of other texts to influence meaning, creating multiple continuities and interrelationships.

*Introverted parallelism* Thought veers from the main theme and then returns.

*Irony* Uses words to suggest the opposite of their literal meaning; *dramatic irony* exists when others know what the characters do not know.

*Jahwist (J)* Denotes one of the sources of the Pentateuch, which uses

Yahweh for the name of God. It was probably written in Judah in the tenth or ninth century BCE. J is characterized by anthropomorphism and records of the faithfulness of God to the Patriarchs. Emphasis is on the Davidic dynasty and leaders and the covenant with David, stressing divine blessing. It mentions Mount Sinai and refers to natives in the land as Canaanites.

*Jewish Bible* The Jewish canon, available in many languages, structures itself around twenty-two books. Jewish Bibles today include the Tanak, an acronym derived from the initial consonants of the three main divisions of the Hebrew Bible, the Torah (Law), Nevi'im (Prophets), and Kethuvim (Writings). The first two parts, the Law and the Prophets, were accepted as sacred and authoritative as early as 200 BCE; the third part, the Writings, has been regarded as less authoritative, and the canon, the authorized and accepted list of books belonging to the Bible, less settled.

*Judaism* The monotheistic religion of the Jewish people, based on the laws contained in the Torah and the Talmud.

*Kinsman-redeemer* The kinsman-redeemer, a near relative, served to protect the family. This relative had the first option by law to buy any land being sold, thus allowing it to be kept within the clan (Lev. 25.23–8; Jer. 32.6–10).

*Lament* A song or poem expressing grief, regret, or mourning.

*Law and cultic regulations* Teaching or instruction. The Ten Commandments may be understood as the heart of Israel's covenantal relationship with God. The book of Leviticus lays out many of the cultic rituals and laws that express the early Hebrew people's conviction that God lived in a tabernacle in their midst.

*Legal codes* A set of rules governing behavior.

*Legend* A story handed down in tradition and having some basis in history.

*Leitmotif* A recurrence of a pattern or image (less dominant than a theme), such as "the way of the righteous" and "the way of the ungodly."

*Letters* Documents, usually persuasive, written to substitute for presence. This genre exists in the Christian Bible as a series of books written by Paul and others to guide and influence the early Church.

*Levirate marriage* The custom whereby the brother of a deceased man must marry his sister-in-law in order to keep the dead man's name and his property rights alive.

*List of tribal leaders* A listing such as the one reflected in the first census of Israel in Numbers 1. This census can be compared to the census of the new generation in Numbers 26.

*Literary* Describes a special use of language that intensifies and transforms it from ordinary use. Reading literature poses the special challenge of the subjectivity of the reader and the objectivity of the text.

*Literary present* The present tense, used to describe fictional action so as to imply that it exists in a timeless world.

*Liturgy* An exercise designed to lift the soul in divine service, to unite the many moods of the soul in worship, and to mingle penitence with praise and confession with supplication, such as is found in Psalms 65, 116, and 118.

*Lower (foundational) criticism* Also known as *textual criticism,* the study and analysis of existing manuscripts to determine evidence on which to base a text and to eliminate error.

*Lyric* Poetry originally designed to be sung and accompanied by a lyre. It is melodic, imaginative, emotional, and designed to create a single, unified impression.

*Macro-plot* A larger or overarching plot that encompasses and transcends a group of individual stories such that a single story may not always need its own plot; a narrative process whereby several layers of stories function as a single entity.

*Masoretic text* The only existing representation of the Old Testament in Hebrew. The oldest fragments date from the ninth century CE, but the oldest complete texts come from the tenth and eleventh centuries CE. This is not the original Hebrew or even the Hebrew spoken in the first century CE. Vowel pointings were added to the text to standardize the pronunciation of the words. The Codex Leningrad is one of the surviving Masoretic texts.

*Merism* Brings together parts or opposites into a single totality.

*Meta-narrative* In literal terms, a meta-narrative means a "big story." It represents, in short, an explanation for everything that happens in a society. As a whole, the Bible reveals a loose chronology and overarching meta-narrative that tells a story about the past and the future, with the New Testament reinterpreting the Old Testament.

*Metaphor* An implicit comparison between two things of unlike nature that yet have something in common; a declaration that one thing is or represents another.

*Metonym* A metaphor in which the thing chosen for the metaphorical image is closely associated with (but not an actual part of) the subject with which it is to be compared.

*Mishnah* From a Hebrew word, *gamar,* which means "to complete." A collection of early rabbinic instruction developed and transmitted orally down to the beginning of the third century CE.

*Mitzvot* The 613 commandments that God gave to the Jewish people in the Torah.

*Monarchy* Designates a period around 1000 BCE and refers to the United Kingdom of Israel under Kings Saul, David, and Solomon; the term refers to rule by one king.

*Monolatry* Devotion to a single deity while at the same time accepting the existence of other deities.

*Monomyth* A hero's journey found in literature that follows a basic pattern of separation, initiation, and return.

*Monotheism* Belief that reality's ultimate principle is God – an omnipotent, omniscient goodness that is the creative ground of everything other than itself – and the view that there is only one such God. It exists in two forms: *inclusive*, emphasizing human limitation in the face of a transcendent God, tolerant in degree to other religions, and *exclusive*, characterized by intolerance of other positions.

*Motif* Repeated instances of the same pattern/image so frequently as to set expectations in the minds of readers.

*Myth* Drama or narrative embodying a people's perceptions of the deepest truths.

*Narrative* An accounting of events either in chronological time or arranged by plot and the type of story. A special way of approaching literature includes its *narratology* or analysis of the relations among the parts of a story.

*Narrative criticism* Insists on close reading and looks at complex literary structures such as plot, characterization, and closure in stories.

*Narrator* The voice that controls the story and through which readers learn about the action and people of the narrative. A narrator can speak in *first* (I, we), second (you), or *third* person (he, she, it, they) and may be *omniscient* – being disembodied, witnessing all events, and privy to all things past, present, and future. A narrator whose knowledge is limited to one character, either major or minor, has a limited omniscient point of view. With the *objective point of view*, the writer tells what happens without stating more than can be inferred from the story's action and dialogue, never disclosing anything about what the characters think or feel, and remaining a detached observer. In the third person, the narrator does not participate in the action of the story as one of the characters, but lets the reader know exactly how the characters feel. In the first-person point of view, the narrator does participate in the action of the story. When reading such stories, we need to realize that what the narrator is recounting might not be the objective truth. We should question the trustworthiness of the accounting.

*Necromancy* The practice of consulting with the dead.

*New birth* An inner spiritual renewal as a result of the power of God in a person's life. The phrase "new birth" comes from John 3.3, 7, where Jesus told Nicodemus, "Unless one is born again, he cannot see the kingdom of God." John the Baptist taught repentance and baptism; Christianity has largely defined "new birth" to be an act of regeneration, re-creation, and renewal by the activity of God's Spirit.

*New Covenant* The new agreement God has made with humankind, based on the death and resurrection of Jesus Christ. The concept of a New Covenant originated with the promise of the prophet Jeremiah that God would accomplish for His people what the Old Covenant had failed to do (Jer. 31.31–4). Under this New Covenant, God would write His Law on human hearts. This promised action suggested a new knowledge of the Lord, a restored relationship, and a new level of trust and obedience.

*New creation* Refers to a universal kingdom of righteousness, peace, and joy that will be fully revealed when Christ returns in triumph over all rebellious creatures and God creates a new heaven and earth (1 Cor. 15.20–8).

*New Jerusalem* The heavenly and eternal city of God (Rev. 21.2–22.5). John identifies "the great city, the holy Jerusalem" (Rev. 21.10) as the Church, which he calls "the bride, the Lamb's wife" (Rev. 21.9).

*New Testament* The twenty-seven books that constitute the canonized books of the Bible written in and after the first century CE.

*Novella* An extended prose narrative story or short novel, usually a fictional narrative. Also referred to as a *novelette*.

*Old Testament* A collection of (depending on which Bible you are referring to) fifty-three, forty-nine, forty-six, or thirty-nine ancient Jewish books, including the history of God's interactions with the people of Israel and related literary works from ancient Judaism.

*Orator* A person who formally delivers a speech.

*Ordinances* Civil, social, and sanitation laws.

*Orthodox* Those who hold "right beliefs" as defined by religious tradition.

*Oxymoron* A figure of speech where literal meanings seem incongruous and contradictory but upon examination prove to be words cleverly joined together to say something wise.

*Palestine* The Hebrew people made Canaan, the land later to become Israel, and known after the Babylonian captivity (587–539 BCE) as Palestine, their home.

*Parable* A story using the familiar to illustrate a religious, ethical, or moral point.

*Paradox* An apparent contradiction that, upon analysis, expresses truth.

*Parallelism* Refers to an essential and characteristic feature in Hebrew poetry, the balancing of verse with verse, either by repetition or by antithesis; it sets thought against thought and balances form in order to create meaning.

*Parataxis* As opposed to *hypotaxis*, indicates a style that uses short, simple sentences without the use of coordinating or subordinating conjunctions.

*Parody* A method of criticism that makes use of another creative work.

*Pastoral* The portrayal of rustic life, after the Latin for "shepherd." Psalm 23 expresses one of the most beautiful and moving pastorals.

*Pentateuch* From the Greek (*penta*, "five," and *teukhos*, "scroll"), meaning five volumes after the Jewish designation "the five-fifths of the law, also known as "Torah," and refers to the first five books of the Old Testament.

*Persona* The voice, pose, or attitude assumed by a narrator.

*Personification* Gives human traits (feelings, characteristics, qualities, or actions) to non-living objects (ideas, colors, things).

*Plot* Can be analyzed in terms of its exposition or beginning, an ensuing complication, a crisis or turning point, falling action, and resolution. See also *macro-plot.*

*Plot motif* A set of unfolding motifs that helps to unite and hold together a story. See also *motif.*

*Point of view* The perspective from which the story is told, which can be in the first or third person.

*Prayer* A petition made to God.

*Priestly (P) source* In Documentary Hypothesis, designating the final body of writing integrated into the Pentateuch. It includes the priestly regulations of Leviticus as well as the creation hymn of Genesis 1. P shows a strong interest in boundaries and order, favoring lists or genealogies and schemata (such as seven days) and concern with the priestly family (Aaronid) and temple-based religious system (Gen. 1). Scholars generally give the composition date as pre-Babylonian exile (sixth century BCE) or during and after the exile.

*Primogeniture* The rights and position of the first-born child.

*Primordial* Describes primeval history, the earliest ages of human-kind, first beginnings.

*Prologue* The introduction to a play.

*Prophecy* A biblical genre where the prophet, a spokesperson for God, addresses on behalf of God immediate political or social crises in the covenant community, for example the Assyrian military threat and the Babylonian destruction of Jerusalem; it can be said generally to be the inspired declaration of divine will and purpose, a prediction of something to come.

*Prophet* An individual who has encountered and become a spokesperson for God.

*Protagonist* The central character with whom readers identify and who functions to unify a story; a story can have more than one protagonist.

*Proverb* A short saying in pithy form expressing insights into human affairs, especially of a social and religious nature. See the book of Proverbs.

*Psalm* A lyrical composition of lament or praise.

*Pseudepigrapha* A collection of early Jewish works, composed between *c.*200 BCE and *c.*200 CE, not found in the Bible or rabbinic writings.

*Pseudonymous* Indicating that a work has been written under a false or assumed name.

*Quest* A journey (physical, intellectual, or spiritual) in which a character searches for destiny. Archetypes include the quest to remain safe or to regain safety, the quest to win, to help others, to search for a better life, to gain love and happiness, to metamorphose, to gain identity, to create order, to enjoy life, to transform, or to gain truth.

*Quotation* A direct quotation is an exact word-by-word transfer of part of one text into another, given in quotation marks. An *indirect quotation* reports what was said without repeating the exact words.

*Rabbinic tradition* Consists of texts by and about rabbis living during and after the first century CE.

*Recursion* A process where the author intentionally shapes material by repeating key elements from one narrative in another.

*Redactors* Individuals who edited parts of the Bible. Redaction criticism attempts to separate the actual literary contribution of the editors from the works they edit.

*Refrain* The repetition of line or lines in music or verse; the "chorus" of a song.

*Remnant theology* Deals with that part of a group which has escaped (e.g. exile, Jer. 24.8) or will not be destroyed (Amos 5.14–15) or which has remained faithful under trials.

*Repetition* A favorite Hebrew literary device in both prose narrative and poetry in which words and phrases, actions, images, motifs, themes, and ideas are repeated and become the central focus.

*Resolution* The part of a story that sums up or brings the conflicts to their conclusion; also refers to a decision that provides a solution or an answer to a problem.

*Retributive justice* A theological view where obedience results in blessings while disobedience results in punishment; may be contrasted to distributive justice.

*Rhetorical question* A figure of speech in the form of a question posed for its persuasive effect without the expectation of a reply.

*Rhetorical strategy* The use of devices that provide additional force, more life, intensified feeling, and greater emphasis to the manifold forms, words, and sentences in the Bible.

*Rising action* In narrative, includes everything that leads up to the climax.

*Round character* A character who embodies a number of qualities and traits and who has considerable intellectual and emotional depth; such a character is complex and three-dimensional and is included in a story to help the reader understand the scene in a way that advances the action.

*Sagen* Sometimes referred to as legend or folklore, consists of prose narratives about famous historical heroes, notable families, or the exploits of kings and warriors.

*Satire* Used in the Bible as a form of protest that holds evil or folly in contempt by means of ridicule or irony.

*Scene* The division of an act.

*Schema* An outline; refers to a deviation from the ordinary pattern or arrangement of words.

*Scripture* A term restricted to those books recognized as canonical.

*Second Temple period* The second Temple was erected in Jerusalem by the returnees from the Babylonian captivity, led by Zerubbabel, and was consecrated around 516 BCE.

*Seer* A person who acquires knowledge through clairvoyance or special psychic powers.

*Septuagint (LXX)* A collection of up to fifty-three books of ancient Jewish Scripture translated into Greek by seventy-two elders (as requested by Ptolemy II (285–247 BCE), who, according to legend, presented identical versions although each was working in solitary confinement. The collection includes all twenty-four books of the Hebrew Bible. The LXX rearranges, renames, subdivides, and/or expands some of the books (thus fifty-three books in four main divisions: Pentateuch, Historical, Prophetic, and Poetic or Writings).

*Sermon* A speech or teaching. See the Sermon on the Mount in Matthew 5–7 and Luke 6.20–3. Among other Christian sermons are Peter's in Acts 3.12–26 and Stephen's speech in Acts 7.2–53.

*Setting* The total environment for the action of a fictional work, including the period and its social, political, and spiritual realities.

*Shema* The first word of Deuteronomy 6.4, "Hear," and the central statement of Jewish faith.

*Sign* An actual occurrence that carries significance beyond its surface meaning.

*Simile* An explicit comparison (using words such as "like" or "as") between two things of unlike nature that yet have something in common.

*Soliloquy* A dramatic or literary form of discourse in which a character talks to himself or herself or reveals his or her thoughts without addressing a listener.

*Soteriology* The theology of salvation of which the basis is found in the Old Testament; New Testament soteriology teaches that Jesus is the perfect law and savior.

*Source criticism* Looks for underlying sources, generally to a hypothesis that Genesis through 2 Kings can be traced to four original and independent source documents (J, E, P, D) interwoven together. They are usually said to refer to different periods, with J being the oldest, E somewhat later, D as essentially Deuteronomy, composed about 612 BCE, and P as Post-Exile.

*Speech* Formal, stylized discourse to an audience.

*Stanza* A grouping of lines with a set pattern of meter or rhyme.

*Static character* A character who undergoes no or little change.

*Statutes* Royal announcements that guide worship and religious observance.

*Stock character* A character who is so obvious and predictable that their role and personality are clichés. Stories should not be too full of these characters or else they will be boring.

*Story* Contains a plot, a deliberately sequenced set of interrelated events, chronological or not, that make up narrative structure and give it a beginning, a middle, and an end; a factual (account of facts) or fictional (made up imaginatively or false) narrative. Story can be defined as a discrete unit that can stand independent of an entire narrative, which then links episodes into greater wholes.

*Strategy* The management of language to achieve specific effects.

*Strophe* A unit grouping of verse that evidences little regularity, rhyme, or recurrent pattern.

*Style* How something is said or written; the mode of expression, or the manner of expression of an author, or the author's choice and arrangement of words and phrases.

*Supersessionism* A theology (Augustine, fifth century; Luther, sixteenth century) that suggests the covenantal relationship with Israel was abrogated, to be taken up by the Church, and that the Mosaic Law was annulled, replaced by the law of Christ.

*Syncretism* The blending of religious beliefs and practices.

*Synecdoche* A figure of speech in which the whole is represented by one of its parts (genus named for species), or vice versa (species named for genus); see Psalm 35.10.

*Synonymous parallelism* The second line reinforces the thought of the first by using similar words and concepts (see Job 38.7; Pss. 3.1; 25.4; 49.1; Prov. 11.7, 25; 12.28).

*Synthetic parallelism* The second line adds to or completes the idea of the first line (see Pss. 1.1–2; 23.1, 5; 95.3; Prov. 4.23).

*Tale* Relates the details of some real or imaginary event, incident, or case. It is a literary composition having the form of a narrative, deriving from an oral tradition.

*Talmud* Discussions and commentaries on the *Mishnah* (the name for the sixty-three tractates which set down Jewish oral laws).

*Tanakh* The Jewish Bible, the Jewish Scriptures. The word *Tanakh* is derived from the letters of the names of its three components: *Torah* (a.k.a. Pentateuch), the Books of Genesis, Exodus, Leviticus, Numbers, and Deuteronony; the *Nevi'im* (a.k.a. Prophets); and the *Ketuvim* (Writings).

*Telos* A Greek word suggesting end, purpose, or goal.

*Tetragrammaton* Represents the four letters (YHWH) which in Hebrew is the personal and proper divine name considered too sacred to pronounce.

*Textual criticism* The study of biblical documents, their copying, transmission, writing style, instruments, etc. It deals with the reconstruction of the original writings through these elements.

*Theme* An organizing principle (idea) that holds together a work; it can be embedded in images, actions, and emotions. Themes may be implied or explicitly stated and usually deal with the fundamental and often universal idea explored by the work.

*Theocracy* God-centered rule.

*Theodicy* A vindication of the divine attributes, particularly holiness and justice, in establishing or allowing the existence of physical and moral evil.

*Theophany* A temporary physical manifestation or revelation of God to a human person, as distinct from a vision.

*Third-person point of view* The narrator is not a character in the story.

Limited third person means the narrator reports the feelings and thoughts of one character. In the omniscient third person, the narrator can enter the minds of different characters at different times.

*Tone* The manner in which an author expresses attitude; the intonation of the voice that expresses meaning.

*Torah* "Five scroll." Genesis, Exodus, Leviticus, Numbers, and Deuteronomy, traditionally believed to have been authored by Moses (also known as the Pentateuch). In a less restricted sense, Torah has sometimes been used to refer to the entire Jewish Bible (the Tanakh or Written Torah for Jews and the Old Testament for Christians). It has also been used to refer to Jewish law and teachings.

*Tragedy* Drama in which human suffering results from a tragic flaw, or defect in character, that arouses pity and fear and leads to catharsis, or purging of the emotions experienced.

*Transcendence* The idea that God is a being who is entirely above the created, physical, and empirical earth.

*Translation* The creation of text in a second language having the same meaning as the written communication in a first language Translation involves interpretation of the meaning of a text and rendering it on a continuum of literal to idiomatic. The text to be translated is the *source* text and the emergent text the translation.

*Trope* A rhetorical figure of speech that deviates from the ordinary pattern or signification of a word (thought).

*Two source hypothesis* The majority opinion among biblical scholars, first proposed in 1855, which stresses Markan priority. Mark was written first, and Matthew and Luke used it as a source. Matthew and Luke also used a second source, usually called "Q" for *Quelle* (German for "source"), and other unique materials (consisting of sayings in Matthew and Luke not included in Mark).

*Type* A symbol, particularly in religious literature, standing for something that is to come and referring to members of the same class who share certain characteristics in common.

*Type-scenes* A literary convention in which scenes repeat with regularity. The narrator uses similarities and differences within the scene to illuminate plot and character development. Robert Alter has identified the betrothal scene as a type-scene present in several stories in the Bible.

*Typology* A way of reading that finds patterns in what has happened in the past (Old Testament) and uses these to anticipate events in the future (the New Testament); the anticipation is called the "type" and the fulfillment the "antitype."

*Undisputed letters of Paul* Scholars generally agree that Paul wrote the letters Romans, 1 and 2 Corinthians, Galatians, Philippians, 1 Thessalonians, and Philemon. Some believe that six others – Colossians, Ephesians, 2 Thessalonians, 1 and 2 Timothy, and Titus, also called deutero-Pauline (or "disputed") letters – were written by

Paul's followers. 1 and 2 Timothy and Titus are generally referred to as pastoral letters.

*U-shaped comedy* A form in which events first descend into potential tragedy and then rise to end happily.

*Variance* Accounts for something being meant that is other than what is literally said.

*Wisdom literature* Literature emphasizing the desirability and elusiveness of true understanding (wisdom).

*YHVH* Proper name of God in Hebrew, also called the Tetragrammaton. Traditionally, vowels added to the Hebrew letters YHVH create the name, which remains unpronounced. For sake of reverence YHV(W)H frequently appears in translations as LORD, LORD your God, Adonai (the Semitic word for LORD), or GOD. The meaning of the name is connected with the verb "to be" or "to become," most likely in a causative sense, "he who comes to be."

*Zoomorphism* An explicit or implicit comparison of God (or other entities) to the lower animals or parts of the lower animals.

# Notes

**PREFACE**

1   Leland Ryken, "The Bible as Literature: A Brief History," in *A Complete Literary Guide to the Bible*, ed. Leland Ryken and Tremper Longman III (Grand Rapids, MI: Zondervan, 1993), 65, 66. Ryken says that viewing the Bible as literature is not new but that obstacles to doing so include the practices of comparing it to familiar classical literature and of viewing it as unique and unlike any other literature. He encourages readers first to accept that the Bible meets the ordinary definition of literature and that a prerequisite to understanding it is talking about form and technique. Part I of this text succinctly reviews developments since the 1970s that have guided what it means to study the Bible as literature, and what, in fact, builds the theoretical basis for a textbook such as this.

2   Chaim Potock, "The Novelist and the Bible," in Ryken and Longman, eds, *A Complete Literary Guide*, 495.

3   Northrop Frye, *Words with Power: Being a Second Study of "The Bible and Literature"* (San Diego: Harcourt Brace Jovanovich, 1990), xiii, describes the central structural principles of literature as deriving from myth, giving it "its communicating power across the centuries" and a "continuity of form that points to an identity of the literary organism."

**CHAPTER 1 READING THE BIBLE AS LITERATURE**

1   David Dewey, *A User's Guide to Bible Translations: Making the Most of Different Versions* (Downers Grove, IL: InterVarsity Press, 2004), 204, provides a useful overview of versions of the Bible.

2   Marc Zvi Brettler, *How to Read the Bible* (Philadelphia: Jewish Publication Society, 2005), 1–12, makes the point that academic scholars "generally prefer not to take sides in the debate as to which covenant with God is in force."

3   Patrick Alexander et al., eds, *The SBL Handbook of Style: For Ancient Near Eastern Biblical and Early Christian Studies* (Peabody, MA: Hendrickson, 1999), 17, suggest that authors be "aware of the connotations of alternative expressions such as . . . Hebrew Bible [and] Old Testament" and use them without prescribing the use of either.

   Walter Brueggemann, *An Introduction to the Old Testament: The Canon and Christian Imagination* (Louisville, KY: John Knox Press, 2003), 2, says the church has always found the two collections close and intimate, that the Christian faith "is both continuous and discontinuous from it [Old Testament], and that the matter admits of no easy articulation."

   Frank McConnell, ed., *The Bible and the Narrative Tradition* (New York: Oxford University Press, 1991) (Questia, www.questia.com/read/34320683?title=The%20Bible%20and%20the%20Narrative%20Tradition, 6), quotes Frank Kermode's *The Genesis of Secrecy* to say "that only once in the history of culture has a book had its entire meaning altered simply by renaming it, . . . to be specific, the 'Old Testament.'"

4   L. Michael White, *From Jesus to Christianity: How Four Generations of Visionaries & Storytellers Created the Old Testament and Christian Faith* (San Francisco:

HarperSanFrancisco, 2004), 445, 457, and 394, explains how the Scriptures were assembled.

5 David Norton, *A History of the Bible as Literature: From 1700 to the Present Day*, vol. 2 (Cambridge: Cambridge University Press, 1993), 392, quotes Robert Alter, co-editor with Frank Kermode of *The Literary Guide to the Bible*, from *The Art of Biblical Narrative* about the difficulty of setting the two bodies of ancient literature comfortably in the same critical framework.

  Gabriele Boccaccini, *Roots of Rabbinic Judaism: An Intellectual History from Ezekiel to Daniel* (Grand Rapids, MI: William B. Eerdmans, 2002), 28–9, states that the major obstacle to the study of ancient Jewish thought stems "from denominationally determined corpora, or canons (the Hebrew Bible or Old Testament, the New Testament, the Apocrypha and Pseudepigrapha, the Dead Sea Scrolls, etc.)." Boccaccini insists scholarly study now requires looking at Christian and Jewish sources in relation to each other.

  Marshall D. Johnson, *Making Sense of the Bible: Literary Type as an Approach to Understanding* (Grand Rapids, MI: William B. Eerdmans, 2002), 2, believes contemporary non-experts can learn "to appreciate much of what the ancient writers were about."

6 Brueggemann, *Introduction to the Old Testament*, 2, cautions readers to keep in mind "how far and in what ways we may read with Jews, and in what ways we read in different directions and apart from Jews."

7 Boccaccini, *Roots of Rabbinic Judaism*, 4, understands Christian and Jewish traditions as advancing the theological model of "one Judaism" that has impeded critical scholarship. He says study requires looking at Christian and Jewish sources in relation to each other.

8 J. H. Gardiner, *The Bible as English Literature* (New York: Charles Scribner's Sons, 1906), 3, insists that Christianity is deeply rooted in the religion of Israel; the same earnestness runs throughout; its story is that of a chosen people and the fulfillment of promise, and it presents throughout a God of justice.

9 Brettler, *How to Read the Bible*, 29, says chapter divisions first appeared in the Vulgate – thus relatively recently.

10 Norton, *History of the Bible*, 401, 436, laments the standard (KJV, 1611) that creates a classic "perpetually and inescapably encountered by all of us."

11 Everett Fox, *The Five Books of Moses* (New York: Schocken, 1983), xii.

  Robert Alter, *Genesis: Translation and Commentary* (New York: W. W. Norton, 1996), notes that returning readers to the original Hebrew language can reduce readability.

12 Ibid., 183, 186.

13 Mart Väljataga, "Why Study Literature," *Eurozine*, 15 August 2008 (www.euro-zine.com/articles/2005-10-05-valjataga-en.html), explains that literary studies justify themselves as a science as a practical matter of jobs and money.

14 Leland Ryken and Philip Graham Ryken, in their preface to the Literary Study Bible, English standard version (Wheaton, IL: Crossway, 2007), focus the literary study of the Bible on genres, subject matter (human experience itself), archetypes and motifs, stylistics and rhetoric, and artistry.

15 Richard Elliott Friedman, *Who Wrote the Bible?* (San Francisco: HarperSanFrancisco, 1997), 15, begins his discussion by extolling the impact the Bible has made, making note of religious, moral, literary, and historical approaches, while pointing to the obvious fact that readers do not have easily available the traditional approach of asking about the author and the author's life.

  Bart D. Ehrman, *Lost Christianities: The Battles for Scripture and the Faiths We Never Knew* (New York: Oxford University Press, 2003), 249, describes the New Testament canon as "the victory of the proto-orthodox" and wonders what would have happened if another group had won.

Norton, *History of the Bible*, 271, provides an excellent academic discussion of the many tensions that have surrounded reading the Bible, noting that approaching it as a literary work became strong in the eighteenth century.

16  Thomas L. Thompson, *The Mythic Past: Biblical Archaeology and the Myth of Israel* (New York: Basic Books, 1999), 29, talks about Israel as playing a role within a morality story.

Northrope Frye, *Words with Power: Being a Second Study of "The Bible and Literature"* (San Diego: Harcourt Brace Jovanovich, 1990), xiv–xv, 99, says that, although the Bible is "written in the literature of myth and metaphor" and may be described as "a work of literature plus," calling it by a post-biblical term would be "an abuse of language."

17  James L. Kugel, *How to Read the Bible: A Guide to Scripture Then and Now* (New York: Free Press, 2007), 685, describes "Scripture [in Judaism] as the beginning of a manual entitled *To Serve God*."

18  Norton, *History of the Bible*, 378, 385, 380, states that Robert Alter's *The Art of Biblical Narrative* (New York: Basic Books, 1981) accommodates belief and engages discussion of what in the Bible is "historicized fiction" and "fictionalized history."

19  Kenneth R. R. Gros Louis and Willard Van Antwerpen, "Joshua and Judges," in Leland Ryken and Tremper Longman III, eds, *A Complete Literary Guide to the Bible* (Grand Rapids, MI: Zondervan, 1993), 138, advance the revelatory nature of the Bible as asking the "largest of human questions" and presenting "embodied human experience."

Charles Allen Dinsmore, *The English Bible as Literature* (Boston: Houghton Mifflin, 1931) (Questia, www.questia.com/read/24729938?title=The%20English%20Bible%20as%20Literature, v), describes the Bible as giving us human experience with all its emotions – love, hate, revenge, thirst for God – "these are permanent, and upon these unchanging feelings the enduring literature rears its stately structure."

20  Norton, *History of the Bible*, 262–7, looks at the nineteenth-century school Bible-reading agenda as contrasting religious and secular literature.

21  John B. Gabel, Charles B. Wheeler, and Anthony D. York, eds, *The Bible as Literature: An Introduction* (New York: Oxford University Press, 1990), 1, regard the Bible as a product of the human mind, a collection of writings produced by real people who lived in actual historical times.

Norton, *History of the Bible*, 272, 407, says "the book contains almost nothing of what ought to be basic to a literary discussion of the Bible," faults it as engaging in a "tiptoeing neutrality," and points out that NKJV has not been "designed to be read as literature, introducing the possibility that the common, religious reader will still prefer sacred text to literature and that publishers provide what sells."

22  Leland Ryken and Tremper Longman III, "Introduction," in *A Complete Literary Guide to the Bible*, 24, quote John Reichert in urging readers to cut through esoteric terms prevalent in approaches to reading the Bible and return to simple procedures.

F. J. P. Fokkelman, *Reading Biblical Narrative: An Introductory Guide*, trans. Ineke Smit (Louisville, KY: Westminster John Knox Press, 1999 [originally pubd as *Vertelkunst in de bijbel: een handleiding bij literair lezen*, Zoetermeer: Boekencentrum, 1995]), 207–9, recommends "grasping the overall shape of a text and in reading from within." He quotes an old rule: "The whole is more than the sum of its parts."

23  Norton, *History of the Bible*, 274, explains that keeping the Bible before the learner as a whole may present "too much to grasp" and makes "the fruitful use of the Bible [he has in mind the King James Version], as literature, . . . almost impossible."

Frye, *Words with Power*, xvi, xvii, 101–2, repeats the point several times that "Coherence is a preliminary intuition or assumption about criticism . . ., a heuristic assumption . . .," remarking that criticism, while different from litera-ture, equally requires creativity and performs the important work of "defining and opening the boundaries of literature." Frye identifies the mythical and metaphorical also from the primary language of criticism.

24 Kugel, *How to Read the Bible*, 686, describes a shift in the way readers read the Bible – from learning from the Bible to learning about it.

25 Leland Ryken, "The Bible as Literature: A Brief History," in *A Complete Literary Guide*, 61–5, remarks that "Most current literary [as opposed to traditional] criticism presupposes an audience whose interest in the Bible is academic rather than religious." This contrasts to Mary Ellen Chase, who called for the Bible to be made accessible to the common reader.

Johnson, *Making Sense of the Bible*, 2, 142, describes fresh reading as reading "with the intent of discovering at least something of the thought-world and mind of the writer."

Fokkelman, *Reading Biblical Narrative*, 206, defines reading as active puzzle-solving.

26 David M. Gunn and Danna Noland Fewell, *Narrative in the Hebrew Bible* (New York: Oxford University Press, 1993), 19, point to a way of reading that finds multivalent and contextual meanings "inescapably bound up with their interpreters."

Frye, *Words with Power*, 75, explains reading as an act that requires readers to go beyond the piece of literature confronting them, to go beyond the object, and also to study the act of reading.

Johnson, *Making Sense of the Bible*, 24–5, explains that the act of reading requires at least two levels of meaning: the text that contains meaning and the reader who understands meaning.

27 Friedman, *Who Wrote the Bible?*, 241, notes that we have, in a sense, come full circle, back to dealing with the Bible as a whole.

28 Thompson, *Mythic Past*, 31, describes the Bible as "survival literature," explaining that people in the Hellenistic period understood themselves as the "children of Israel," a surviving remnant from old Israel, or as a resurrected or reborn Israel.

29 Norton, *History of the Bible*, 393, states "There is, in short, arbitrariness or an act of faith involved in any conception of the Bible as a unity."

Notes in the New Interpreter's Study Bible, 2261, illustrate how knowl-edge of the Hebrew Scriptures is critical to making New Testament writings intelligible.

McConnell, *The Bible and the Narrative Tradition* (Questia, 8), says, "'Intertextuality' is a phrase much bandied – or shuttlecocked – among critics with a yen for the fashionable these days. Like most such phrases it is not only phonetically ugly but, semantically, virtually null."

30 Leland Ryken, "The Literary Impulse," in *A Complete Literary Guide*, 362–5, acknowledges the Bible as "unique" but makes the point that it impacts and affects readers existentially, as does other literature.

31 Kugel, *How to Read the Bible*, distinguishes typology from allegory, explaining that typology works on the horizontal level to see people and events of the Old Testament as foreshadowings or types of people in the New Testament; allegory works on the vertical level, moving from the concrete to the abstract.

32 Thompson, *Mythic Past*, 57, counters the traditional notion of prophets as messengers, understanding them rather to function as catalysts to a hardening of hearts and an ultimate rejection of the Torah.

33 Gabel, Wheeler, and York, *The Bible as Literature*, 158, consider God's breaking into history the distinguishing feature of apocalyptic literature, as contrasted to prophecy, with its concern with "this world" and "with real offenses committed against real people and with obvious violations of time-honored principles of religion and right conduct."

34  Stephen B. Chapman, *The Law and the Prophets: A Study in the Old Testament Canon Formation* (Tübingen: Mohr Siebeck, 2000), 276, insists that "the initial placement of the Torah in the canon has more to do with 'story' rather than 'status.'"

35  Boccaccini, *Roots of Rabbinic Judaism*, 2, describes the "so-called Christian fulfillment . . . [as] estrangement, if not treachery and betrayal."

36  Gunn and Fewell, *Narrative in the Hebrew Bible*, 29, suggest a way of reading the Bible that places a large narrative (Genesis to 2 Kings) into the context of the larger Hebrew Bible.
    Marcus J. Borg, *Meeting Jesus Again for the First Time* (San Francisco: HarperSanFrancisco, 1994), 123, finds "three macro-stories at the heart of Scripture that shape the Bible as a whole": the story of Exodus, the story of the exile and return from Babylon, and the Priestly story, "grounded not in the history of ancient Israel but an institution – namely, the temple, priesthood, and sacrifice."

37  Fokkelman, *Reading Biblical Narrative*, 162, demonstrates how structurally Genesis uses toledoth to organize the book as generations or early history.

38  Marcus J. Borg and N. T. Wright, *The Meaning of Jesus: Two Visions* (San Francisco: HarperSanFrancisco, 1999), 10, depict this view as reducing reality "to the space–time world of matter and energy, thereby making the notion of God problematic and doubtful."

39  Ibid., 61, describes the mystical state as "a sense of descending (or ascending) beyond the ordinary level of the self to a level where one experiences communion or union with God."

40  Ibid., "Images of Jesus," 139.

41  Ibid., 149.

42  Ibid., 183.

43  Ibid., 74–5.

44  Frye, *Words with Power*, xvi, xvii, 101–2.
    Marcus J. Borg and John Dominic Crossan, *The First Paul: Reclaiming the Radical Visionary behind the Church's Conservative Icon* (New York: HarperOne, 2009), 21, describe enlightenment "as a transformed way of seeing," a "moving from darkness to light, from blindness to sight, from sleeping to being awake."

45  Borg and Wright, *The Meaning of Jesus*, 260.

46  The "Introduction" to the HarperCollins Study Bible, xxiii, says that, "Despite the Bible's diversity, most readers do feel that as a whole it somehow makes sense."
    Alter, *Genesis*, xl, counsels that "the biblical conception of a book was clearly far more open-ended than any notion current in our own culture" and that readers essentially should bracket the modern sense of "book."

47  Ryken and Longman, "Introduction," in *A Complete Literary Guide*, 35, have gained distinction for taking readers through the various literary forms of the Bible; they describe it as containing narrative unity in a loosely chronological arrangement.

48  N. T. Wright, "How Can the Bible Be Authoritative?" *Vox Evangelica*, 21 (1991), 7–32.

49  Gunn and Fewell, *Narrative in the Hebrew Bible*, 2, distinguish the broader term "story" from "narrative" and say that defining narrative in terms of character, plot, and word-play is a preliminary step in the exploration of stories.

50  Thompson, *Mythic Past*, 18: "Being like God, and obedience hardly a divine virtue, nothing less could be expected."

51  Thompson, ibid., 30, says: "We do not have an origin tradition that closes with a sense of belonging . . . That Israel never came to be."

52  David Leeming, *The Oxford Companion to World Mythology* (New York: Oxford University Press, 2005), presents an alphabetized list of mythical characters, including biblical representation.

53 Frye, *Words with Power*, 5–12, xv, identifies the verbal modes as descriptive (perceptions, facts, experience), logical (concepts, dialectical opposites), rhetorical (persuasion, convention, and ideology), and poetic (metaphorical and mythical), explaining that modern thinking has favored descriptive, logical, and rhetorical modes even though mythology preceded them.

54 Robert Alter and Frank Kermode, *The Literary Guide to the Bible* (Cambridge, MA: Belknap Press, 1987), 2–3, remark that the Bible "is probably the most important single source of all our literature," but that its neglect in secularized times has led to a general ignorance that impoverishes the study of literature itself.

55 Edgar Whitaker Work, *The Bible in English Literature* (London and Edinburgh: Fleming H. Revell, 1917), 33, says the Bible has "sharpened and determined the very genius of the English-speaking peoples."

56 Alter and Kermode, *The Literary Guide to the Bible*, 5, recognize "an urgent need to try to learn how to read the Bible again."

57 Leland Ryken, "The Literary Influence of the Bible," in *A Complete Literary Guide*, 473–88, 485, concludes, "Usually the story of biblical influence on literature has resembled the history of Western literature itself."

58 Leland Ryken, *How to Read the Bible as Literature . . . and Get More out of It* (Grand Rapids, MI: Zondervan, 1984), 11–31, explains the literary approach as looking at imaginative literature or creative writing, admitting that the Bible is a mixed book containing both literary and non-literary writing.

59 Leland Ryken, James C. Wilhoit, and Tremper Longman III, *The Dictionary of Biblical Imagery* (Downers Grove, IL: InterVarsity Press, 1998), xiv, xxi.

60 Ryken, *How to Read the Bible*, 15.

61 Ryken, Wilhoit, and Longman, *Dictionary of Biblical Imagery*, xiii.
   Frye, *Words with Power*, xv, argues that "the beginning of the response to the Bible must be a literary response."
   Borg and Wright, *The Meaning of Jesus*, 5, point out that, "though metaphorical language is not literally true, it can be powerfully true in a nonliteral sense."

62 Ryken, *How to Read the Bible*, 21, explains that "literature conveys a sense of life – a sense of how the writer thinks and feels about what really exists, what is right and wrong, what is valuable and worthless."

63 Ibid., 11, 30, makes the point that the focus of literature must always be on finished wholes rather than "a patchwork of fragments."

64 Ryken, Wilhoit, and Longman, *Dictionary of Biblical Imagery*, xiii, quote H. Richard Niebuhr: "We are far more image-making and image-using creatures than we usually think ourselves to be and . . . are guided and formed by images in our minds."

65 Bruce M. Metzer and Michael Coogan, *The Oxford Companion to the Bible* (New York: Oxford University Press, 1993), 516, defines the ultimate goal of human life as being "to conform to the image of God."

66 Thomas Cahill, *The Gifts of the Jews: How a Tribe of Desert Nomads Changed the Way Everyone Thinks and Feels* (New York: Nan A. Talese/Anchor Books, 1998), 47–50, says metaphor, founded on correspondence, forms the basis of language and poetry, and that "the need for correspondence derives from the human urge to perceive itself as belonging to the cosmos."

67 The New Testament generally uses a Deuteronomic theology emphasizing covenant (internal) and a deliverer (Christ).

68 Metzer and Coogan, *Oxford Companion to the Bible*, 515, 516, state that the unknown must be expressed in terms of the known: "the language about God must be figurative."

69 Ibid., 403.

70 Ryken and Longman, "Introduction," in *A Complete Literary Guide*, 59, describe 1900–75 as a time when two traditions – the teaching of the Bible in college

literature courses and the work of liberal scholarship – converged to produce the current interest in the Bible as literature.

Frye, *Words with Power*, 100–3, 139, says "the concept of 'literature' is really post-Biblical, even if much of what we now call literature is earlier."

71  Gabel, Wheeler, and York, *The Bible as Literature*, 12–13, distinguish between the literature of the Bible and the Bible as literature. They argue that the literature of the Bible approach fails to account for the usefulness of the extracted narratives for religion and, while "recognizing the literary status and characteristics of individual portions of the Bible, denies this recognition to the Bible as a whole." Norton, *History of the Bible*, 162.

72  Ryken, "The Bible as Literature: A Brief History," in *A Complete Literary Guide*, provides specimen titles: *The English Bible, Being a Book of Selections from the King James Version* (ed. Wilbur O. Sypherd, 1923); *The Bible Designed to be Read as Living Literature* (ed. Ernest S. Bates, 1936); *The Bible for Students of Literature and Art* (ed. G. B. Harrison, 1964); and *The Bible: Selections from the King James Version for Study as Literature* (ed. Roland M. Frye, 1965).

73  Cullen Schippe and Chuck Stetson, eds, *The Bible and its Influence* (New York: Bible Literacy Project, 2006), offer a textbook designed as "secularly acceptable" for use in public schools (now in use in thirty) and describe it as representing both the Bible in literature – the way later writers have used the Bible – and the Bible as literature – addressing aesthetic categories, the broad genres of narrative and poetry, the use of language, symbolism, and motifs. See www.bibleliteracy.org/Site/Case/index.htm (accessed 22 May 2007).

74  David Damrosch, *The Narrative Covenant: Transformations of Genre in the Growth of Biblical Literature* (Ithaca, NY: Cornell University Press, 1987), 5, argues that the "difficulty of dealing with textual history leads in one of two directions. A critic can ignore the history of the text altogether and carry out close readings and structural analyses of the overall text without reference to its complex compositional history . . . Or the critic can bow before history in silence, confining the analysis to some small, discrete unit, preferably one with an uncomplicated compositional background."

75  James Kugel, "Appendix 1: Apologetics and Biblical Criticism," www.jameskugel. com/read.php, 18–24, remarks that "Apologetics have also tinged another modern method of analyzing Scripture, today's 'literary' approach to biblical texts. Unbeknownst to some of its current practitioners, this approach actually has deep roots, going back to antiquity and various early Christian thinkers" (accessed 4 February 2008).

76  Norton, *History of the Bible*, 262–7, regards the use of the "long history of Bible reading in schools as consistently an attempt to take pupils across this line [secular and sectarian]." Norton summarizes a 1963 Supreme Court decision as supporting the Bible in schools only if it is approached as something other than religion; he calls this "encouragement to camouflage, noting that Gabel, Wheeler, and York, in *The Bible as Literature*, follow this approach, since they do not present commentary, impose an interpretive scheme, or advocate moral instruction; rather they present the Bible as a "fascinating human document."

Phyllis Trimble, in the New Interpreter's Study Bible, New Revised Standard Version with Apocrypha (Nashville: Abingdon Press, 2003), 2248, says that "Traditionally the phrase [Word of God] has meant that the Bible is the word of God . . .. For some believers, this idea assumed literal form."

77  Leland Ryken, "The Literary Influence of the Bible," in *A Complete Literary Guide*, 473, remarks on this relationship between the Bible and Western literature and says: "No sharp distinction can be made between the Bible as literature and the Bible in literature: our acquaintance with imaginative literature influences how we talk about the Bible as literature, and the Bible itself has influenced Western literature since the Middle Ages."

78  Friedman, *Who Wrote the Bible?*, 16.

Fokkelman, *Reading Biblical Narrative*, 21, 25, 27, criticizes the threefold alienation of the reader from the Bible that comes from the historical-critical school.

79 Norton, *History of the Bible*, 272, 276.

80 Richard G. Moulton, *The Literary Study of the Bible: An Account of the Leading Forms of Literature Represented in the Sacred Writings Intended for English Readers* (Boston: Heath, 1909), xii.

81 Ryken, *How to Read the Bible*, 11, 29. Ryken defines "the growing awareness that the Bible is a work of literature" as "a quiet revolution going on in the study of the Bible."
Friedman, *Who Wrote the Bible?*, 215, in talking about historical and literary approaches, makes the important point that the writers of the Bible had no words for history or literature and that, to them, it represented a book.

82 *Church Symbolism: An Explanation of the More Important Symbols of the Old and New Testament, the Primitive, the Mediaeval and the Modern Church*, 2nd edn (Cleveland: J. H. Jansen, 1938).

83 This text includes an essay by Leland Ryken, "The Bible as Literature: A Brief History," which explores several approaches.

84 Norton, *History of the Bible*, Vol. 1, 1x, begins by quoting the minor poet and critic John Husbands (1706–32): "Yet how beautiful do the holy writings appear, under all the disadvantages of an old prose translation?" Norton interprets Husbands's remark as identifying three disadvantages: (1) it is old; (2) it is prose; and (3) it is a translation. The New Revised Standard Version refers to the King James Bible, the noblest monument of English prose that has contributed more than any other single book to the "making of the personal character and the public institutions of the English-speaking people. We owe it an incalculable debt." Norton concludes that "no translation will become what the KJB has been to the English-speaking world."

85 Ryken and Longman, *A Complete Literary Guide*, 65.

86 Stephen L. Harris, *Understanding the Bible*, 5th edn (Mountain View, CA: Mayfield, 2000).

87 *From Adam to Armageddon*, 4th edn (Belmont, CA: Wadsworth, 1994).

88 Ryken and Longman, *A Complete Literary Guide*, 15–39.

89 Gabel, Wheeler, and York, *The Bible as Literature*, 10, warn that the holistic approach to the Bible as a unified and homogeneous work forces readers "to ignore what is known about its origin and composition but also to explain away a host of textual problems – duplications of material, omissions, interpolations, contradictions – that are most sensibly accounted for as the result of multiple authorship over a long period of time."

90 Ryken and Longman, *A Complete Literary Guide*, 59.

91 Norton, *History of the Bible*, 391, calls these discussions of large-scale unity "expressions of belief," arguing that it makes a difference what books are read and in which order. One attempt to discover such large-scale unity is Gabriel Josipovici's *The Book of God* (New Haven, CT: Yale University Press, 1988). Fokkelman, in *Reading Biblical Narrative*, 188–205, makes a case for finding unity and coherence between the Old and New Testaments.

92 Northrop Frye, *The Great Code: The Bible and Literature* (San Diego: Harcourt Brace Jovanovich, 1983), presents the Bible as redeeming history with a visionary poetic perspective held together by myth, metaphor, and thematic units.
Michael Dolzani, in his edition of Frye's *Words with Power* (Toronto: University of Toronto Press, 2008), xxi, describes the Bible as telling a story from creation to apocalypse, "a single pattern of meaning expressed in a cluster of metaphorical images."

93 Paul J. Achtemeier, ed., with the Society of Biblical Literature, *The HarperCollins Bible Dictionary*, rev. edn (San Francisco: HarperSanFrancisco, 1996) provides a glossary of critical approaches to the study of the Bible.

94  It should be noted that "**lower criticism**" or "textual criticism" has taken on a much broader context than the methodology that selects, after examination of all available material, the most trustworthy evidence on which to base a text or the attempt to eliminate the errors which are found even in the best manuscripts.

Gabel, Wheeler, and York, *The Bible as Literature*, 14, identify themselves as representing higher criticism.

Brettler, *How to Read the Bible*, 3, explains that "historical" refers "to the view that the main context for interpretation is the place and time in which the text was composed" and that "'critical' simply means reading the text independently of religious norms or interpretative traditions – as opposed to accepting them uncritically."

Damrosch, *The Narrative Covenant*, discusses the complex "quest for history in textual analysis" in his first chapter, faulting the historical-critical method as "dealing the last blow to any hopes for . . . literary history."

95  John R. Donahue, in the New Interpreter's Study Bible, 2261, 2264, points out that "Biblical criticism as we know it today is a 19th century child of the Enlightenment."

96  John Barton and John Muddiman, eds, *The Oxford Bible Commentary* (New York: Oxford University Press, 2000), 1–4, provide a succinct overview of approaches to biblical criticism.

Gunn and Fewell, *Narrative in the Hebrew Bible*, 2, after distinguishing the broader term "story" from "narrative," go on to suggest strategies for reading and finding meaning in texts.

97  James Barr, *Holy Scripture: Canon, Authority, Criticism* (Oxford: Clarendon Press, 1983), makes the important point that "the world within the Bible is very different from the world as perceived when the Bible, already formed and demarcated, is taken as a unitary body of material uniquely authoritative as controlling criterion for faith."

98  Borg and Crossan, *The First Paul*, 13, describe a traditional way of reading the Bible that sees it "unlike other books . . . inerrant and infallible," and suggest the alternative of seeing it as "a historical product."

Bart D. Ehrman, *Jesus Interrupted: Revealing the Hidden Contradictions in the Bible (and Why We Don't Know about Them)* (New York: HarperOne, 2009), 4, describes the "historical-critical approach" as asking about original historical context, authorship, circumstances under which the Bible texts were written and issues addressed, how authors were affected by historical and cultural assumptions, what sources they used and when these were produced, differences in perspective, and meaning in original context.

99  Gunn and Fewell, *Narrative in the Hebrew Bible*, 7–13, identify these as "crippling disadvantages" that have contributed to a lack of agreement, though they share similarities in approach among the practitioners of historical criticism. They criticize reliance upon a view of truth as external and approached through reason and science with a result of searching for a single, right meaning for a text. They also find fault with the approach for denying the reader's contribution to making meaning.

100  George Aichele, *The Postmodern Bible* (New Haven, CT: Yale University Press, 1995), 1, describes the scientific method as having a "desire for doing away with ambivalence and uncertainty once and for all by effectively isolating the text and its criticism from the reader's cultural context, values, and interests" and effectively turning "the Bible into an historical relic, an antiquarian artifact." *The Postmodern Bible* introduces, illustrates, and critiques seven prominent strategies of reading the Bible, including rhetorical criticism, structuralism and narratology, reader-response criticism, and feminist criticism.

101  Gabel, Wheeler, and York, *The Bible as Literature*, 114–15, become poetic in describing documentary theory as "an immense mountain looming before us, a perpetual source of awe, inspiration, and challenge." They believe that,

digging into it, readers can find "a vivid record of the past," and suggest that the view from the summit is "improved by our knowledge of what had to take place before we could stand there."

Friedman, *Who Wrote the Bible?*, 241, concludes, "The Bible is thus a synthesis of history and literature, sometimes in harmony and sometimes in tension, but utterly inseparable."

Brettler's *How to Read the Bible* advocates a historical-critical approach that requires reading the Bible (Jewish Scriptures) as would an ancient Israelite, including understanding genres and conventions. He demonstrates how reading the Jewish Bible in a historical-critical manner and understanding its proper rules or genres can help readers better understand and appreciate its foundational role in the Jewish faith.

102 Ryken and Longman, *A Complete Literary Guide*, 35. Ryken describes the Bible as being "an amazingly unified book," with much of this achieved through its narrative unity.

103 Norton, *History of the Bible*, 393, remarks that "any conception of the Bible as a unity" comes from arbitrariness of an act of faith, although he concedes that literary and theological continuities exist and identifies typology as one means of presenting this continuity.

Thompson, *Mythic Past*, 1–33, 30, argues against continuity as an arbitrary act of faith, pointing out, rather, that the Bible as we have it came through an interpretive process in successive reiterative histories in which a later tradition supersedes and moves forward a new Israel. He calls this "survival literature."

Friedman, *Who Wrote the Bible?*, 241, demonstrates a remarkable narrative unity in the Bible when it is read as a whole. He says scholarship has often been "a tearing-down without a putting-back-together."

Fokkelman, *Reading Biblical Narrative*, 207, insists "the whole is more than the sum of its parts" and that "grasping the overall shape" of a text enhances readers' understanding.

104 Fokkelman, ibid., uses such a narrative approach, identifying the Old Testament as taken up by two extensive narrative complexes.

Gunn and Fewell, *Narrative in the Hebrew Bible*, organize their book about strategies for reading, narratives and stories, characters and narrators, and the lure of language.

105 Gunn and Fewell, ibid., 12, remark that "The history of the interpretation of biblical narrative is a play of continuity and discontinuity over two millennia."

106 Ibid., 27.

107 Victor H. Matthews, *Manners and Customs in the Bible: An Illustrated Guide to Daily Life in Bible Times*, rev. edn (Peabody, MA: Hendrickson, 1991), xxii. This text provides a very readable summary of the people throughout these periods.

108 The NIV Archaeological Study Bible (Grand Rapids, MI: Zondervan, 2005), 3.

109 Brettler, *How to Read the Bible*, 44–7, summarizes: "The Garden Story is about immortality lost and sexuality gained," and credits this idea to several other scholars.

110 James VanderKam, "Culture and Religion among the Ancient Israelites," in the New Interpreter's Study Bible, 2224–79, provides the material and structure for this discussion.

111 Johnson, *Making Sense of the Bible*, 16, 18, footnotes the "spiritual impasse" idea as attributable to E. A. Speiser (*The Jewish Experience*, 1976). Johnson says that "Abraham's compulsion was religious: he responded to an urge he believed came from a great and all-powerful, ubiquitous God . . . though the monotheistic concept was not fully developed in his mind, he was a man striving towards it."

112 Cahill, *The Gifts of the Jews*, 94, 88, describes Abraham's history as "real history and irreversible, not the early dramatization of a heavenly exemplar" and "an impersonal manipulation by means of ritual prescriptions."

113 Thompson, *Mythic Past*, 32, understands monotheism as evolving from ancient worlds (Persian and Hellenistic) that were "becoming increasingly integrated by the political and economic controls of empire – already at work in the Assyrian period – [leading to] ideas about the gods began to change accordingly." Polytheism, which had its roots in the complexity of life as well as in the many different groups interacting within any single society, began to give way to an increasingly integrated sense of divine power that was transcendent, beyond human understanding, and apart from people as well as peoples.

114 Cahill, *The Gifts of the Jews*, 41, 83.

115 The NIV Archaeological Study Bible, 5, in comparing the ancient creation stories from Mesopotamia, Egypt, and Syria-Palestine, makes the point that the Genesis account presents a universal God, Elohim, more generic than Yahweh, with no need to establish supremacy over other deities, questioning the interpretation of Exodus 6.2–3, which, some argue, supports Yahweh as being known first by Abraham.

116 Paul Johnson, *A History of the Jews* (New York: HarperPerennial, 1988), explains that the Bible mostly makes a theological statement: "an account of the direct, often intimate, relationship between the leaders of the people and God, . . . [presenting] Abraham as the founder of the nation."

117 Harris, *Understanding the Bible*, 76–80, provides these facts about the land and a good overview of the land of Canaan.

## CHAPTER 2 STYLE, TONE, AND RHETORICAL STRATEGY

1 George Lakoff and Mark Johnson, *Philosophy in the Flesh: The Embodied Mind and its Challenge to Western Thought* (New York: Basic Books, 1999), 379, 3, makes a case for a conceptual system in which the mind is embodied, thought is mostly unconscious, and abstract concepts are largely metaphorical.

2 Leland Ryken, in *How to Read the Bible as Literature. . . and Get More Out of It* (Grand Rapids, MI: Zondervan, 1984), makes exactly this point about the amazing unity of the Bible, and Kenneth Barker, in his introduction to *The NIV: The Making of a Contemporary Translation* (Grand Rapids, MI: Academie Books, 1986), 11, remarks how John Donne (*Sermons*, VII, 65) describes God as a poet, expressing the inexpressible in metaphorical and figurative language.

3 E. W. Bullinger, *Figures of Speech Used in the Bible: Explained and Illustrated* (1898; Grand Rapids, MI: Baker Book House, 1968), vi, says that, "in the use of these figures, we have, as it were, the Holy Spirit's own markings of our Bible."

4 Northrop Frye, *Words with Power: Being a Second Study of "The Bible and Literature"* (San Diego: Harcourt Brace Jovanovich, 1990), xiv, understands the Bible, with some exceptions, as being "written in the literary language of myth and metaphor."

5 Bullinger, *Figures of Speech Used in the Bible*, provides the definitive source for figures of speech used in the Bible.

A. E. Knoch, "Introduction," in *Concordant Literal New Testament with Keyword Concordance*, 6th edn (Santa Clarita, CA: Concordant, 1983) (available at www.peterwade.com/articles/other/knoch01.shtml [accessed 20 August 2009]), remarks on the necessity of understanding the literal meaning of a word as well as recognizing when the word is intended to be interpreted figuratively.

6 Barker, *The NIV*, 9, calls the question of why we can't have a direct translation of the original "naïve because literary style intricately permeates the Bible, as it does all literature."

7 Robert Alter, "To the Reader," in *Genesis: Translation and Commentary* (New York: W. W. Norton, 1996), xii–xlvii, identifies concreteness and parataxis as distinguishing features of biblical writing and describes the use of language as "deliberately limited" and "nuanced.".

8 J. P. Fokkelman, *Reading Biblical Narrative: An Introductory Guide*, trans. Ineke Smit (Louisville, KY: Westminster John Knox Press, 1999), 156.

9  Figures taken from Knoch, "Introduction."

10  Bullinger, *Figures of Speech Used in the Bible*, 375, writes that "the simile gently states that one thing is like or resembles another" and that metaphor "boldly and warmly declares that one thing IS the other."

11  Knoch, "Introduction," remarks on "the vast importance of figures of speech in interpretation," pointing out that "In the Reformation a single metaphor, 'this is My body,' led to conflicts and divisions which would never have arisen if there had been even an elementary knowledge of figurative language."

    Calvin, *Institutes*, IV, 10, vii, 20–2, boils the dispute down to taking a figurative (versus literalist) approach.

12  Bullinger, *Figures of Speech Used in the Bible*, 736, says that to mistake metaphor, "representation," as simile, or "resembles," leads to a mistake in interpreting "This is my body" (Matt. 26.26).

13  Rachel Strasser, "An Anomalous Genesis: Metaphor and Implication in the Creation of the Golem," www.csua.berkeley.edu/~ether/thesistext.html (accessed 10 March 2007), suggests that the metaphorical structures in Genesis "indicate an imperfect reflex, a broken mirroring of the act of Creation."

14  Such conceptions as light and darkness, life and death, high and low, are freely used as figures. Marcus J. Borg and N. T. Wright, *The Meaning of Jesus: Two Visions* (San Francisco: HarperSanFrancisco, 1999), 5, define metaphor broadly "to include symbol and story," pointing out that metaphor, while "not literally true . . . can be powerfully true in a nonliteral sense."

15  Knoch, "Introduction," says, "The point to press in figures of likeness is that they depend upon unlikeness."

16  Jack Miles, *God: A Biography* (New York: Alfred A. Knopf, 1995), 4, 5, says that God has come alive as a character in the way that no other character has – whether on stage, page, or screen; everyone has heard of God, and everyone can tell you something about God.

17  Zvi Brettler, *How to Read the Bible* (Philadelphia: Jewish Publication Society, 2005), 45, demonstrates the disastrous result that would come from immortal human beings who were also procreative.

18  Bullinger, *Figures of Speech Used in the Bible*, 779, insists that the "Holy Spirit quotes in the New Testament those Scriptures which He had before inspired in the Old" and calls for "regard to the great and important fact that the Bible has only one author, and that 'Holy men of God spake as they were moved by the Holy Ghost' (2 Peter 1.21)."

    Frye, *Words with Power*, 139, provides another way of talking about the New Testament when he suggests that it expresses the realities for which the Old Testament provided the types. He qualifies this by remarking that both books are mythological in expressing spiritual understanding.

19  Bullinger, *Figures of Speech Used in the Bible*, 782, makes the case that the Holy Spirit, as the author of the Bible, does what "any and every human writer may do . . . constantly repeat, refer to, and quote what they have previously written and spoken."

20  Leland Ryken (quoting Austin Farrer), "Revelation," in Leland Ryken and Tremper Longman III, eds, *A Complete Literary Guide to the Bible* (Grand Rapids, MI: Zondervan, 1993), 465.

21  Ryken and Longman, *A Complete Literary Guide*, 7.

    Marcus J. Borg, *Meeting Jesus Again for the First Time: The Historical Jesus and the Heart of Contemporary Faith* (New York: HarperCollins, 1994), finds a coherence in the three main stories that shine through the Bible as a whole: the Exodus story, the story of the exile and return, and the Priestly story.

    Robert Alter, "Putting Together Biblical Narrative" (Berkeley: University of California, Department of Classics, 1990), http://repositories.cdlib.org/cgi/viewcontent.cgi?article=1009&context=ucbclassics (accessed 10 August 2009), remarks on the pervasiveness of allusion in the Bible and calls it "an indispensable mechanism of all literature."

22 Alter, ibid. describes allusion as the "indispensable mechanism of all literature" and says that the Bible demonstrates "remarkable density of such allusion," describing the power of this technique as the "activation of one text by another." The examples in the next immediate paragraphs come from Alter.

23 Introduction to the New Oxford Annotated Bible, 316.

24 L. Michael White, *From Jesus to Christianity: How Four Generations of Visionaries & Storytellers Created the Old Testament and Christian Faith* (San Francisco: HarperSanFrancisco, 2004), 323.

25 Robert Alter, *The Art of Biblical Narrative* (New York: Basic Books, 1992), 95–100, says the Bible has two sets of questions: one asked by the limited creature, relentlessly drilling in on suffering, and another asked by God, affirming the splendor and vastness of life.

26 Bullinger, *Figures of Speech Used in the Bible*, 808, calls this a "Divine Sarcasm on all scientists who profess to understand and tell us all about the earth, its size, and its shape, and its weight, etc., etc."

27 According to Bullinger, ibid., 405, amplifications are "not superfluous when used by the Holy Spirit, nor are they idle or useless."

28 The New Oxford Annotated Bible, 335.

29 David M. Gunn and Danna Noland Fewell, *Narrative in the Hebrew Bible* (New York: Oxford University Press, 1993), 157–8.

30 Leland Ryken, "Revelation," in *A Complete Literary Guide*, 467.

31 John H. Sailhamer, "Genesis," in *A Complete Literary Guide*, 117, calls this "narrative typology," a technique whereby the author shows that the events of the past are pointers to those of the future.

32 Robert Alter, *The Art of Biblical Narrative*, 62, concludes that much of the art of the Bible lies "in the shifting aperture between the shadowy foreimage in the anticipating mind of the observer and the realized revelatory image in the work itself."

33 Tremper Longman III, *How to Read the Psalms* (Downers Grove, IL: InterVarsity Press, 1988), 107.

34 Brettler, *How to Read the Bible*, 32–4.

35 David L. Ulansey, "The Heavenly Veil 'Inclusion,'" *Journal of Biblical Literature*, 110/1 (1991), 123–5, identifies a cluster of motifs at the baptism and death of Jesus: tearing of the veil, a voice heard from heaven, a descending, the presence of Elijah, and the presence of the spirit.

36 Watson E. Mills and Roger Aubry Bullard, *Mercer Dictionary of the Bible*, 3rd edn (Macon, GA: Mercer University Press, 1998), 41.

37 Tremper Longman III, "The Literature of the Old Testament," in *A Complete Literary Guide*, 99, provides a chiasm from J. P. Fokkelman's *Narrative Art in Genesis*.

38 David Miller, "The Bible as Metaphor," *Touchstone*, 58/6 (2003), http://www.touchstonemag.com/archives/article.php?id=15-10-019-v, describes John Spong, author of *Rescuing the Bible from Fundamentalism*, writing that "Jesus was a man 'alive, totally alive, and in that vibrant vital life God was experienced.' (But not alive any more, of course, except in the minds of people who are totally alive, etc.)"

## CHAPTER 3 IMAGE, METAPHOR, SYMBOL, AND ARCHETYPE

1 Northrop Frye, *Words with Power: Being a Second Study of "The Bible and Literature,"* ed. Michael Dolzani (Toronto: University of Toronto Press, 2008), xxiii, introduces a sequence of five modes of language: fact and evidence; logic and demonstration; social belief and values; language of the imagination; and the revelation.

2 Frye, *Words with Power* (San Diego: Harcourt Brace Jovanovich, 1990), xiii, devotes a good deal of attention to the connections between literature and religion.

3 Leland Ryken and Philip Graham Ryken, in their preface to the Literary Study Bible, English standard version (Wheaton, IL: Crossway, 2007), describe the meaning of the Bible as conveyed through form and genres.

4 Leland Ryken, James C. Wilhoit, and Tremper Longman III, eds, *The Dictionary of Biblical Imagery* (Downers Grove, IL: InterVarsity Press, 1998), xiii–xvii, define and provide the examples of image, metaphor, symbol, and archetype immediately following.

5 Leland Ryken and Tremper Longman III, eds, *A Complete Literary Guide to the Bible* (Grand Rapids, MI: Zondervan, 1993), 37, describe archetype (master image) as falling into three categories: plot motif (e.g. quest, initiation, rescue), character types (e.g. hero, villain, tempter), and images (e.g. light, darkness, mountaintops).

6 George Lakoff and Mark Johnson, *Philosophy in the Flesh: The Embodied Mind and its Challenge to Western Thought* (New York: Basic Books, 1999),77, question this common-sense notion of the world. They argue for "the centrality of conceptualization and reason of imaginative processes, especially metaphor, imagery, metonymy, prototype, frames, mental spaces, and radical categories."

7 Frye, *Words with Power*, xiii.

8 Ryken, Wilhoit, and Longman, *Dictionary of Biblical Imagery*, 512.

Frye, *Words with Power*, xx, 155, 23, describes the canonical unity of the Bible present in themes of ascent and descent (stairs, mountains, and trees). He points to Jacob's vision of angels descending and ascending, the prophecy of Jesus (John 1.51), involving the heavens opened and the angels of God ascending and descending, and the Incarnation as "the descent of the Word in flesh." Species of myth can be identified as the biblical creation, fall, exodus, and migration, destruction of the human race in the past (deluge) or the future (apocalypse), and redemption in this life or an afterlife.

9 Ryken, Wilhoit, and Longman, *Dictionary of Biblical Imagery*, 509.

10 Ibid., 99.

11 Marcus Borg, *Meeting Jesus Again for the First Time: The Historical Jesus and the Heart of Contemporary Faith* (San Francisco: HarperSanFrancisco, 1994), 24, 76.

12 Ryken, Wilhoit, and Longman, *Dictionary of Biblical Imagery*, 512, advance a central thesis: "Light in its varied meanings is at the heart of . . . central biblical themes." Light transforms the earthly and human sphere with a transcendent splendor.

Frye, *Words with Power*, 23, calls "these" species of myth.

13 Ryken, Wilhoit, and Longman, *Dictionary of Biblical Imagery*, 929.

14 Ibid., 73, says that John is much like Elijah, who parts the Jordan River, and Elisha, who has the Gentile Naaman wash in the Jordan for his healing.

15 Ibid., 931, 73.

16 Frye's *Words with Power*, ed. Dolzani, xxiii, describes metaphor as annihilating the alienating distance between A and B by identifying them.

17 Bruce M. Metzer and Michael Coogan, *The Oxford Companion to the Bible* (New York: Oxford University Press, 1993), 516.

Christine Hayes, "Introduction to the Old Testament (Hebrew Bible): Lecture 14," Yale University, 2006, http://oyc.yale.edu/religious-studies/introduction-to-the-old-testament-hebrew-bible/content/transcripts/transcript14.html (accessed 26 June 2008), argues that a misunderstanding of the metaphorical nature of sonship leads to the literal Christian understanding that Jesus is the literal son of God.

18  Ryken, Wilhoit, and Longman, *Dictionary of Biblical Imagery*, xiv, xvii.

19  Metzer and Coogan, *Oxford Companion to the Bible*, 413.
   Frye, *Words with Power*, 163, points to the imagery of the rising and falling tower as signifying "the aspect of history known as imperialism, the human effort to unite human resources by force that organizes larger and larger social units, and eventually exalts some king into a world ruler, a parody representative of God" (this comes fully into focus in Daniel).

20  Ryken, Wilhoit, and Longman, *Dictionary of Biblical Imagery*, identifies the Kingdom of God as a central motif related to the imagery of the throne (occurring 135 times in the Old Testament and 61 times in the New Testament).

21  Ibid., 868.

22  Frye, *Words with Power*, 129, sees the Bible "framed within a gigantic metaphor of a court trial, ending in a last judgment, with an accuser and defender."

23  Ryken, Wilhoit, and Longman, *Dictionary of Biblical Imagery*, 471, states that God is held as the ultimate authority, the ultimate justice.

24  Ibid., 538.

25  The New Interpreter's Study Bible, 389, prefers the two requests – marriage for Ruth and redemption for Naomi – over the traditional interpretation of asking Boaz to fulfill the Levirate marriage custom.

26  Metzer and Coogan, *Oxford Companion to the Bible*, 496, likens the covenantal relationship between Yahweh and Israel to a covenanted marriage.

27  Frye, *Words with Power*, 191, 193, understands the connection of this imagery to myth and the recurrent Mother Nature and the earth goddess of pre-biblical Eastern religions. "Clearly one intention in the Eden story is to transfer all spiritual ascendancy of the pre-Biblical earth goddess to a symbolically male Father-God associated with the heavens."

28  Ibid., 209, makes the point that the bride and bridegroom imagery of Revelation should be connected with apocalypse, the end of space and time, and suggests an image of redemption, restoration, and unity.

29  Ryken, Wilhoit, and Longman, *Dictionary of Biblical Imagery*, 273, describes fatherhood as an ideal of "good "created by God himself.

30  Ibid., 274–5.

31  Ibid., 805.

32  Ibid., 273.

33  Ibid., 274.

34  Frye, *Words with Power*, 118, speaks of capitalized terms such as God, Word, Spirit, and Father as pure projections. But, as the subject–object cleavage becomes increasingly unsatisfactory, subject and object merge in an intermediate verbal world.

35  Ryken, Wilhoit, and Longman, *Dictionary of Biblical Imagery*, 572–4.

36  Ibid., 573–4.

37  Frye, *Words with Power*, 152, says, "The altar is also an image of a connection between earth and heaven, but one that subordinates the human side of the connection."

38  Ryken, Wilhoit, and Longman, *Dictionary of Biblical Imagery*, 749–50.

39  Marcus J. Borg and John Dominic Crossan, *The First Paul: Reclaiming the Visionary behind the Church's Conservative Icon* (New York: HarperOne, 2009), 130, opposing the theology of the death of Jesus as substitutionary, introduce this broader sense of atonement as "at-one-ment."

40  Ryken, Wilhoit, and Longman, *Dictionary of Biblical Imagery*, 184, describe the cross as signifying "an all-encompassing reconciliation."

41  Ibid., 889–92.

42  Ibid., 889.

43  Ibid., 890, states that "the cross of salvation is the ultimate ground of both curse and blessing, judgment and healing."

44 Frye, *Words with Power*, 166, makes such a connection when he states, "The Ascension is a New Testament antitype."

## CHAPTER 4 MAJOR GENRES

1 R. W. L. Moberly, "Story in the Old Testament," in James Phelan and Peter Rabinowitz, eds, *A Companion to Narrative Theory* (Oxford: Wiley-Blackwell, 2005).

2 Richard G. Moulton, *The Literary Study of the Bible* (Boston: Heath, 1898), 74–82, presents the four "cardinal points" of literature: description, presentation, poetry, and prose.

3 Leland Ryken, "The Literature of the New Testament," in *A Complete Literary Guide to the Bible*, 363, notes a tendency in the direction of a "mixed-genre format."

4 Ryken, "Introduction," ibid., 18: "Northrop Frye sounds the keynote when he says that the 'right' interpretation is the one 'that conforms to the intentionality of the book itself and to the conventions it assumes and requires.'"

5 Leland Ryken and Tremper Longman III, eds, *A Complete Literary Guide to the Bible* (Grand Rapids, MI: Zondervan, 1993), 21, say that poetry, drama, and narrative (terms that did not exist for biblical writers) are still "the best critical terms" available to help understand the Bible as literature.

6 Steven L. McKenzie, *How to Read the Bible: History, Prophecy, Literature – Why Modern Readers Need to Know the Difference, and What it Means for Faith Today* (New York: Oxford University Press, 2005), 1, 21, identifies five genres in the Bible: historiography, prophecy, wisdom, apocalyptic, and letter.

7 Ryken and Longman, *A Complete Literary Guide*, 69, warn against making "hard and fast distinctions between them [poetry and drama]."

   Moulton, *Literary Study of the Bible*, 76, 80, explains poetry as mostly conveyed in verse.

8 David M. Gunn and Danna Nolan Fewell, *Narrative in the Hebrew Bible* (New York: Oxford University Press, 1993), 2, define "story" as a broad term and "narrative" as a generic term.

9 Marcus J. Borg and N. T. Wright, *The Meaning of Jesus: Two Visions* (San Francisco: HarperSanFrancisco, 1999), 5, make the important distinction between "history remembered" and "history metaphorized" and insist that metaphor "can be powerfully true in a nonliteral sense."

   Ryken, "Introduction," in *A Complete Literary Guide*, 27, describes the nature of narrative as "historicized fiction" or "fictional history."

10 Moberly, "Story in the Old Testament," 77–82.

11 Tremper Longman III, "Biblical Narrative," in *A Complete Literary Guide*, 70.

   J. P. Fokkelman, *Reading Biblical Narrative: An Introductory Guide*, trans. Ineke Smit (Louisville, KY: Westminster John Knox Press, 1999), 171, points out that plot-arranged material uses "two ordering principles, sequentiality and thematics."

12 Longman, "Biblical Narrative," 76–8.

13 Robert Stam, *Film Theory* (Oxford: Blackwell, 2000), 14.

14 Gunn and Fewell, *Narrative in the Hebrew Bible*, 7–10, present these two views, the "serious" and the "rhetorical," and intentionally position themselves on the side of the rhetorical: discovering texts as multivalent and their meanings as contextual and bound up with their interpreters, the meaning of texts inherently unstable and language as always slipping, their reader-response and deconstructive reading acknowledges subjectivity as a strength. They point out three disadvantages to historical criticism: the paucity of external controls (datable literary texts or historical records of ancient Israel); the use of arbitrary and rarely acknowledged aesthetic principles; and according privilege to the "original" over "final" canonical text.

15 The HarperCollins Study Bible, xviii, explains that the variety in the Bible

accounts for richness but causes puzzlement and leads to investigating the
origins of the literature.

16 Benjamin Wisner Bacon, *The Triple Tradition of the Exodus: A Study of the
Structure of the Later Pentateuchal Books, Reproducing the Sources of the
Narrative, and Further Illustrating the Presence of Bibles within the Bible*
(Hartford, CT: Student Publishing Co., 1894), xx, makes the point that Genesis
to Joshua (in the Priestly writing) is a complete work.

17 Moulton, *Literary Study of the Bible*, vi, says "Its allegiance is not to literature,
but to Semitic Studies, in which literary questions are inextricably interwoven
with questions of language and history. It goes beyond the text of Scripture to a
further inquiry into the authority of the existing text, its mode of composition,
the dates and surrounding conditions of authorship."

18 David Damrosch, *The Narrative Covenant: Transformations of Genre in the
Growth of Biblical Literature* (Ithaca, NY: Cornell University Press, 1987), 41,
suggests that the Bible's historical writing can best be read "as the result of a
far-reaching transformation of earlier genres." The impetus to transform stems
from two historical events (monarchy, 1000 BCE) and exile to Babylon (587–520
BCE).

19 The New Interpreter's Study Bible, New Revised Standard Version with
Apocrypha (Nashville: Abingdon Press, 2003), 2, states that "It is less important
to date these authors precisely than to recognize how they told stories of their
origins in order to explain these later realities with which they were familiar."
The HarperCollins Study Bible introduces Genesis as the foundation for Jewish
and Christian theology, describing the book as laying "the foundation for the
relationship between God and humanity" – a book that is the historical and the
conceptual starting point for both religions.

20 Richard Elliott Friedman, *Who Wrote the Bible?* (San Francisco:
HarperSanFrancisco, 1997); *The Hidden Book in the Bible* (San Francisco:
HarperSanFrancisco, 1998); *The Bible with Sources Revealed* (San Francisco:
HarperSanFrancisco, 2003). In *Who Wrote the Bible?*, Friedman advances his
own theory about origins.
     In *The Book of J* (New York: Grove Weidenfeld, 1990), Harold Bloom and
David Rosenberg reconstruct Yahwist writings and suggest that the author may
have been a woman.

21 John Barton and John Muddiman, eds, *The Oxford Bible Commentary* (New
York: Oxford University Press, 2000), 15–20, discuss the logic of source criticism, identify the four documentary hypotheses, provide an example of such
analysis of the flood story in Genesis and an analysis of the Pentateuch, and give
approximate dates for each source.

22 Ryken, "Introduction," in *A Complete Literary Guide*, 35, outlines the overall
narrative shape of the Bible and the associated genres, loosely chronological, as
the beginning of human history – creation, fall, and covenant (story of origins);
exodus (law); monarchy (wisdom literature and psalms); exile and return
(prophecy); life of Christ (Gospel); Christian church (Acts and Epistles); and
consummation of history (apocalypse).

23 The HarperCollins Study Bible, xxiii, emphasizes an "odd concentricity" in the
Bible, its tensions held in check by some common framework.

24 Maud Elma Kingsley and Frank Herbert Palmer, eds, *Narrative Episodes from
the Old Testament* (Boston: Palmer, 1910), organize the Old Testament into
thirty-two familiar episodes.

25 Barry McWilliams, "Discerning the Story Structures in the Narrative Literature
of the Bible," www.eldrbarry.net/mous/bibl/narr.htm (accessed 25 March
2009).

26 Michael Travers, "Luke," in *A Complete Literary Guide*, 402.

27 Fokkelman, *Reading Biblical Narrative*, 10.

28 Marcus J. Borg and John Dominic Crossan, *The First Paul: Reclaiming the*

*Radical Visionary behind the Church's Conservative Icon* (New York: HarperOne, 2009), 31–45.

29  Robert Alter, *Genesis: Translation and Commentary* (New York: W. W. Norton, 1996), xlii.

30  Steven Weitzman, "David's Lament and Poetics of Grief in 2 Samuel," *Jewish Quarterly Review*, 85/3–4 (1995), 341–60.

31  Ibid., 356.

32  Robert Alter, "Putting Together Biblical Narrative" (Berkeley: University of California, Department of Classics, 1990), http://repositories.cdlib.org/cgi/viewcontent.cgi?article=1009&context=ucbclassics, 117–29.

33  Robert M. Price, "New Testament Narrative as Old Testament Midrash," www.robertmprice.mindvendor.com/art_midrash1.htm (accessed 2 April 2009), provides these examples of midrashic expansion.

34  Gunn and Fewell, *Narrative in the Hebrew Bible*, 3, 4.

35  Ryken, "Introduction," in *A Complete Literary Guide*, 35.

36  Marcus J. Borg, *Meeting Jesus Again for the First Time: The Historical Jesus and the Heart of Contemporary Faith* (San Francisco: HarperSanFrancisco, 1994), 120, says that "story theology" has remarked on this single story.

37  Ibid., 122–33, finds all three stories as "imaging the religious life" and addressing the human condition and its need for liberation, homecoming, and acceptance.

38  The Interpreter's Study Bible, 2.

39  Fokkelman, *Reading Biblical Narrative*, 172, 174, in "The Collaboration of Prose and Poetry," makes these distinctions and says: "Biblical Israel is rather conspicuous by not having written and left any epic poetry," where epic poetry is defined as narrative in verse. Rather, biblical writers embedded poetry in narrative, gradually fading over from prose to poetry – poetry most clearly a distinct genre in the oracles and prophecies.

40  Alter, *Genesis*, ix–xlvii, identifies formal symmetries, refrainlike repetitions, parallelisms, and other rhetorical devices as elevating the language of Genesis and imparting to it the dignity of epic poetry.

41  Gunn and Fewell, *Narrative in the Hebrew Bible*, 88, suggest a lack of consideration for Isaac or Sarah in the way that the narrator tells the story of the near sacrifice that points to a "dark" or "fallible" side to God's nature.

42  Thomas L. Thompson, *The Mythic Past: Biblical Archaeology and the Myth of Israel* (New York: Basic Books, 1999), 31.

43  Alter, *Genesis*, xlii.

44  HarperCollins Study Bible, 5.

45  Leland Ryken, *How to Read the Bible as Literature . . . and Get More Out of It* (Grand Rapids, MI: Zondervan, 1984), 34.

46  The HarperCollins Study Bible, 6, continues the musical analogy, saying that "like a musical theme with variations, the story shows the world gradually becoming more mobile and complex, until, by the sixth day, it is ready for self-perpetuation through procreation."

47  Stephen L. Harris, *Understanding the Bible*, 5th edn (Mountain View, CA: Mayfield, 2000), 100–1.

48  Fokkelman, *Reading Biblical Narrative*, 178.

49  Ibid., 181.

50  Ibid.

51  Ibid.

52  Ibid., 156, makes this observation, naming this grouping of stories an "act." Fokkelman defines an act as bringing together five to six stories; on another level, the cycle brings together three to five acts and, occasionally, an entire book comprised of acts.

53  Ibid., 22, says: "Comparative philology offers a useful strategy for constructing a reading that says nothing about possible theological issues or themes (e.g.

theodicy, sin, and judgment), nothing about the individual characters and their intentions or emotions, nothing even about Speiser's own claim that the story really depicts a social rather than individual conflict," and concludes: "Still, we do learn that in Akkadia dogs 'have experience' of other dogs."

54  Alter, *Genesis*, xliii.

55  Fokkelman, *Reading Biblical Narrative*, 156, 161, suggests beginning with the lowest levels – sounds, words, and sentences (traditional grammar) – then moving from the sentence to the story, paying attention to paragraphs with narrator's text or speeches, then to scenes or story segments, and finally on to act, cycle, and the composition of the book. The writer is always concerned with the whole so that each element "has been put there . . . with an eye to its contribution to the whole, chosen for reasons of thematic and effective communication."

56  Fokkelman, *Reading Biblical Narrative*, 207.

57  Robert Alter, *The Art of Biblical Poetry* (New York: Basic Books, 1985), concludes his exploration of narrative by making words, actions, dialogue, and narration the rubrics or tools that will help readers take scrutiny of representative texts forward "through a broad spectrum of other texts."

58  Fokkelman, *Reading Biblical Narrative*, 156.

59  Fokkelman, ibid., makes the point that "hardly a story in the Bible stands on its own" but, rather, five or six stories belong together as an "act," and the Bible contains "cycles" of stories consisting of three to five acts. More rarely, an entire book will be comprised of acts. For this reason, the story does not always require a plot of its own.

60  Ibid., 162, explains, "A sound interpretation of a biblical text must start by taking all these levels seriously and sound them out one by one . . . and then relate the various layers 'vertically' to each other in order to understand how they work together as a single entity (synthesis) . . . the macroplot."

61  Ibid., 162–7.

62  Richard G. Moulton, *A Short Introduction to the Literature of the Bible* (Boston: D. C. Heath, 1901), 3–41, identifies varieties of literary form in Job – drama, philosophical discussion, philosophy and science, and art of rhetoric, to name a few.

63  Marshall Johnson, *Making Sense of the Bible: Literary Type as an Approach to Understanding* (Grand Rapids, MI: William. B. Eerdmans, 2002), 4, 2, 25, after making these observations, says, "The book of Job is the magnum opus of wisdom literature."

64  Robert Sutherland, *Putting God on Trial: The Biblical Book of Job* (Victoria, CA: Trafford, 2004), describes Job as a theodicy and lawsuit drama in which entities are put on trial: God → Job (twice); Satan → God; Job's friends → Job; Job → friends; and the climatic Job → God.

65  Jerry A. Gladson, "Job," in Ryken and Longman, eds, *A Complete Literary Guide*, 240.

66  Fokkelman, *Reading Biblical Narrative*, 108–9, noting the folktale beginning, says the prose ending suggests that prosperity and well-being are the rewards of the righteous, whereas the poetry (and dialogues) argue that suffering is not necessarily punishment for sin.

67  Moulton, *A Short Introduction*, 164–86.

68  Gladson, "Job," 243, describes Job as one of the "Bible's superb examples of symbiotic interaction of the beauties of language and the drama of the human encounter with God that lies at the core of the Judeo-Christian tradition."

69  Moulton, *Literary Study of the Bible*, 25, calls Job "magnificent drama," with scenic effect, the ash mound a stage, a crowd of spectators first silent then presenting their sentiments in chorus, a dramatic background of sky and atmosphere, and a transition from brilliant sunshine to a thunderstorm, the reader watching and a part of the whole.

70  Alter, *Art of Biblical Poetry*, 87. Alter's language, which is echoed in the next immediate section, itself soars to exquisite poetry.

71 Ibid., 89, 110.
72 Ibid., 95–110.
73 Ibid., 96.
74 Ibid., 97.
75 Ibid., 98.
76 Ibid., 99–103.
77 Ibid., 100, summarizes the distance between man's and God's world as the difference between inseminator, body, and actual birth.
78 Ibid., 96, 100.
79 Ibid., 110.
80 Richard G. Moulton, *The Modern Reader's Bible: The Books of the Bible with Three Books of the Apocrypha Presented in Modern Literary Form* (New York: Macmillan, 1963), 1518, explains that rhythm based upon feet and syllables belongs to the original Hebrew and remains a discussion of Hebraists.
81 Moulton, *Literary Study of the Bible*, 45, says: "The Bible is the worst-printed book in the world."
82 James L. Kugel, *The Idea of Biblical Poetry: Parallelism and its History* (New Haven, CT: Yale University Press, 1981), 57–8, makes this point: "All parallelism is really 'synthetic'; it consists of A, a pause, and A's continuation, B."
83 Moulton, *Modern Reader's Bible*, 1518.
84 Alter, *Art of Biblical Poetry*, 107.
85 Barton and Muddiman, *The Oxford Bible Commentary*, 331, describe the poetry as rejecting the retributive position of the prose.
86 McKenzie, *How to Read the Bible*, 109, argues that a lack of clear resolution for the problem of suffering characterizes wisdom literature and that the ending of Job suggests that, indeed, God rewards righteousness and, by extension, punishes sin through suffering.
87 Katharine Dell, "Reviewing Recent Research on the Wisdom Literature," *Expository Times*, 119/6 (2008), 267, refers to J. L. Crenshaw's magisterial work on theodicy in the Bible and points out that Job gets "pride of place as providing the most profound airing of theodicy in the Bible."
88 John. H. Augustine, "Mark," in Ryken and Longman, eds, *A Complete Literary Guide*, 387–97, describes the initiation motif in Mark.
89 Moulton, *Modern Reader's Bible*, 1492, describes this God as being one not of Infinite Inaccessibility, as Job thought, but of Infinite Sympathy.

## CHAPTER 5 SUB-GENRES

1 Richard G. Moulton, *The Literary Study of the Bible* (Boston: Heath, 1898), 75, identifies four "cardinal points" of literature: description, presentation, prose, and poetry. Moulton describes prose as moving mostly in the region limited by facts.

George Lakoff and Mark Johnson, *Philosophy in the Flesh: The Embodied Mind and its Challenge to Western Thought* (New York: Basic Books, 1999), 545, question the Classical reliance upon disembodied reason, replacing it with embodied imaginative reason and metaphor as the tools we use to understand abstract domains and to extend our knowledge.

Kenneth Burke, *A Grammar of Motives* (Berkeley: University of California Press, 1969), examines human motives in terms of action and ends in the creation of discourse, the heuristic known as "Pentad."

2 Robert M. Grant and David Noel Freedman, *The Secret Sayings of Jesus* (New York: Barnes & Noble, 1960), 22–3, insist that, for the gospels, including the Gospel of Thomas, fact and faith in the minds of the early writers could not be divorced.

3 Leland Ryken and Philip Graham Ryken, eds, preface to the Literary Study Bible, English standard version (Wheaton, IL: Crossway, 2007).

4  Moulton, *Literary Study of the Bible*, vi, xi, describes literary investigation as focusing on form, with the structural coming before other analysis.

5  Ibid., 83, calls a focus upon isolated sentences, isolated texts, and isolated verses an "imperfect reading," a habit hanging on from medieval days.

6  Bart D. Ehrman, *Lost Christianities: The Battles for Scriptures and the Faiths We Never Knew* (New York: Oxford University Press, 2003), 249, calls the literal a "commonsensical approach to the text" that marginalizes the figurative and belongs to an orthodox dominance.

   James L. Kugel, *The Bible as it Was* (Cambridge, MA: Harvard University Press, 1997), 17–22, 49, makes a compelling case that traditions in exegesis have influenced the interpretation of the Bible in ways that are not always literal and that emphasize cryptic, implied and hinted-at meaning, perfection and harmony, and divine inspiration.

7  Leland Ryken, *How to Read the Bible as Literature . . . and Get More Out of It* (Grand Rapids, MI: Zondervan, 1984), 25.

8  Leland Ryken and Tremper Longman III, "Introduction," in *A Complete Literary Guide to the Bible* (Grand Rapids, MI: Zondervan, 1993), 23, quoting John Sider, outline traditional criticism as relying upon the general and familiar genres, regarding their traits as universal tendencies, and then raising these to the level of archetypes.

9  John B. Gable and Charles B. Wheeler, eds, *The Bible as Literature: An Introduction*, 4th edn (New York: Oxford University Press, 1990), 14, make the point that "every piece of writing is a kind of something" and that it "takes place within a particular formal tradition and in itself exemplifies that tradition."

10  Moulton, *Literary Study of the Bible*, 83, explains that readers read for "Higher Unity" rather than just clauses, verses, and stanzas.

11  Ibid., iv, remarks that "one person is willing to read the Bible for every ten who are ready to read about it."

12  John H. Sailhamer, "Genesis," in Ryken and Longman, eds, *A Complete Literary Guide*, 108–9.

13  Wilson H. Baroody and William F. Gentrup, "Exodus, Leviticus, Numbers, and Deuteronomy," ibid., 122–3.

14  Kenneth R. R. Gros Louis and Willard Van Antwerpen, Jr., "Joshua and Judges," ibid., 137–50.

15  These ideas have been drawn from the collection of essays in Ryken and Longman, eds, *A Complete Literary Guide*.

16  Anthony Billington, "Christian Cartography: Mapping Biblical Literature and Theology with Kevin Vanhoozer," *The Glass*, 13 (2000), www.scu.supanet.com/html/m.htm (accessed 30 October 2009).

17  David Damrosch, *The Narrative Covenant: Transformations of Genre in the Growth of Biblical Literature* (Ithaca, NY: Cornell University Press, 1987), 38–9, identifies three general categories of genre: epic, chronicle, and history.

18  John Sider, "The Parables," in *A Complete Literary Guide*, 364, suggests beginning with genres, noting their hybrid nature, then moving to other features such as images, characters, events, the re-creation of experience, the imagistic and the figurative, and self-conscious artifice.

   Marshall Johnson, *Making Sense of the Bible* (Grand Rapids, MI: William B. Eerdmans, 2002), 3, says: "Recognizing that there are diverse kinds of literature within the Bible, each with distinctive perspectives, can be an effective first step in making sense of what many readers have found to be confusing, arcane, or contradictory."

19  Moulton, *Literary Study of the Bible*, 75, says "we can never be clear as to the contents of a piece of literature unless we have settled the external form."

20  Damrosch, *The Narrative Covenant*, 32–3, warns that, when the Bible is read as literature, temptation exists to read "novelistically and to skim over larger stretches of legal, priestly materials."

21  Damrosch, ibid., 36, advises thinking of genres as formed by the merging of formerly separate genres.

22  Moulton, *Literary Study of the Bible*, 74.
      Damrosch, *The Narrative Covenant*, 2, defines genre as "the narrative covenant between author and reader, the framework of norms and expectations shaping both the composition and the reception of a text."

23  Damrosch, ibid., 36, 7, considers the study of genre fundamental to the construction of the meaning in texts but subject to constant alteration, both deliberate and inadvertent, which results in theoretical problems.

24  Damrosch, ibid., 32–3 reminds readers that "very few of the Biblical writers seem to have thought they were writing literature" and that "much of the Bible reads like rather 'poor' literature."

25  Kugel, *The Bible as it Was*, 94, 70, describes biblical poetry as using complex heightening effects in combinations and intensities and not simply as a matter of metrics and parallelism.

26  Johannes C. de Moor and Wilfred G. E. Watson, eds, *Verse in Ancient Near Eastern Prose* (Kevelaer: Butzon & Bercker, 1993), 345–58, provide a full discussion of inset verse.

27  Moulton, *Literary Study of the Bible*, 137–42, provides an antiphonal layout for Deborah's poem.

28  Moulton, ibid., 133, 142–3 describes this song under the genre of biblical ode, a form of poetry that he says soars highest and "remains longest on the wing."

29  John Barton and John Muddiman, *The Oxford Bible Commentary* (New York: Oxford University Press, 2001), 181, describe the composition as characterized by "a parallelistic variety of repetition whereby imagery unfolds in a beautifully layered or impressionistic style . . . so that the parallel line adds color, nuance, or contrast to its neighboring description."

30  Emil G. Hirsch and George A. Barton, "Song of Moses," www.jewishencyclopedia.com/view.jsp?artid=967&letter=S (accessed 2 February 2007).

31  "Miriam's Song: The Womanly Note in the Song of History," www.meaningfullife.com/torah/parsha/shmot/beshalach/MiriamDIVs_Song.php (accessed February 2007).

32  According to the New Advent Catholic Encyclopedia, the Magnificat is "fulfillment of the olden prophecy and prophesying anew until the end of time," www.newadvent.org/cathen/09534a.htm (accessed 2 January 2007).

33  Barton and Muddiman, *Oxford Bible Commentary*, 927, explain that the angel's visit to Zechariah is the prelude to that to Mary.

34  John Sider, "The Parables," in *A Complete Literary Guide*, 423–4.

35  E. W. Bullinger, *Figures of Speech Used in the Bible: Explained and Illustrated* (1898; Grand Rapids, MI: Baker Book House, 1968), 749.

36  Ryken, *How to Read the Bible*, 199. Ryken explains "aversion to the arbitrary allegorizing of the Bible" as growing in part from a desire to read the Bible literally as "fact" and to resist the nature of language as a complex system of inter-functioning symbols

37  Lloyd Carr, "Song of Songs," in Ryken and Longman, eds, *A Complete Literary Guide*, 283–9, makes a compelling case for reading the Song of Solomon as a love poem.

38  The New Interpreter's Study Bible, 1051–2, explains Jeremiah's life as "a symbol of the nation's demise and restoration."

39  L. Michael White, *From Jesus to Christianity: How Four Generations of Visionaries & Storytellers Created the New Testament and Christian Faith* (San Francisco: HarperSanFrancisco, 2004), 264–9.

40  Ryken, "Revelation," in *A Complete Literary Guide*, 460.

41  Marcus J. Borg and N. T. Wright, *The Meaning of Jesus: Two Visions* (San Francisco: HarperSanFrancisco, 1999), 68. Borg says that Jesus used aphorisms

and parables to "invite hearers to enter the world of the story and to see something differently because of the story."

42 Ryken, *How to Read the Bible*, 202.

43 John Sider, "The Parables,"*A Complete Literary Guide*, 423.

44 Samuel E. Balentine, *Prayer in the Hebrew Bible: The Drama of Divine–Human Dialogue* (Minneapolis: Fortress Press, 1993), uses literary methods to show that prayers embrace a dialogic in which characters appear differently before prayer than they do afterward.

45 Bruce M. Metzger and Michael D. Coogan, eds, *The Oxford Companion to the Bible* (New York: Oxford University Press, 1993), 607.

46 Ibid., 667, says the sacrifice of Christ "definitively secures for the whole of humanity the effects (atonement, fellowship with God) that older sacrifice brought about only temporarily."

47 Ibid., 607.

48 "The Shemoneh Esrei: Reciting the Weekday Amidah Prayers," www. hebrew4christians.com/Prayers/Daily_Prayers/Shemoneh_Esrei/shemoneh_ esrei.html (accessed 7 September 2009).

49 N. T. Wright, "The Lord's Prayer as a Paradigm of Christian Prayer," in R. L. Longnecker, ed., *God's Presence: Prayer in the New Testament* (Grand Rapids, MI: Eerdmans, 2001), 132–54, makes the point that "the Lord's Prayer is the 'true Exodus' prayer of God's people"; www.ntwrightpage.com/Wright_ Christian_Prayer.htm (accessed 19 February 2007).

## CHAPTER 6 CHARACTER

1 Leland Ryken, *How to Read the Bible as Literature . . . and Get More Out of It* (Grand Rapids, MI: Zonderman, 1984), 37.

2 Robert Alter, *The Art of Biblical Narrative* (New York: Basic Books, 1981), 117, outlines this scale of means in presenting characters.

3 Alter, ibid., 39, 129, describes biblical characters as "unpredictable, impenetrable, constantly emerging from and slipping back into a penumbra of ambiguity."

4 Ryken, *How to Read the Bible*, 58, defines reality as what really exists; morality as what constitutes good and bad behavior; and values as what really matters, and what matters most.

5 Alter, *The Art of Biblical Narrative*, 189, 157, 46, 158, describes the characters as finite personages created by omniscient narrators.

6 Frederick Buechner, "The Bible as Literature," in Leland Ryken and Tremper Longman III, eds, *A Complete Literary Guide to the Bible* (Grand Rapids, MI: Zondervan, 1993), 42, states, "The central character, of course – the one who dominates everything and around whom all the others revolve – is God himself."

7 As Alter, *The Art of Biblical Narrative*, remarks, characters in the Bible present a vision of human beings "enjoying or suffering all the consequences of human freedom."

8 Ryken, *How to Read the Bible*, 44, quoting Flannery O'Connor.

9 Bruce M. Metzger and Michael D. Coogan, eds, *The Oxford Companion to the Bible* (New York: Oxford University Press, 1993), 301, explain that the effort to express the full presence of God in Jesus led to the conclusion that this specific mode of presence had existed prior to the life of Jesus.

10 Alter, *The Art of Biblical Narrative*, 3–22.

11 Ibid., 20.

12 Leland Ryken and Tremper Longman III, "Introduction," in *A Complete Literary Guide*, 17.

13 Ryken, *How to Read the Bible*, 51, calls this the threefold principle of structure: antecedents, occurrence, and consequences.

14 David M. Gunn and Danna Nolan Fewell, *Narrative in the Hebrew Bible* (New

York: Oxford University Press, 1993), 47, state that "The power of narrative lies in its ability to imitate life."

15 These character descriptions are taken from essays in Ryken and Longman, eds, *A Complete Literary Guide.*

16 Leland Ryken, James C. Wilhoit, and Tremper Longman III, *Dictionary of Biblical Imagery* (Downers Grove, IL: InterVarsity Press, 1998), 782.

17 Presenting the Bible's characters individually has been the work of authors Sue and Larry Richards in *Every Man in the Bible* and *Every Woman in the Bible* (Nashville: Thomas Nelson, 1999).

Edith Deen, in her introduction to *All of the Women of the Bible* (New York: Harper, 1955), xxi, says she will provide a feminine portrait gallery of 150 named women and more than 100 unnamed women in the Bible, less familiar characters than their male counterparts.

18 J. P. Fokkelman, *Reading Biblical Narrative: An Introductory Guide* (Louisville, KY: Westminster John Knox Press, 1999), 63, describes the narrator as above the material and outside the story and the character as inside the story.

19 Robert Polzin, *Samuel and the Deuteronomist: 1 Samuel* (Bloomington: Indiana University Press, 1993), 11, reviews the historical critical work of scholars Noth and Cross and asks, "Why have we chosen to apply our considerable skills to reconstructing a supposed prior text and to determining its theological intention and probable date of composition, without employing as much sympathetic care and effort in determining the global meaning of the very text . . .?"

The New Interpreter's Study Bible, 392, observes that the sources include one expressing approval of the move from confederacy to monarchy and another expressing disapproval of the monarchy.

Joel Rosenberg, "1 and 2 Samuel," in Robert Alter and Frank Kermode, eds, *The Literary Guide to the Bible* (Cambridge, MA: Belknap Press, 1987), 122, makes the point that 1 and 2 Samuel have been "deprived of their autonomy as books and of the commonality of texture and perspective that unites them with most other books of the Hebrew Bible."

Walter Brueggemann, *An Introduction to the Old Testament: The Canon and Christian Imagination* (Louisville, KY: Westminster John Knox Press, 2003), 131, argues 1 and 2 Samuel make one canonical entry.

G. N. Knoppers, "Is There a Future for the Deuteronomistic History?," in *The Future of Deuteronomistic Theology*, ed. T. Römer (Leuven: Peeters, 2000), objects to the proposal for a continuous Deuteronomistic history.

Alter, *The Art of Biblical Narrative*, 11, says that students have more to learn from the tradition that assumes the text is intricately connected.

20 The Interpreter's Study Bible, 404, describes God's reaction to the demand for a king as making clear that "the institution of monarchy is wrong."

21 Fokkelman, *Reading Biblical Narrative*, 59–61.

22 The Interpreter's Study Bible, 405, suggests Saul may have been chosen as first king based upon his physical characteristics, his being a Benjamite and a warrior, and because the people wanted such a warrior.

23 Ibid.

24 Richard Elliott Friedman, *Who Wrote the Bible?* (San Francisco: HarperSanFrancisco, 1989), 238–40, explains that the Priestly source stressed the divine aspect of justice and that transgressors get what they deserve, leading to the retributive justice formula: obedience is rewarded; transgression is punished.

25 Excursus, Interpreter's Study Bible, 314. Holy war invokes the metaphor of the Lord going into battle as the divine warrior at the head of the troops, highlighting God's intervention in human events.

26 The New Oxford Annotated Bible, 361, points out that Saul's consultation with the medium here further depicts him as a "moral and religious reprobate."

27  The Interpreter's Study Bible, 434, describes Saul as anxious and physically and spiritually unprepared for battle.

28  Fokkelman, *Reading Biblical Narrative*, 63.

29  Richard L. Pratt, "First and Second Chronicles," in Ryken and Longman, eds, *A Complete Literary Guide*, 197–205.

30  Ibid., 198.

31  Ryken and Longman, "Introduction," in *A Complete Literary Guide*, 17.

32  Edith Deen, *All of the Women of the Bible*, 144, concludes that Huldah must be a woman of some distinction in Jerusalem to be sought out by the priest.

33  Phyllis Trimble, "Authority of the Bible," in the Interpreter's Study Bible, 2248–53, lists seven features of authority.

34  Loring W. Batten, *The Hebrew Prophet* (New York: Macmillan, 1905), 3, 4, insists theology made a fatal mistake by admitting the line of demarcation between the natural and the supernatural, a mistake not made by the Hebrew prophet.

35  James N. Rhodes, *The Epistle of Barnabas and the Deuteronomic Tradition* (Tübingen: Mohr Siebeck, 2004), 144, describes Stephen's speech as "a Christian appropriation of the Deuteronomistic view of history."

David P. Moessner, *Lord of the Banquet: The Literary and Theological Significance of the Lukan Travel Narrative* (Minneapolis: Trinity International Press, 1998), describes Luke as advancing a Deuteronomistic view.

Paul Nadim Tarazi, *Luke and Acts*, Vol. 2 (Crestwood, NY: St Vladimir's Seminary Press, 2001), 12, says, "The story in the Deuteronomistic History unfolds in a series of clearly defined states: perfection (Joshua) and close adherence to the Law; a gradual falling away; the coming of prophets; the people's rejection of the prophets' message; God's rejection of Jerusalem as a result; and finally the rebirth of God's prophetic word in the Gentile land of Babylon."

36  The Interpreter's Study Bible, 1967, 1969, explains Stephen's critique of the Jerusalem Temple as "a denunciation of what is made by human hands."

Rhodes, *The Epistle of Barnabas*, 144, points out that Stephen considers the Temple which Solomon has built "an idolatrous innovation."

37  Metzger and Coogan, *Oxford Companion to the Bible*, 55–6, provide a useful introduction to the history of the ark.

38  The Interpreter's Study Bible, 1153, says that Ezekiel has the task of explaining "Israel's defeat, Jerusalem's destruction, and massive deportation in the light of a vision of divine glory."

39  Deen, *All of the Women of the Bible*, 193.

40  Deen, ibid., 238, describes Timothy, Eunice, and Lois as "the strongest spiritual trio from the maternal line of any family group in the New Testament."

41  The New Oxford Annotated Bible takes the position that circumcision was not inconsistent, and the New Interpreter's Bible, 2089, says that Paul showed his awareness of Jewish sensitivities.

42  Santiago Guijarro, in "Why Does the Gospel of Mark Begin as it Does?" *Biblical Theology Bulletin*, 33/1 (2003), 28–38, says Mark evidences the characteristics of the kind of biography familiar in the Roman and Hellenistic "lives."

43  Guijarro, ibid., 35, provides the full argument for emphasizing not Jesus' human ancestry, but his true identity as the Son of God.

## CHAPTER 7 THEMES AND MOTIFS

1  N. T. Wright, *The New Testament and the People of God* (London: SPCK, 1992), 42, 135–9.

2  John B. Gabel, Charles B. Wheeler, and Anthony D. York, eds, *The Bible as Literature: An Introduction* (New York: Oxford University Press, 1990), 10, describe the Bible as an anthology, a library of religious and national writing.

David Perkins, "Literary Histories and the Themes of Literature," in Werner Sollors, ed., *The Return of Thematic Criticism* (Cambridge, MA: Harvard University Press, 1993), 111, 113, 22, makes the point that literary histories tend to group authors and texts in this manner.

3  Werner Sollors, "'Theme' as a Theme," ibid., 18, 11, and "Introduction," ibid., xi, notes that "thematic criticism was given a first-class funeral a few years ago" but survives as a neothematism "passed through the filter of structuralist criticism."

   Sidney Greidanus, "The Value of a Literary Approach for Preaching," in Leland Ryken and Tremper Longman III, eds, *A Complete Literary Guide to the Bible* (Grand Rapids, MI: Zondervan, 1923), 512, makes the point that theme is an abstraction from narration.

   Frederick Buechner, "The Bible as Literature," ibid., 40, says the common reader experiences in an introductory approach to the Bible something that holds it together.

   James Steele, "Reconstructing Structuralism: The Theme-Text Model of Literary Language and F. R. Scott's 'Lakeshore,'" in John Moss, ed., *Future Indicative: Literary Theory and Canadian Literature* (Ottawa: University of Ottawa Press, 1987), 153, 156, describes the theme-text model (credited to Alexander Zholkovsky and J. K. Scheglov) as resting on "a productive middle ground [structuralists and post-structuralists], its structure identical with the text itself yet derivable from an invariant, proto-formative theme."

   Heather Murray, "Reading for Contradiction in the Literature of Colonial Space," ibid., 74, 75, suggests reading for contradiction as the corollary for reading for coherence, this and close reading an outcome of objectivist New Criticism.

4  Thomas L. Thompson, *The Messiah Myth: The Near Eastern Roots of James and David* (New York: Basic Books, 2005), proves a useful background for the study of themes of motifs.

5  M. H. Abrams, *A Glossary of Literary Terms*, 5th edn (New York: Holt, Rinehart & Winston, 1988), 110.

6  Claude Bremond, "Concept and Theme," in Werner Sollors, ed., *The Return of Thematic Criticism*, 50, presents Gerald Prince's distinction "that the difference is more one of degree than of nature."

7  Willian Freedman, "The Literary Motif: A Definition and Evaluation," *Novel: A Forum on Fiction*, 4/2 (1971), 123–31, describes motif as "a recurrent theme, character, or verbal pattern, . . . a family or associational cluster of literal or figurative references to a given class of concepts or objects, . . . generally symbolic – that is, . . . [carrying] meaning beyond the literal one immediately apparent."

   Ryken,"Introduction," in *A Complete Literary Guide*, 22, 36, suggests that, amid analysis, the Bible presents itself as a coherent, unified text.

8  Leland Ryken, James C. Wilhoit, and Tremper Longman III, *Dictionary of Biblical Imagery* (Downers Grove, IL: InterVarsity Press, 1998), xv.

9  Thompson, *Messiah Myth*, 23.

10  Robert Alter, *The Art of Biblical Narrative* (New York: Basic Books, 1981), 51.

11  Thompson, *Messiah Myth*, 23.

12  Leland Ryken, *How to Read the Bible as Literature . . . and Get More Out of It* (Grand Rapids, MI: Zondervan, 1984), 177–97, devotes an entire chapter to "The Literary Unity of the Bible."

13  Sollors,"Introduction" to *The Return of Thematic Criticism*, xi, counts the number of the Modern Language Association's sessions referencing themes and shows twenty-four sessions in 1977, thirty-four in 1979, and only eight in 1990.

14  Nancy Armstrong, "A Brief Genealogy of Theme," ibid., 38–45, traces this "inside–outside" controversy back to Locke's epistemology.

15  Øyunn Hestetun, "Text, Context, and Culture in Literary Studies," *American Studies in Scandinavia*, 25 (1993), 27–36.

16  David H. Richter, ed., *The Critical Tradition: Classic Texts and Contemporary Trends*, 2nd edn (New York: Bedford Books, 1998), introduces classic texts and provides an oversight of contemporary trends useful to understanding general critical literary traditions.

17  F. J. P. Fokkelman, *Reading Biblical Narrative: An Introductory Guide*, trans. Ineke Smit (Louisville, KY: Westminster John Knox Press, 1999), 26, 27, insists that how a text is constructed produces more enhanced understanding than the question about what it says.

18  Thomas Pavel, "Thematics and Historical Evidence," in Werner Sollors, ed., *The Return of Thematic Criticism*, 127–8, 135, describes the observation of themes as biased and not decisively arguable, further remarking that the three assumptions – reader's bias, the relativity of relevance, and ideological determinism – all constrain the critic's interpretive attention.

19  Menachem Brinker, "Theme and Interpretation," ibid., 22.

20  Claude Bremond, "Concept and Theme," ibid., 49, 54, 56, defines thematization as consisting "of an indefinite series of variations on a theme whose conceptualization, far from being preordained, still remains to be completed."

21  Ryken, *How to Read the Bible*, 180, quotes C. S. Lewis to the effect that the Bible is "remorselessly and continuously sacred" and Erich Auerbach's suggestion that the Bible is tyrannical in insisting that it describes the only real world.

22  Thompson, *Messiah Myth*, 237, cautions that "we are pursuing an impossible dream" if we think we can reconstruct the past.

Willis Barnstone, ed., *The Other Bible* (San Francisco: Harper & Row, 1984), xix, describes the New Testament as "a small and highly repetitive canon" that excluded the Christian Apocrypha and all Gnostic scriptures, giving us "a highly censored and distorted version of ancient religious literature."

23  Thompson, *Messiah Myth*, 210, succinctly argues that the Bible is about traditions and themes, not history and events.

David M. Gunn and Danna Nolan Fewell, *Narrative in the Hebrew Bible* (New York: Oxford University Press, 1993), 3–5, summarize the plot of the Bible as consisting of a "God, who attempts to establish and sustain a relationship of trust with human kind" and humans, in search of their place and identity, who become lost by failing to "take seriously their own story and to respond to God."

24  Thompson, *Messiah Myth*, 234, suggests that old Israel is a metaphor representing "a negative theological concept and a faithless lost."

25  Walter Brueggemann, *An Introduction to the Old Testament: The Canon and Christian Imagination* (Louisville, KY: Westminster John Knox Press, 2003), 15.

26  Fokkelman, *Reading Biblical Narrative*, 9.

27  Richard Elliott Friedman, *Who Wrote the Bible?* (San Francisco: HarperSanFrancisco, 1997), 231–2, gives credit to David Noel Freedman as identifying an eleven-book continuity in the Old Testament.

Zvi Brettler, *How to Read the Bible* (Philadelphia: Jewish Publication Society, 2005), 100, credits the German biblical scholar Martin Noth (1943) for proposing that a Deuteronomistic historian put together the books of Deuteronomy, Joshua, Judges, Samuel, and Kings.

28  Friedman, *Who Wrote the Bible?*, 83.

29  Brueggemann, *An Introduction to the Old Testament*, 85.

30  The New Interpreter's Study Bible, new revised standard version with Apocrypha (Nashville: Abingdon Press, 2003), 252, points out that Deuteronomy distinguishes carefully between three covenants: the promise made to the ancestors (Gen. 15.1–21), the covenant at Horeb or Sinai (Deut. 2.2), and the covenant made in the plains of Moab (Deut. 29.1), all related to the continuing purpose of God for Israel.

Friedman, *Who Wrote the Bible?*, characterizes the Deuteronomistic historian as shaping the history of Israel around four themes: fidelity to Yahweh, the
Davidic Covenant, the centralization of religion at the Temple in Jerusalem, and
the Torah.

31  Bruce M. Metzer and Michael D. Coogan, *The Oxford Companion to the Bible*
(New York: Oxford University Press, 1993), 163–8.

32  Brettler, *How to Read the Bible*, 64–7, understands the Decalogue as comprised
of as many as thirteen separate statements.

33  Friedman, *Who Wrote the Bible?*, 226, 229, credits a late redactor (whom he
identifies as Ezra) as combining alternative versions of the same stories into
one.

34  James L. Kugel, *How to Read the Bible: A Guide to Scripture Then and Now* (New
York: Free Press, 2007), 243, makes this distinction.

35  David Noel Freedman, *The Nine Commandments: Uncovering a Hidden Pattern
of Crime and Punishment in the Hebrew Bible* (New York: Doubleday, 2000),
91.
    Marshall D. Johnson, *Making Sense of the Bible: Literary Type as an Approach
to Understanding* (Grand Rapids, MI: William B. Eerdmans, 2002), 67, explains
that "Reference to the commandments being written on two stone 'tablets'
or 'tables' (Ex. 24.12; 34.1) has led many readers to distinguish two kinds of
commands," the first referring to worship of YHWH and the second half dealing
with interhuman relationships.
    Kugel, *How to Read the Bible*, 255, traces this explanation of structure to
Philo.

36  Joseph Telushkin, *Biblical Literacy: The Most Important People, Events and
Ideas of the Hebrew Bible* (New York: William Morrow, 1997), 423.

37  Wayne Dosick, *Living Judaism: The Complete Guide to Jewish Belief, Tradition
and Practice* (San Francisco: HarperSanFrancisco, 1995), 36, points out that,
while other codes for human behavior have come and gone, Judaism's ethical
monotheism has endured.

38  Barnstone, *The Other Bible*, xxii, explains how three conflicting views present
Jesus: after he is crucified, Jews think of him as a man and go on seeking the
Messiah; Christians proclaim Jesus Christ as both God and man; and the
Docetic view suggests Jesus only appeared to be on the cross, arguing for his
being merely an image or representation of Jesus.

39  Ibid., xvii.

40  Friedman, *Who Wrote the Bible?*, 139, links apostasy to exile in the writings of
the Deuteronomistic history.

41  Brueggemann, *An Introduction to the Old Testament*, 86–7.

42  Marcus J. Borg and John Dominic Crossan, *The First Paul: Reclaiming the
Radical Visionary behind the Church's Conservative Icon* (New York: HarperOne,
2009), 160, 161, make the case that both Jesus and Paul were passionate about
distributive justice.

43  Brueggemann, *An Introduction to the Old Testament*, 86–7.

44  The cover to Freedman's *The Nine Commandments* describes him as charting
"the violation of the first nine commandments one by one."

45  Kugel, *How to Read the Bible*, 108–18, describing these two ways of perceiving
God, points out that the earlier model can be found in many of the narratives of Genesis, Exodus, Joshua, and Judges, as well as in Psalms, prophecies, and laws; the later model, he explains, dates from as early as the sixth
century BCE and became fully developed only near the end of the biblical
period.

46  Thompson, *Messiah Myth*, 300, explains that "Yahweh became the name and
reflection of the divine. He was God for Israel: Immanuel. God belonged now
only to a human world."

47  Dosick, *Living Judaism*, 8.

48  Thompson, *Messiah Myth*, 23, discusses how many of the Bible's early stories interweave successive pairs, a structural device using the themes of echoing and competition.

49  Thompson, ibid., 322, says, "In this form of inclusive monotheism, there is but one God for Israel, the God of heaven."

50  Ibid., 295–301.

51  Freedman, *The Nine Commandments*, 17, says, "Thus, with the opening statement, . . . Yahweh sets forth the reason why Israel should worship and obey him. In essence, Yahweh argues, 'Because I have released you from Egyptian slavery, you shall keep my commandments. Therefore, you shall have no other gods before me.'"

52  Brettler, *How to Read the Bible*, 93, states that Deuteronomy commands love not as an emotion but as a set of concrete actions.

53  Ibid., 155.

54  Freedman, *The Nine Commandments*, 1, 161, says this "Master Weaver or Editor . . . has skillfully woven into Israel's history a message to a community in exile that their present condition is not the result of God abandoning them, but of their abandoning God through their complete disregard for their covenant obligations . . ."

55  Christine Hayes, "Introduction to the Old Testament (Hebrew Bible): Lecture 14," Yale University, 2006, http://oyc.yale.edu/religious-studies/introduction-to-the-old-testament-hebrew-bible/content/transcripts/transcript14.html (accessed 26 June 2008), references Jon Levenson's *Sinai and Zion* as describing a "deep tension between the covenant theology and the royal ideology. . . . the royal ideology fostered . . . a belief in the inviolability, the impregnable nature of David's house."

56  Friedman, *Who Wrote the Bible?*, 104, finds the concept of covenant critical to any discussion of who wrote the Bible.

    Kugel, *How to Read the Bible*, 103–6, describes covenant as a biblical institution and the word itself as a fancy way of meaning agreement or treaty.

57  Thompson, *Messiah Myth*, 18, identifying the God of creation as the only completely autonomous being, says, "The unbridgeable difference between what God sees and what humans see as good is present already at the creation. The whole of biblical history is sketched in terms of human fate implicit in the way we are. There is nothing new under the sun, and the long narrative which sets out in Genesis is but an ever expanding illustration of this eternal conflict of will as the divine Father struggles with his children; even his first-born Israel."

    Gabriele Boccaccini, *Roots of Rabbinic Judaism: An Intellectual History from Ezekiel to Daniel* (Grand Rapids, MI: William B. Eerdmans, 2002), xii, 120, outlines three traditions leading from ancient Judaism to the second century BCE: the Sapiental or Wisdom tradition, the Zadokite or Priestly tradition (coming largely out of the J tradition), and the Enochic tradition.

58  Thompson, *Messiah Myth*, 19, says this history of reiteration "can best be seen through the many stories that present the recurrent theme of new creation, new beginning, new hope. All play out their contrast to the stories of human willfulness."

59  Friedman, *Who Wrote the Bible?*, 236–41.

60  The New Interpreter's Study Bible, 14–22, pulls apart the Yahwist and Priestly accounts of the flood, noting that the Priestly account concerns itself with boundaries, order, and ritual. It credits Genesis 4.17 as the Yahwist generation of those who lived before the flood and chapter 5 as the Priestly account of generations both before and after the flood.

61  Friedman, *Who Wrote the Bible?*, 62, contrasting the J source to E, calls attention to the Patriarch Abraham as living in Hebron, the principal city of Judah, the capital of Judah under King David, the city of the chief priest Zadok.

62  Friedman, ibid., points out that P presents only four stories of any length: the

creation; the flood, culminating in the covenant with Noah; the covenant with Abraham; and the death of Aaron's sons Nadab and Abihu. He concludes of the writer, "Apparently he was in a hurry to get to Sinai."

63  Ibid., 105.

64  The New Interpreter's Study Bible, 113, 1313, provides an excursus on covenant as well as on marriage as covenant.

65  Friedman, *Who Wrote the Bible?*, 130–2, describes the Deuteronomist writer as active in the time of King Josiah and assembling one continuous history out of the earlier sources (J, E, and another tradition combining the two) that extends from the arrival in the land to Josiah in the 600s BCE.

66  Ibid., 133.

67  Ibid., 141–3.
    James D. Tabor, *The Jesus Dynasty* (New York: Simon & Schuster, 2006), 51–6, accounts for two branches in the royal family of David, one used by Matthew that traces Jesus through Joseph back to Solomon, and one in Luke that traces Jesus from Mary, back to Nathan, the brother of Solomon.

68  Tabor, ibid., 48, suggests that Matthew calls attention to the irregularity in the birth of Jesus.

69  Ibid., 48–57.

70  Friedman, *Who Wrote the Bible?*, makes a bold identification of the Deuteronomist as Jeremiah.

71  Friedman, ibid., 30, uses source theory to account for why the Bible presents "a deity torn between divine justice and divine mercy," evidencing a tension between punishment and forgiveness.

72  Tabor, *The Jesus Dynasty*, 73, 110, makes these observations and describes Christianity as "a set of universal ethics that superseded the legalistic ways of Judaism," also labeling it as Christian anti-Semitism.

73  Kugel, *How to Read the Bible*, 353–5, credits William L. Moran for seeing in Deuteronomy the use of love to mean political loyalty related to the vassal treaty.

74  Kugel, ibid., 362, understands the third-, second-, and first-century BCE interpreters as viewing the Pentateuch as "divine wisdom in written form, one great book of legal and ethical instruction."

75  Friedman, *Who Wrote the Bible?*, 238, makes the case that source P never uses the words "mercy," "grace" or "repentance," but rather emphasizes the divine aspect of justice, in contrast to J and E sources that emphasize mercy – the word occurring about seventy times in J, E, and D. A redactor combined sources, creating a new formula, in which justice and mercy stood in balance.

76  Friedman, ibid., says, "There is a constant tension in Yahweh between his justice and his mercy. They are not easily reconcilable. When should one predominate, and when should the other?" He suggests readers must read both parts of the formula: justice (P) and love (J, E, D).
    Gunn and Fewell, *Narrative in the Hebrew Bible*, 89, describe coming to understand the character of YHWH as "one of the great challenges of the Hebrew Bible."

77  Dosick, *Living Judaism*, 249–52. Judaism has no word for "charity," an English word derived from the Latin *caritas*, meaning "charity." Judaism prefers *tzedakah*, which means "just" and "righteous" and refers to obligation.

78  Tabor, *The Jesus Dynasty*, 74.

79  Gunn and Fewell, *Narrative in the Hebrew Bible*, 81–9, describe the Old Testament's presentation of God as a character who is sometimes present implicitly and who guides all of human activity providentially; this God can bring evil upon one character in order to promote covenantal outcomes.

80  Northrop Frye, *Anatomy of Criticism* (Princeton, NJ: Princeton University Press, 1957). Other works important to understanding this archetypal theme include

Joseph Campbell, *The Hero with a Thousand Faces* (New York: World, 1956) and Carl Jung, ed., *Man and his Symbols* (Garden City, NY: Doubleday, 1964).

Frye's *Words with Power: Being a Second Study of "The Bible and Literature,"* ed. Michael Dolzani (Toronto: University of Toronto Press, 2008), xxiii, argues that we get to the spiritual through the imagination, with plot being the typical quest journey that moves participants to another world and to a greater reality.

81  Thompson, *Messiah Myth*, 31, says: "'Exile' is the means by which those who identify themselves with the tradition can understand themselves as saved."

82  Thompson, ibid., 15–33, remarks that Genesis reiterates themes through successive heroic pairs, each following a plot of "peoples whose lands have been promised to them by their deity since the earliest times."

83  Fokkelman, *Reading Biblical Narrative*, 164, calls this macro-plot and describes the life of Abraham as a quest "which supposes that the object of value at the end of its trajectory is the arrival of a physical son to Abraham and Sarah." Once Abraham arrives in Palestine, the desired object is attainment of Canaan (Gen. 13.14–17).

84  Fokkelman, ibid., 163, identifies the macro-plot of Genesis 12–25 as connecting the Patriarchs in the quest for dynasty.

85  Fokkelman, ibid., 157, says that, after the searchlight hits the person of Abraham, "this concentration of election by God determines the focus of attention until the end of the Hebrew Bible."

86  Kugel, *How to Read the Bible*, 244–7.

# Index

Aaron 46, 73, 135, 142
Abiathar 115
Abimelech 98–9
Abraham 33, 34, 36, 201
   allusion, use of 7, 97, 121
   covenants 75, 97, 105, 106, 133,
      135, 137, 138, 139–40
   heroic quest 147, 202
   and Isaac 34, 58, 60, 75, 79–80,
      140, 189
   journey into Egypt 33, 38
   relationship with God 18, 58, 80,
      105, 106, 181–2
Absalom 71, 145–6
Achan 135
acts 78, 153, 190
Acts of the Apostles 35, 47, 122,
   125
Adam 8, 12, 27, 57, 102, 147
   and Eve 11, 55, 77, 138, 139
Adonai 3
Ahab 135
allegory 68, 92, 93, 98–103, 153,
   175, 193
allusion 7–8, 32–3, 68, 72, 80, 94,
   96–7, 121–2, 153, 183–4
alpha and omega 31, 37, 76
altars 60, 186
Alter, Robert 14, 15, 71, 75
Amalekites 115, 116
ambiguity 68, 87, 116
ambition 124
Amos 48
amplification 36, 153, 184
analogy 98, 103, 153
ancestry 9, 78, 79, 80, 107, 139, 142,
   147, 160
  Jesus 56, 78, 126, 142, 196, 201
angels 112
animal images 29, 100, 112
annunciation 97–8, 130, 193

anthology 130, 197
anthropomorphism 28–9, 153
Antiochus IV Epiphanes 19
antiphonal arrangement 93, 94–5,
   153
aphorism 103, 154, 194
apocalypse 8, 37, 107, 154, 175
Apocrypha (deuterocanonical) 2,
   19, 134, 154, 157
apostasy 100, 154
apostrophe 68, 95, 154
appelation 25, 154
archetype 44, 57, 58, 59–62, 130–1,
   132, 146, 154, 185, 192
argument 90, 154
ark of the covenant 121
Arnold, Matthew 14
ascent and descent 58, 185
Asian myth 11
association 25–6
Assyria 101
atonement 60, 61, 186

Babel, Tower of 29
Babylon 7, 9, 19, 100, 101, 103, 105,
   115, 134
Balaam's ass 112
baptism 8, 11, 49–50, 140
Barak 54
barrenness 100, 105, 130, 140, 147
Bathsheba 53–4, 104, 135, 142, 146
battle 115, 196
Behemoth 86, 112
belittlement 26
bias 131, 198
Bible
   influence on other literature
      11–12, 13, 177–9
   interpretation 15–17, 23, 144,
      180
   as literature vi–viii, 13–17, 172

Bible (*cont.*)
  origins and manuscripts 2, 3, 4,
       173
  reading the Bible 91, 111, 131,
       174–5, 190, 191–3, 197
    American teaching 14, 178
    and Christianity 6, 131
    literary approach 6–7, 131–2
    readership 6, 173–4
    *see also* history
  sanctity of 131, 198
  translations 4–5, 24–5, 182–3
    King James Version vi, 4, 24,
       173, 179
    New Oxford Annotated (NRSV)
       vi, 4, 5, 24, 74
  unity 23, 58, 62, 147–8, 182, 187
  *see also* Apocrypha; New
       Testament; Old Testament
Bible, Hebrew *see* Old Testament
       (Hebrew Bible)
Bible, Jewish *see* Old Testament
       (Hebrew Bible)
biography 126, 154–5, 196
birth 10, 83–4, 103, 131, 164–5, 191
birthright 140, 147
blessing 62, 99, 120, 187
blindness 47, 83
blood 60, 61, 139
Bloom, Harold 69
Boaz 55–6
bramble 98, 99
bride/bridegroom *see* marriage

Cain 37, 38, 103, 139
  and Abel 105, 139
calf, fatted 116
Canaan 18–19, 147, 165
Catholicism 133
chaos, primeval 83–4
character and characterization 67,
       110–28, 153, 159, 167, 169,
       194
  Chronicles I 114–15, 117, 118
  Jesus 111, 194
charity 145, 201
chiasm 39, 86, 155
choice 40, 120, 138, 155, 184
Christ, types of 8
Christianity 10–11, 32–3, 47, 50,
       155

and baptism 50, 140
and death 37, 50
and Judaism 143, 201
and justice 144, 173
New Covenant 137, 142
and prophecy 8, 32–3
and reading Bible 6, 131
relationship with God 100, 143
Chronicles I 92, 132, 145–6
  characterization 114–15, 117,
       118
Chronicles II 92, 132
circumcision 49, 105, 125, 140, 143,
       155, 196
circumlocution 25, 155
cisterns 49
Clement 3
cognates 94, 95, 156
colloquies 82, 156
comedy 81, 156, 171, 191
commandments 139
  Great Commandment 46, 125,
       143–4
  Ten Commandments 50, 59–60,
       132–6, 137, 138, 143–4, 156,
       199, 200
    Moses 59–60, 132–3, 138, 141,
       144
comparison 25–6, 27, 68, 98
complication 77
Convent of the Pater Noster 106
convention 140
Corinthians I 31, 61, 145
Corinthians II 48
covenants 122, 137–42, 156, 200,
       201
  between author and reader 93,
       193
  covenant relationships 50–1, 75,
       132, 186
  New Covenant 60, 137, 140, 142,
       165
  Old Testament (Hebrew Bible) 2,
       56, 98–9, 100, 101–2, 119–20,
       137–42, 148
    Abraham 75, 79, 80, 105, 133,
       135, 137, 139–40, 199
    David 8, 51, 97, 133, 141–2,
       145
    Deuteronomy 50–1, 133,
       140–1, 143–4

Genesis 138, 139–40
  Moses 132, 133, 140–1, 145,
    199
  Noah 133, 139, 199
covetousness 135
creation 10, 27, 37, 38, 45–6, 48,
    131, 183
  myth of 10, 11, 58, 185
  as a story 70, 76–7
cross/crucifixion 60–2, 122, 187
culture 17–20
curse 62, 120, 187
cycles 12, 18, 79, 141, 142, 156, 190

Dagon 121
Daniel 8, 132
David 61, 121
  and Absalom 71, 145
  and Bathsheba 53–4, 104, 135,
    142, 146
  Davidic covenant 8, 51, 97, 133,
    138, 141–2, 200
  and justice 51, 53–4, 145–6
  King David's Song 97
  kingship 47, 51, 115, 138, 200
  parent–child relationship 57–8,
    117
death 11, 36–7, 83, 120, 122–3, 131
Deborah, Song of 54, 94–5, 96, 97,
    105, 193
debt 71–2, 136
Decalogue *see* commandments,
    Ten Commandments
deliverance 96, 141, 143
description 125, 191
deserts 130
destruction of the human race 48,
    58, 185
deuterocanonical *see* Apocrypha
Deuteronomic tradition 69, 113,
    132–3, 157, 195, 196, 198
Deuteronomy 141, 201
  characterization 116, 120
  covenants 50–1, 133, 140–1,
    143–4
  justice 54, 115, 135–6, 195–6
  law 116, 140–1
  literary devices 7, 30, 38, 62, 102
  love 102, 143, 200, 201
  Shema 105, 136
dialect 24

dialogue 68, 70, 157
*Dictionary of Biblical Imagery* 14
Dinsmore, Charles Allen 14
disciples 73
divorce 54, 100
Documentary Hypothesis 69–70,
    75, 157
double meaning 26, 157
dragons 103
drama 67, 68, 80–7, 92, 99, 187,
    191

eagles 112
Ecclesiastes 38, 137, 148
Eden 7, 18, 28, 30, 37, 38, 48–9,
    77–8, 181
Egypt 19, 33, 38
'elect lady' 125
Eli 57, 121, 135
Elijah 59, 71, 72–3, 82, 135
Elisha 70, 72–3, 112
Elizabeth 140
Elohim 3, 157
Elohist tradition 69, 79, 132–3, 143,
    157–8
Enoch 139
Ephesians 30–1, 61, 102
Ephraim 102, 147
epic 67, 92, 158, 189
epilogue 81, 158
epiphany 130, 158
episodes 70–4, 158
Esau 5, 147
eschatology 46, 158
Esther 132
Estienne, Robert 4
Eunice 124–5, 196
euphemism 36–7, 159
Eve 11, 27, 55, 77, 99, 138, 139
evil/sin 81, 84, 87, 103, 107, 191
exile 37, 147, 202
  Assyria 7, 9
  Babylon 7, 9, 19, 74, 100, 101
  Egypt 38
exodus 8, 48, 49, 58, 74, 185
Exodus, Book of 7, 9, 46, 59–60,
    116, 133, 143–4, 146
Ezekiel 30, 48, 49, 52, 55, 100–1,
    112, 122–3, 196
Ezekiel's wife 122–3
Ezra 54, 132

fable 77, 107, 159
fact 90, 191, 192
faith 90, 192
faithfulness 101–2, 199
    see also infidelity
family life 141
fatherhood 57–8, 186
favor, divine 140
fear 79, 84, 143
feeding of the 5,000 32, 73
fertility 56–7, 100
fiction 67–8, 187
fig tree 98, 103
fire 46, 60
first-born children 140, 166
flesh 77, 139
folktales 75, 81, 158–9
food, provision of 32, 70–1, 72–3,
    107, 130, 139
foreshadowing 32–3, 121–2, 140,
    159–60
Fox, Everett 5
Friedman, Richard Elliott 69
Frost, Robert 12
Frye, Northrop 58

Gabel, John B. 15
Galatians 62
gardens 130
    see also Eden
gems 84
genealogy see ancestry
Genesis 17–18
    covenants 138, 139–40
    literary devices 28, 37–8, 39
        heroic quest 147, 202
        imagery 45–6, 48–9, 62
        merism 30, 31
        metaphor and simile 27, 28,
            183
        narrative/storytelling 9, 74–80,
            92, 176
    poetry 74, 189
    see also Abraham; Adam; Isaac;
        Jacob; Noah
genre 66–109, 160, 187, 192–3
    sub-genres 90–109
Gentiles 61, 102
Gibeah 47
Gideon 51
Gnosticism 136, 160

God 48, 87, 92, 140
    character of 50, 75, 142–8, 183,
        189, 201, 202
        central character 111, 194
        human characteristics of 29,
            142, 146
        New Testament (Christian)
            143
        Old Testament (Hebrew Bible)
            3, 146
    Church of God 59, 100, 102, 143
    Creator 34–5, 76
    image of 12, 29, 176, 177
    justice 87, 102, 115, 123, 144–5,
        201
    Kingdom of God 9, 51–2, 186
    love of 102, 106, 142, 143
    man's perception of 136, 138,
        199, 200
    mercy of 122, 123, 141, 142,
        143–4, 201
    names for 3, 200
    'oneness' 132, 136–9
    relationship with man 50–9, 76,
        77, 79, 132–6, 198, 200
        Abraham 18, 58, 80, 105, 106,
            181–2
        bride–bridegroom relationship
            10, 57, 103, 186
        Christians 100, 143
        husband–wife relationship 12,
            55–7, 100, 102, 186
        Israel 57, 100, 101–2, 143–4
        Jeremiah 100, 142, 194, 201
        justice 52–4, 87, 102, 115
        king–subject relationship
            50–2, 186
        love 102, 143–4
        parent–child relationship
            57–8, 137, 143–4, 186
goddesses 11
Golgotha 59, 60–2
Gomer 101
Greek myth 11, 74

Habakkuk 97
Hagar 79–80, 139, 140
Hammurabi 134
Hannah 94, 97, 105, 140
Harris, Stephen L. 15
heaven 23, 107

Hebrew history 144
Hebrew language 5, 173
Hebrew tradition 137, 143, 167
Hebrews, Book of 32–3, 34, 60, 61
hell 11, 23
Herod dynasty 19–20
heroes 10, 92, 103, 132, 140, 146,
    160–1
heroic quest 146–8, 167, 202
Hezekiah 133
Hilkiah 119, 120
historical dates (BC, BCE, CE, AD)
    3–4, 154
historiography 74, 161
history
  historical fact in the Bible 6, 11,
      66, 67, 69, 99, 174, 180–1,
      187, 188
    Genesis 74–5, 92
    Hebrew history 18, 120, 121
    New Testament (Christian)
        90
  history of the Bible itself 16–17,
      180–1
Horeb, Mount 59–60, 82, 133
Hosea 12, 32, 55, 100, 101–2, 105–6
Huldah 119–20, 196
humans
  human behavior 137, 141, 145
  human experience 6, 12–13, 35,
      91, 112, 174
  in image of God 12, 29, 176,
      177
  relationship with each other 132,
      138, 143
  relationship with God 50–9, 76,
      77, 79, 132–6, 198, 200
    bride–bridegroom relationship
    10, 57, 103, 186
    Christians 100, 143
    husband–wife relationship 12,
    55–7, 100, 102, 186
    Jeremiah 100, 142, 194, 201
    justice 52–4, 87, 102, 115
    king–subject relationship
    50–2, 186
    love 102, 143–4
    parent–child relationship 12,
    57–8, 137, 143–4, 186
    *see also* covenants
  hunger 38, 130

husband–wife relationship 55–7,
    100, 102, 186
hymns 92, 94, 161

idols, worship of 62, 100–1, 106,
    119, 133, 135
imagery 12, 44, 68, 94, 95, 161, 177
  unifying 45–50, 60, 131, 185
immortality 30, 62, 183
impulsiveness 114–15
inclusio 38, 161
incongruity 26, 161
Indo-European myth 11
infidelity 100, 101, 114, 117, 133,
    135
  adultery 100, 101, 134
  *see also* faithfulness
inheritance 140, 144, 147
initiation 132
intertextuality 7, 161
irony 26, 33–4, 68, 114, 115, 116,
    157, 162
Isaac 34, 47, 57–8, 105, 139, 147,
    189
Isaiah 18
  God–man relationship 12, 52,
      55, 56, 100
  literary devices 28, 32, 35, 39, 97
    imagery 45, 48, 62
Ishmael 79–80, 139, 147
Islam 6
Israel
  history of 10, 37, 98, 120
  kings of 117, 141–2
  as metaphor 132, 198
  relationship with God 57, 100,
      101–2, 143–4

Jabin 95
Jacob 5, 36, 47, 58, 75, 122, 130, 147
Jael 54, 96
Jairus 73
James 38, 124, 143
Jeconiah 142
Jehovah 3
Jephthah 53, 94
Jereboam 115
Jeremiah 30, 31, 71–2
  God–man relationship 100, 142,
      194, 201
  imagery 48, 49, 61–2

Jerusalem 10, 19, 100, 101, 112, 121
  New 45, 46, 165
Jesus 10, 33, 49, 58, 105, 134, 143
  ancestry 56, 78, 126, 142, 196, 201
  baptism 38, 184
  character 111, 194
  death 38, 59, 60–2, 184, 186
  divinity 12–13, 134, 199
  and justice, retributive 143, 199
  rejection 73, 121–2
  teaching of 103, 194
  temptation 59, 120
Jewish Study Bible 98
Jezebel 59, 82
Job 12, 47, 71–2, 97, 145
  covenants 137, 148
  drama 80–7, 92, 112, 144–5, 190–1
  and justice 81, 87
  literary devices 28, 30, 34, 36
    rhetorical question 34, 35
John, disciple 124
John, Gospel of 12, 32, 46
John I 45, 46, 48, 61
John II 125
John the Baptist 97, 126
Jonah 8, 12, 73, 112, 132
Jonathan 71, 146
Joseph, husband of Mary 55, 56, 57–8
Joseph, son of Jacob 36, 38, 75
  foreshadowing 33, 121
Joshua 7, 37, 92, 97, 112, 121–2
  characterization 113, 135
Josiah 119, 120, 133
journeying 9, 79, 82, 130
Judah 73, 100–2, 117, 119, 120, 142, 147
Judaism 6, 19, 162
  and Christianity 102, 201
  and God 28, 100, 131, 137, 143, 144
  law 134, 199
  prayers 105, 106
  ritual 49, 125, 140, 196
Judas 39
judge–litigant relationship 52–4, 186
Judges 32, 47, 53–4, 92, 112, 113

Jung, Carl 13
justice 52–4, 102, 118, 132, 141, 186, 187, 201
  and Christianity 144, 173
  and David 51, 53–4, 145–6
  Deuteronomy 54, 115, 135–6, 195–6
  God's 52–4, 81, 87, 102, 115, 122, 123, 144–6, 201
  and Jesus 143, 199
  and Job 81, 87, 145
  retributive justice 46, 81, 114, 115, 135–6, 143, 145, 167, 199, 201

Kent, Foster 14
Kethuvim 2
king–subject relationship 50–2
Kings I 71, 73, 92, 113, 117, 118, 135
Kings II 71, 73, 92, 112, 113, 145
kingship 98–9, 113–15, 117–18, 119, 121, 135, 141, 164, 195
kinship 56, 92, 162
knowledge, tree of 62

lambs 12, 112
Lamech 139
lampstand 62
land 130, 140, 141, 144, 147
Langton, Stephen 4
language 9–10, 23, 86, 182
law 60, 62, 81, 92, 133–4, 143–4, 162, 201
  Deuteronomy 116, 140–1
  Judaism 134, 199
  see also commandments
leitmotif 130, 162
letters/epistles 66, 107, 158, 162
Leviathan 83, 86, 112
Levirate marriage custom 55–6, 162, 186
Leviticus, Book of 46, 61
life 31, 56, 62, 92, 120
  water of life 11, 48–9
light and darkness 9, 27, 30, 46, 47–8, 83, 176, 183, 185
lions 112
literary traditions 69
  see also Deuteronomic tradition;

Elohist tradition; Priestly
    tradition; Yahwist tradition
literature, English 11–12, 177
literature, Western 13, 14, 178–9
Lois 124–5, 196
'Lord is my Shepherd' 26–7
Lord's Prayer 9, 57, 106–7, 194
Lot 49, 140, 147
love 142
    New Testament (Christian)
        102–3, 107, 125, 137, 143,
        145
        Great Commandment 46, 124,
            143
        Old Testament (Hebrew Bible)
            99–100, 101, 102, 106, 107,
            143, 200
Luke, Gospel of 46–7, 59, 69, 97–8,
    104, 142
lyric 67, 163

Maccabean revolt 19
Macleish, Archibald 12
Magnificat 193
Malachi, Book of 58, 97
man, fall of 48, 58, 185
Mark, Gospel of 38, 39, 57, 61, 69,
    72–3, 103–4
    and character 124, 125–6, 196
marriage 10, 55–6, 57, 100–1, 102,
    103, 162, 186
Mary 11, 57, 124, 142
    and the annunciation 97, 193
    Song of 94, 95–6, 97–8, 105
Masoretic text 4, 163
master–servant relationship 58
Mattathias 19
Matthew, Gospel of 56, 69, 123–4,
    134, 142
    imagery 47, 48
    literary devices 8, 30, 31, 32, 35
mercy 122, 123, 132, 141, 142,
    143–4, 201
merism 29–30, 163
Mesopotamian myth 11, 74
metaphor 12, 26–7, 44, 50–9, 92,
    98, 163, 177, 182, 196
    in Genesis 27, 28, 183
    Israel as 132, 198
    in literature vii, 23
meter 68, 85, 191

metonymy 25, 28, 163
Milton, John 12
Miriam, Song of 94, 105
Mitzvot 135, 163
monolatry 133, 164
monologues 82
monomyth 10–11, 164
monotheism 18, 133–4, 137, 158,
    164, 181–2, 200
morality 66, 79, 80–1, 194
Moses 8, 10, 37, 38, 46, 58, 73, 106,
    116, 144
    allusion and foreshadowing 32,
        33, 122, 140
    covenants 132, 133, 140–1, 145,
        199
    and justice 54, 144
    Red Sea crossing 49, 73
    in the reeds 32, 140
Song of Moses 38, 51, 94, 95, 96–7,
    105, 193
    Ten Commandments 59–60,
        132–3, 138, 141, 144
motif 5, 44, 59, 79, 80, 103, 142,
    164, 197
    ancestry 78, 130
    barrenness 105, 130, 140, 147
    betrothal/marriage/love 44, 99,
        103, 130
    birth/baptism 11, 103, 131
    family struggle/sibling rivalry
        105, 147
    Israel 132, 137
    journeying 79, 130
    land 130, 132, 137
    testing 79, 80, 112
    water/wells 11, 44, 48–9, 130,
        140
motion imagery 96
Moulton, Richard Green 14
mountains 59–60
    *see also individual mountains*
mourning 122–3
murder 134
music 76, 93, 189
mythology vii, 11, 23, 58, 96, 164,
    172, 177, 183, 185
    creation 10, 11, 58, 185
    Genesis 74, 182
    Greek 11, 74
    pagan 56, 186

name changing 140
narrative/storytelling 7, 24, 31, 65,
    67, 69–80, 92, 132, 164, 169,
    198
  meta-narrative 10, 163, 176
  narrative voice 67, 76
  primary 7, 73–4
narrators 111, 113, 164, 195
Nathan 4, 53–4, 104, 118, 142, 146
Nehemiah 106, 132
Nevi'im 2
New Interpreter's Study Bible 69
New Testament (Christian) vi, vii,
    3, 10, 31, 66, 130, 131, 134,
    165, 198
  allusion to Old Testament 7, 10,
    31–2, 72–4, 121, 183
  husband–wife relationship 56,
    102
  law 134, 143
  love 102–3, 107, 125, 137, 143,
    145
    Great Commandment 46, 124,
    143
  New Covenant 60, 137, 140, 142,
    165
  prophecy 8, 32–3, 97, 120–1, 142,
    193
Nicodemus 55
Nietzsche 28
Noah 32, 38, 133, 138, 139, 147
Noah's flood 18, 37–8, 46, 49, 140,
    200
Nob 115
Norse myth 11
Norton, David 14
novelette 75, 165
Numbers, Book of 105

obedience 113, 115, 123, 124–5,
    134, 137–42, 143, 144, 176,
    196
Oholah and Oholibah 101
Old Testament (Hebrew Bible) vi,
    31, 105, 198
  character of God 3, 146
  covenants see covenants, Old
    Testament
  love 101, 102, 106, 107, 143, 200
  manuscripts and forms 2–3, 4,
    160, 162, 163, 165, 169, 170

narrative/storytelling 132, 147
  prophecy 92, 114, 117, 119–20,
    175, 196
  quotation in New Testament 7,
    10, 31–2, 72–4, 121, 183
olive tree 98–9
oxen 112
oxymoron 29, 31, 165

paganism 116, 117, 118
pairs 200
Palestine see Canaan
parables 92, 93, 98, 103–4, 116, 124,
    165, 194
paradoxes 68, 142–8, 165, 201
parallelism 85–6, 92, 94, 95–6, 98,
    125, 158, 160, 162, 165
  synthetic 169, 191
parataxis 24, 165
parent–child relationship 12, 57–8,
    117, 137, 143–4, 186
parody 72, 165
Passover 61, 80, 119
Paul 31, 32, 47, 55, 143, 145, 171,
    199
  and Timothy 125, 196
peace offering 61
Pentateuch 69, 92, 144, 166, 188,
    201
Pentecost, Day of 29
personification 28, 68, 166
perspective 67
Peter, disciple 47, 72–3
Peter I 58
Peter II 46, 48
Pharisees 19, 134
Philemon 71
Philistines 121
'Physician, cure yourself!' 104
plan, of God 142
plot 67, 70–1, 137, 166, 187
  macro-plots 9, 78–80, 147, 163,
    176, 190, 202
  unifying 69, 188
poetry 65, 66, 67, 68, 76–7, 80–7,
    94, 99–100, 187, 191
  epic 67, 74, 75, 189
  Genesis 74, 189
  Psalms 92, 105
  songs 93–8, 193
praise 92, 96, 97

prayer 92, 93, 104–7, 166, 194
  Lord's Prayer 9, 57, 106–7, 194
  Shema 55, 105, 133, 136–9
priesthood 74, 115
Priestly tradition 69, 76–7, 132–3,
      136–7, 138, 139, 166, 200, 201
procreation 30, 57, 183
Prodigal Son 116
prologue 81, 125, 166
promises *see* covenants
prophecy 166
  New Testament (Christian) 8,
      32–3, 97, 120–1, 142, 193
  Old Testament (Hebrew Bible)
      92, 114, 117, 119–20, 175, 196
prose 65, 66, 67, 74, 92, 189, 191
prosperity 87
prostitution 100–1, 103, 118
protection 138
Proverbs 31, 57, 92, 137, 148, 166
Psalms, Book of 57, 105, 112, 146,
      167
  genres 92, 97, 98, 137
  literary devices 28, 29, 30, 38
    imagery 46, 62
  poetry 92, 105
Ptolemies 19
punishment 87, 114, 115, 135, 139,
      141, 144, 146, 196, 201

Q (*Quelle*) 69
quotation 7–8, 31–2, 167, 183

reality 9, 12, 23, 45, 67, 68, 176, 194
reason 191
Rebekah 58, 140
rebellion 139
recognition 80
reconciliation 61, 187
recruitment 73
recursion 37–8, 167, 184
Red Sea crossing 49, 73
redemption 10, 48, 58, 96, 97, 101,
      102, 176, 185
Reformation 8
Reheboam 115
rejection 73, 121–2, 135
remnant theology 145, 167
Renaissance 68
repetition 36, 37, 67–8, 71–2, 85,
      96, 167

request 123–4
resolution 70, 77, 167
resurrection 8, 10, 56, 72–3
Revelation, Book of 8, 66
  God–man relationship 52, 58
    marriage 10, 57, 103, 186
  imagery 45, 46, 48, 49
  literary devices 31, 32, 37
  motif 59, 103, 130
  symbolism 39–40, 62, 103, 112
rhetorical strategy 22–4, 26–40, 68,
      167, 183, 184, 187–8
righteousness 87, 146, 191
ritual
  baptism 8, 11, 49–50, 140
  circumcision 49, 105, 125, 140, 143,
      155, 196
  Hebrew tradition 137, 143, 167
  sacrifice 60, 61–2, 105, 115, 122,
      124, 130, 194
Roman occupation 19–20
Romans, Book of 12, 34, 60, 105
Romantics 68
Ruth 36, 55–6, 92, 112, 132, 142
Ryken, Leland 12, 14

Sabbath 133
sacrifice 60, 61–2, 105, 115, 122,
      124, 130, 194
Sadducees 19, 134
sagen 75, 168
Salome 123–4
Samaria and Samaritans 49, 101
Samson 47
Samuel 12, 97, 113–16
Samuel I, 51, 92, 104, 113–16, 135,
      139
Samuel II, 53–4, 71–2, 92, 97, 116,
      118, 135, 142, 145
Sarah 34, 79, 139, 140
sarcasm, divine 34, 184
Satan 59, 81, 120
Saul 51, 71, 73, 113–17, 135, 146,
      195, 196
sayings 92
science 75
Seleucids 19
self-knowledge 110
Septuagint (LXX) 2, 168
serpent 112
service 87, 112, 143, 145

Seth 139
setting 67, 70, 77, 168
seven 37, 75, 82
sexual intimacy 36
sexuality 30, 99–100, 183
Shem 38, 147
Shema 55, 105, 133, 136–9, 168
'Shemoneh Esrei' 106
shepherds and sheep 98, 112
Shunammite widow 70–1, 72–3
sibling rivalry 105, 140
sight 10, 47, 83, 84, 176
signs 39–40, 168
Simeon 46
simile 26–7, 44, 98, 103, 168, 183
sin offering 61
Sinai, Mount 59–60, 82, 133
Sisera 54, 96
Skull, Mount of the see Golgotha
slang 24
slavery 71
Sodom 32, 47, 139
Solomon 53, 58, 115, 117–18, 121,
        135, 138, 142
Song of Songs 97, 99–100, 112, 193
songs 92, 93–8, 193
    Deborah 54, 94–5, 96, 97, 105,
        193
    Mary 94, 95–6, 97–8, 105
    Miriam 94, 105
    Moses 38, 51, 94, 95, 96–7, 105,
        193
    Zechariah 94, 97–8, 193
source criticism 68–9, 87, 144,
        168–9, 188
sower parable 103–4
speeches 31, 107, 169
stanzas 84, 95, 169
Stephen 120–2, 196
stereotype 110, 146
stories, groups of 78–9
storms 73, 81
storytelling see narrative/
        storytelling
strophes 84, 85, 95, 169
structure 43, 68, 86, 125–6, 185, 195
style 23–4, 79, 169
suffering 81, 83, 87, 97, 132, 144,
        190, 191
Sumerian myth 11
Superman 28

supersessionism 3, 169, 172
suzerain treaty 138, 141
symbolism vii, 44, 46, 61, 68, 99,
        130, 171, 193
    Ezekiel 112, 122–3
    Revelation 39–40, 62, 103, 112
syncretism 118, 137, 169
synecdoche 28, 29, 59, 169
Syro-Phoenician woman 72

tabernacle 62
Talmud 3, 135, 169
Tanakh 2, 169
Temple 117, 119, 121, 123, 135,
        168, 196
temptation 59, 73, 107, 120
testing 79, 80, 81–2, 112, 130, 144
thematic analysis 131, 198
themes 37, 129–51, 170, 197
theodicy 80–1, 87, 120, 170, 191
theology 27, 48, 66, 113, 129
theophany 81, 82, 96, 107, 133, 170
thirst 130
'This is my body' 27
Thomas, Gospel of 192
throne image 52, 186
time 112
Timothy 31, 124–5, 196
tolerance 137
tone 23–4, 76, 170
Torah 2, 132, 135, 137, 142, 170
tragedy 81, 170
trees 11, 61–2, 98
triads 11, 31
tribalism 113, 114
tribulation 99
truth 12, 90, 125, 145, 177
Two Source Hypothesis 69, 170–1
typology 7, 8, 71–2, 80, 130, 171,
        175, 184
tzedakah 145, 201

understanding, spiritual 183
unity 102, 125
    Bible 23, 58, 62, 147–8, 182, 187
    unifying images 45–50, 60, 131,
        185
    unifying plot 69, 188

variance 26, 171
verbal modes 177

victory, celebrating 94–5
viewpoint 113, 166, 170
vines 99
violence 139
visions 40
vocabulary 24

wakefulness 10, 176
war 11
water 44, 45–6, 48, 49, 73, 130, 140
    water of life 11, 48–9
Webber, F. R. 14
wells 44, 80, 130
Wheeler, Charles B. 15
White, Benton 15
Wild, Laura H. 14
wilderness 79, 82, 130
wind 82–3, 85
wisdom 84, 107, 144

wisdom tradition 81, 87, 92, 137,
    143, 171, 190, 191
Witch of Endor 114, 116
women 142, 195, 201
words, arrangement of 26
worship 92, 141

Yahwist tradition 69, 77, 79, 137,
    139, 143, 162, 200
YHWH 3, 136–7, 170, 200
York, Anthony D. 15

Zacchaeus 70
Zaraphath, widow of 72–3
Zarathustra 28
Zechariah 32, 94, 97–8, 193
Zedekiah 135
Zion, Mount 59, 100, 112
zoomorphism 29, 171